AF378781

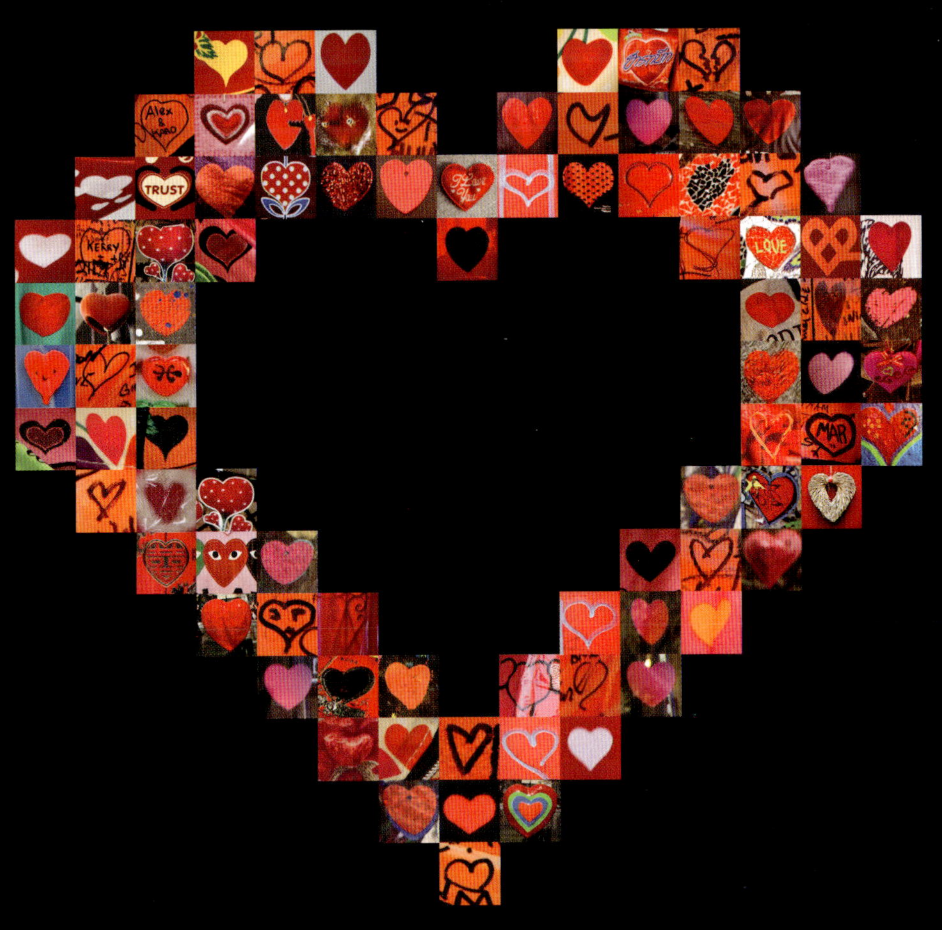

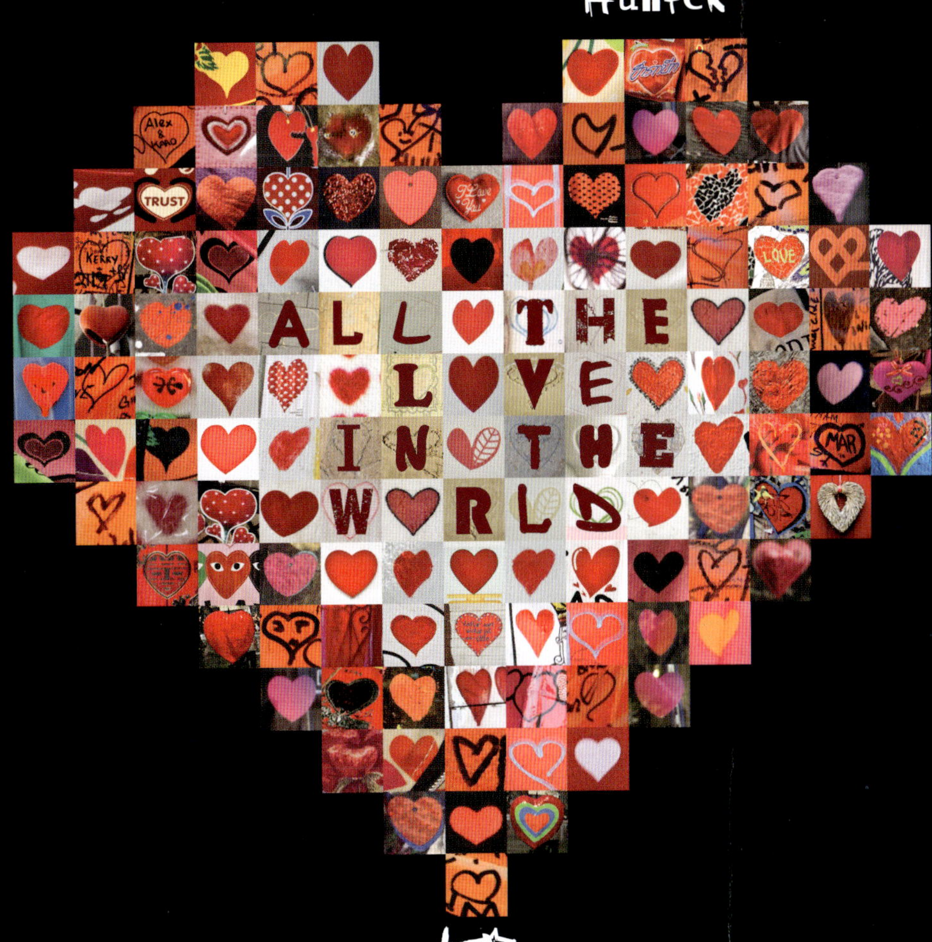

Jesse Hunter

hardie grant books
MELBOURNE · LONDON

Published in 2013 by Hardie Grant Books

Hardie Grant Books (Australia)
Ground Floor, Building 1
658 Church Street
Richmond, Victoria 3121
www.hardiegrant.com.au

Hardie Grant Books (UK)
Dudley House, North Suite
34–35 Southampton Street
London WC2E 7HF
www.hardiegrant.co.uk

Cataloguing-in-Publication data is available from the National Library of Australia.

All the Love in the World
ISBN: 9781742705941

Concept, design and photography: Jesse Hunter
Design liaison: Mikala Robinson-Koss
Proofreading: Kate O'Donnell

www.alltheloveintheworld.co

Colour reproduction by Splitting Image Colour Studio
Printed in China by 1010 Printing International Limited

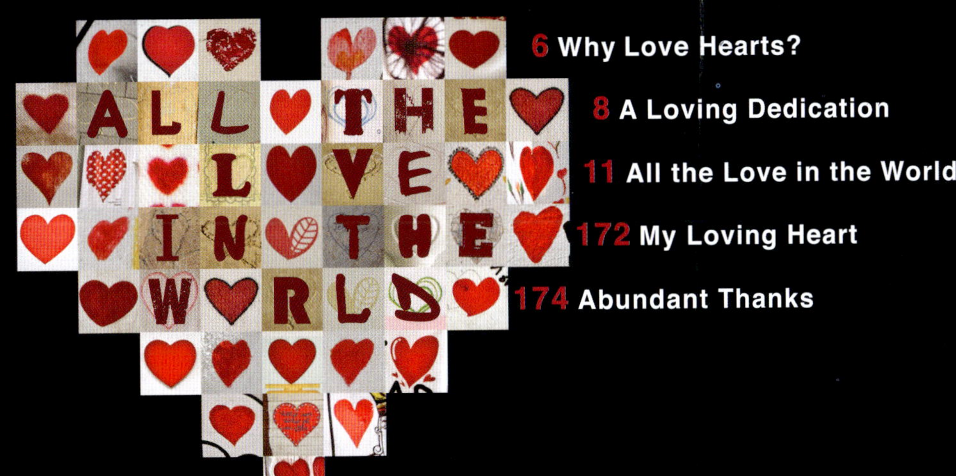

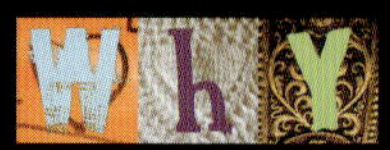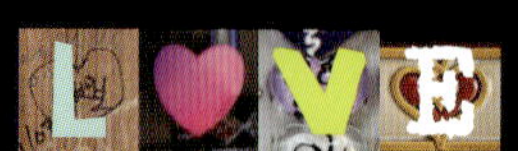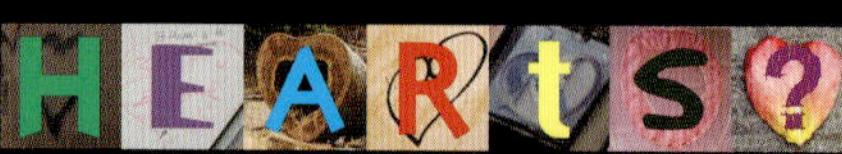
WHY LOVE HEARTS?

In 2010, my partner Mikala
and I embarked on a global
photographic adventure
to frame the world in our
own unique way. For
650 days, we travelled
across 44 countries,
on 6 continents, always
armed with our camera gear.

After a couple of months travelling
around our beautiful globe,
I realised there were certain 'things'
I was photographing again and again.
These 'things', which became
collections — included unique
house numbers, sewer plates,
sporting city names, intriguing
windows and taxi drivers in their
rear-view mirrors.

But the most-photographed
of all my collections were
love hearts. I captured more
than 1000 individual love hearts
during our journey — and a lot
of these can be seen on the cover
of this book.

Basically,
the love hearts
chose me
and I obeyed.

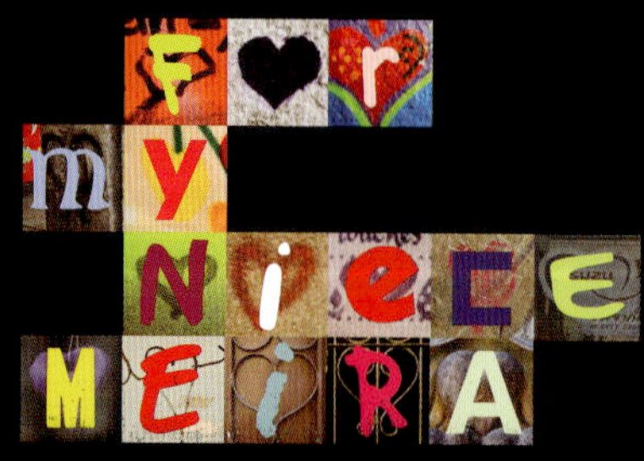

8

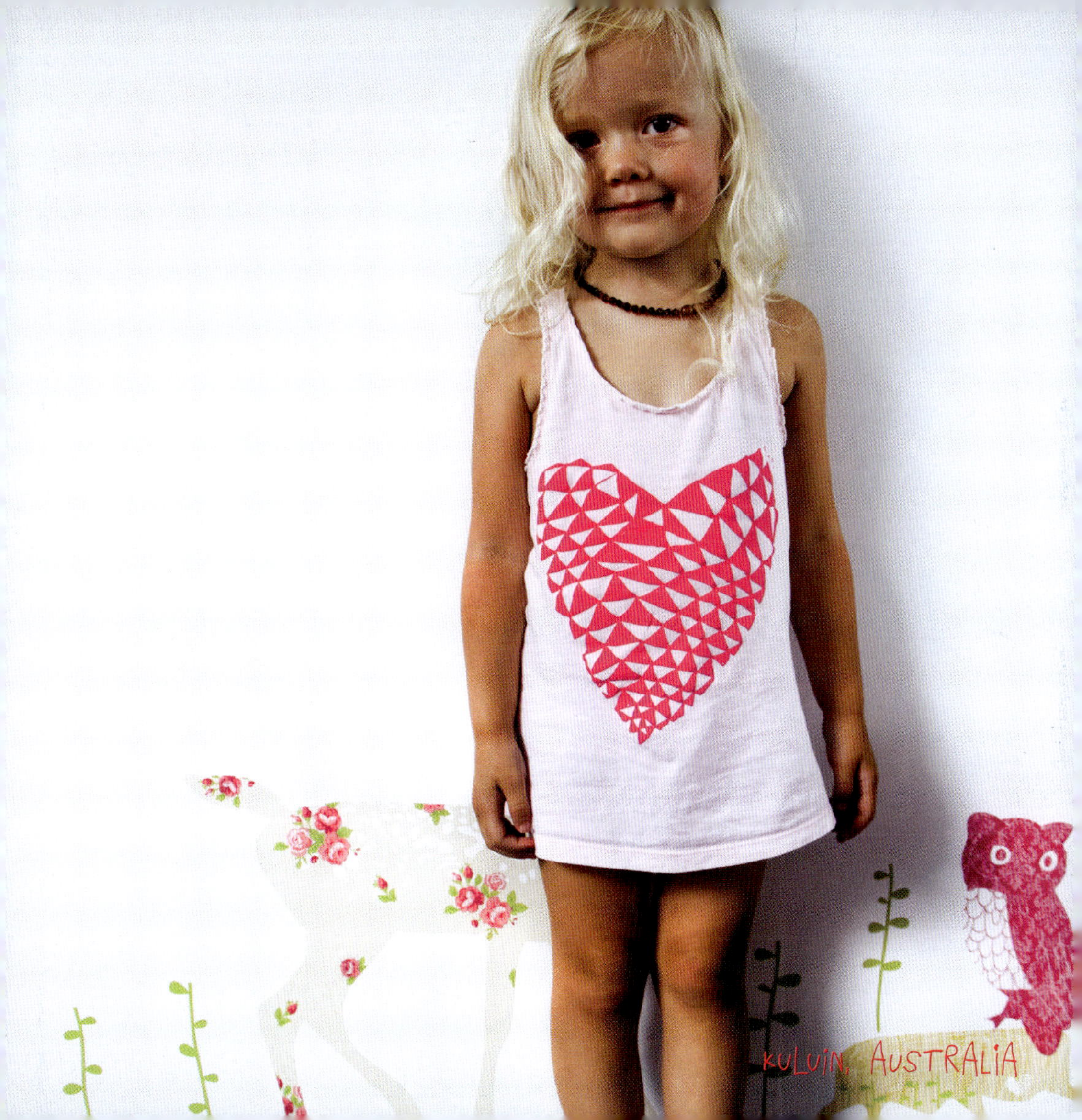
KULUIN, AUSTRALIA

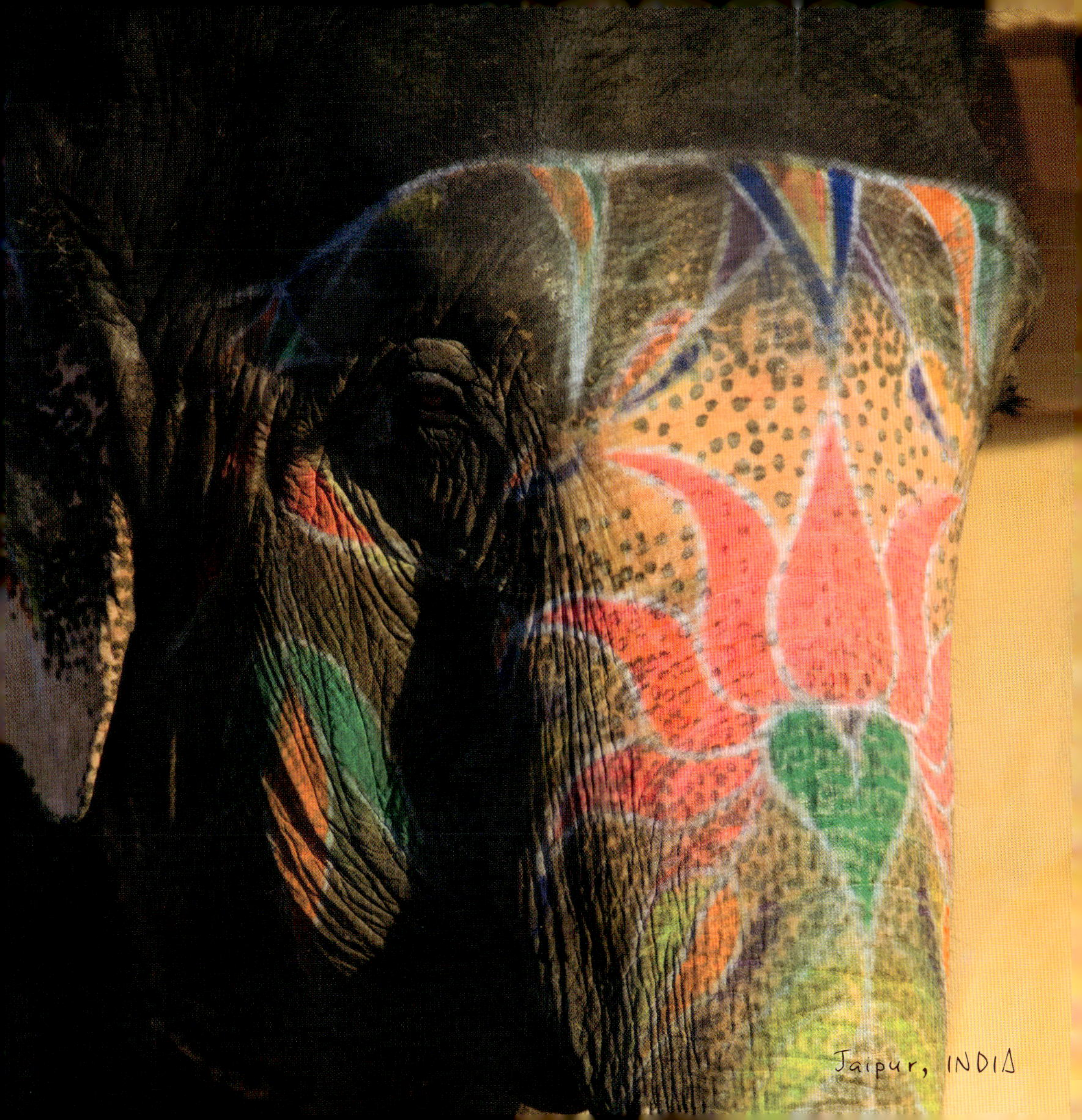
Jaipur, INDIA

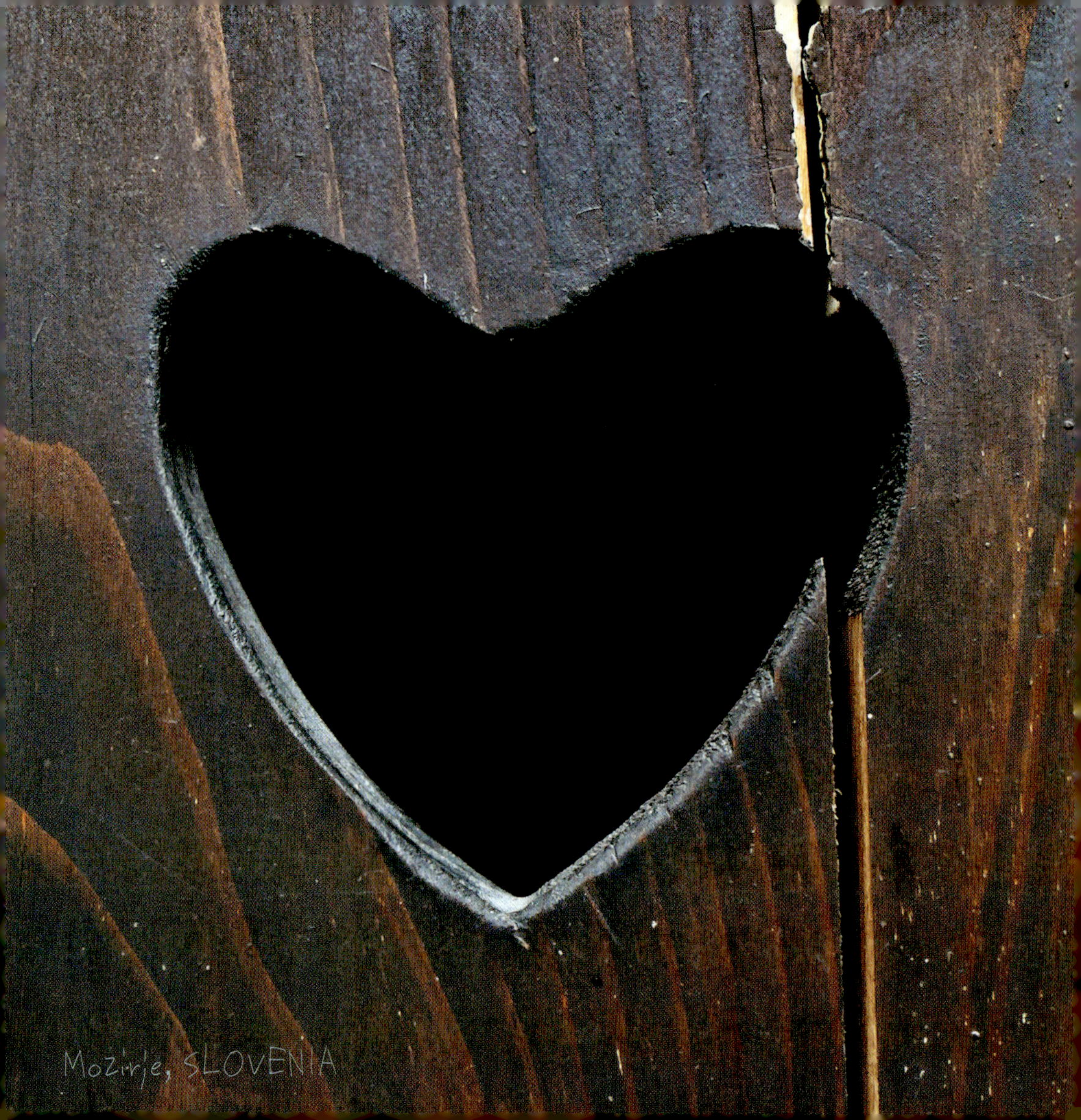
Mozirje, SLOVENIA

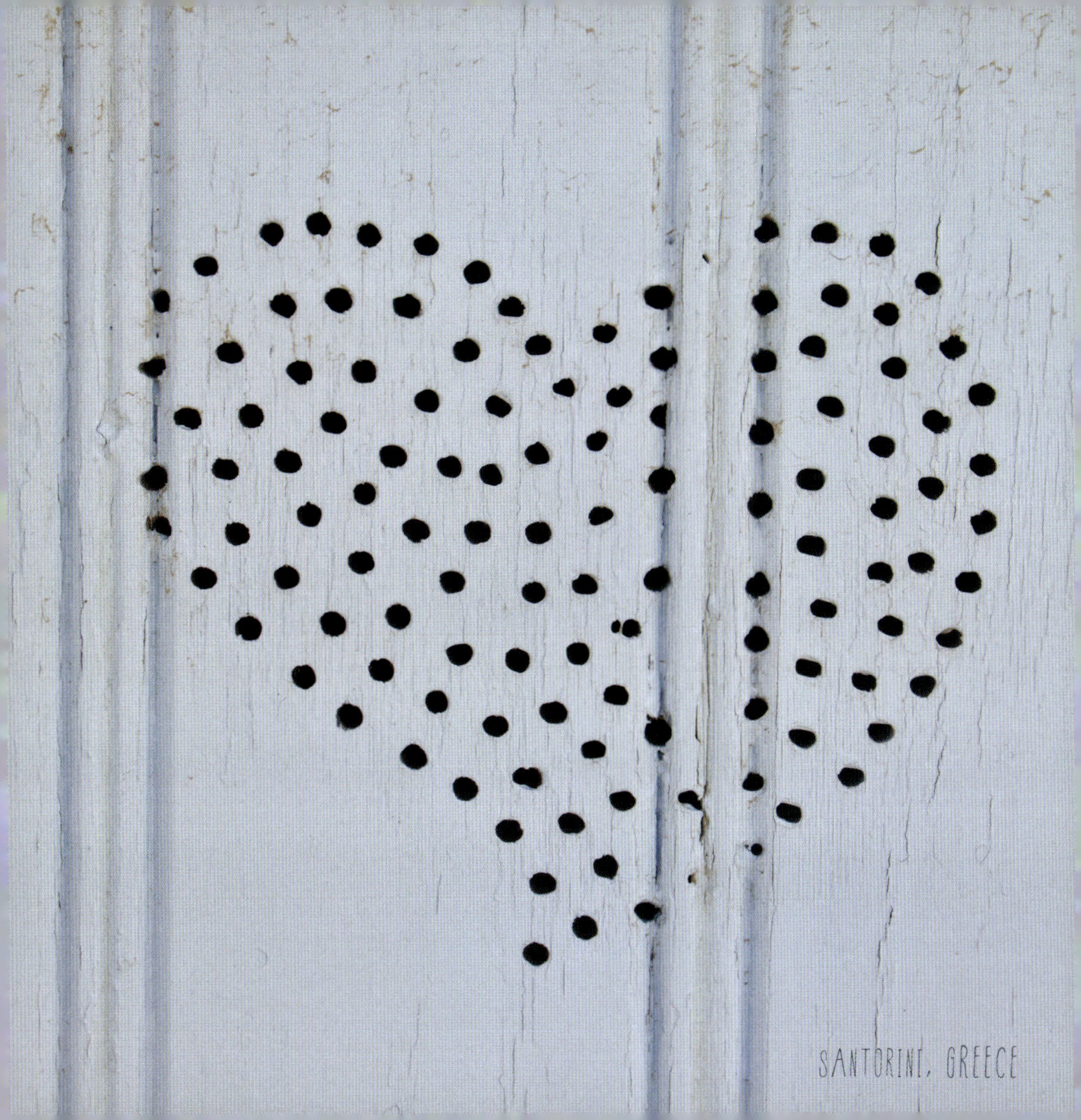

SANTORINI, GREECE

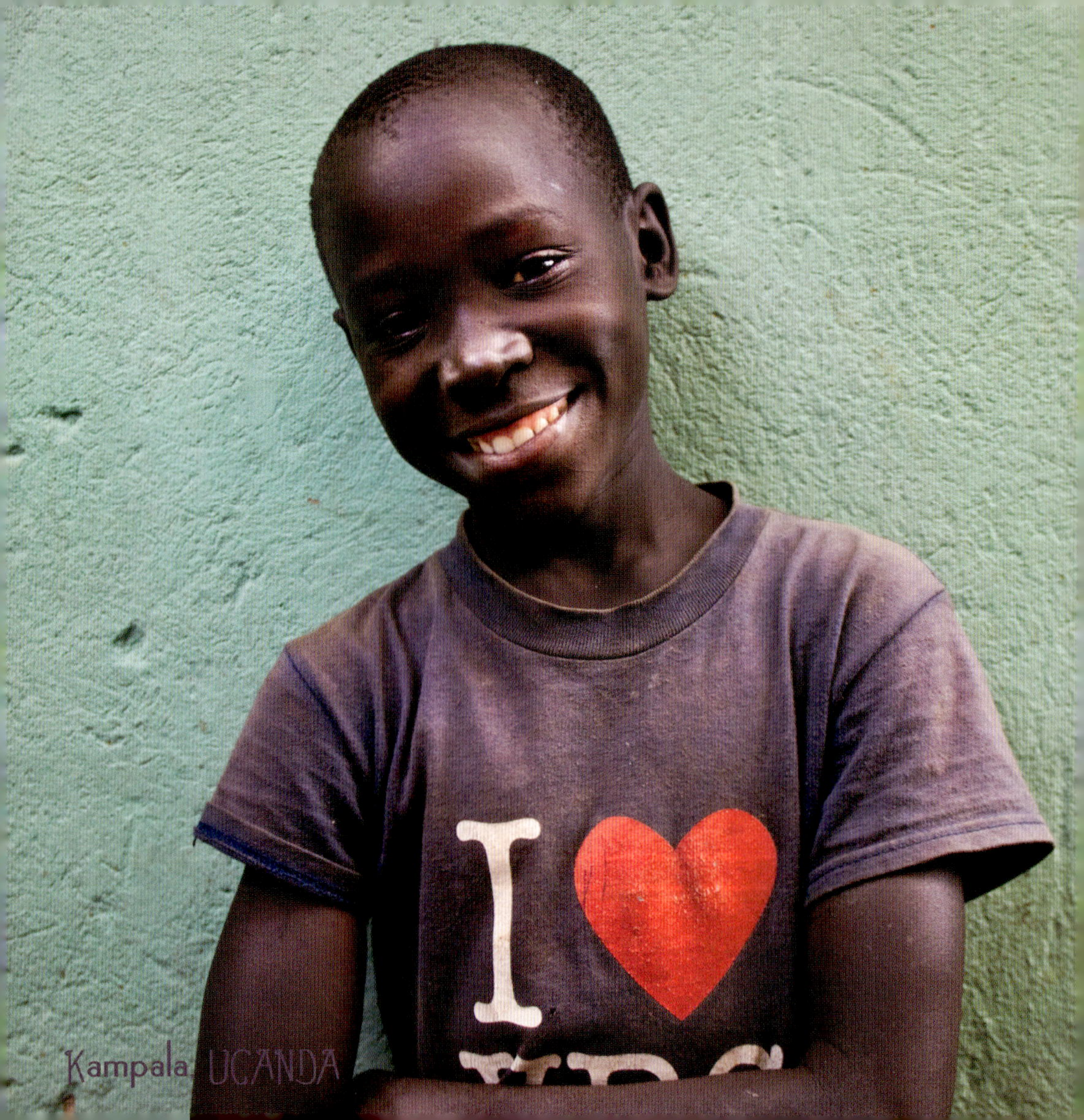
Kampala UGANDA
I ♥

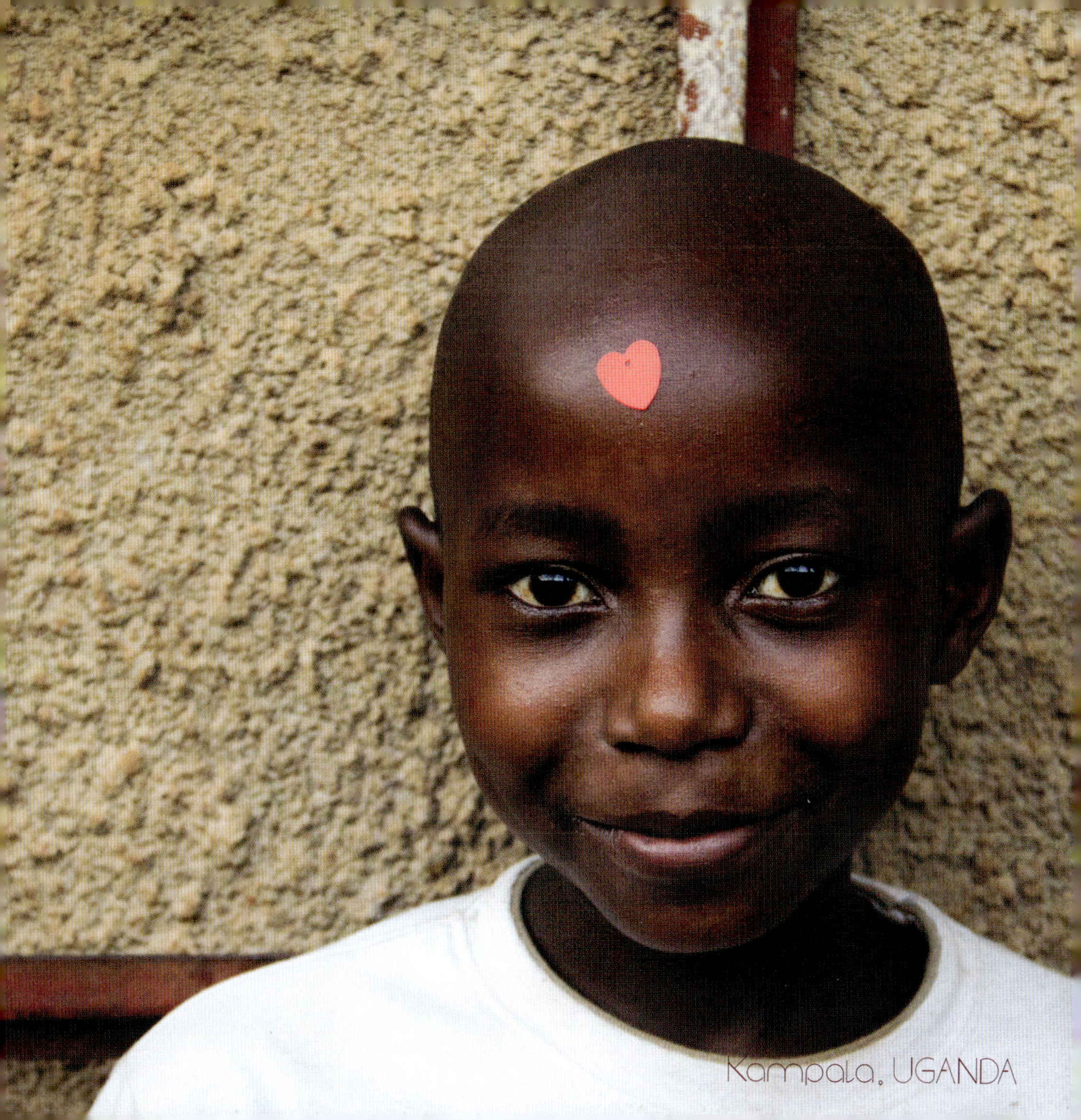
Kampala, UGANDA

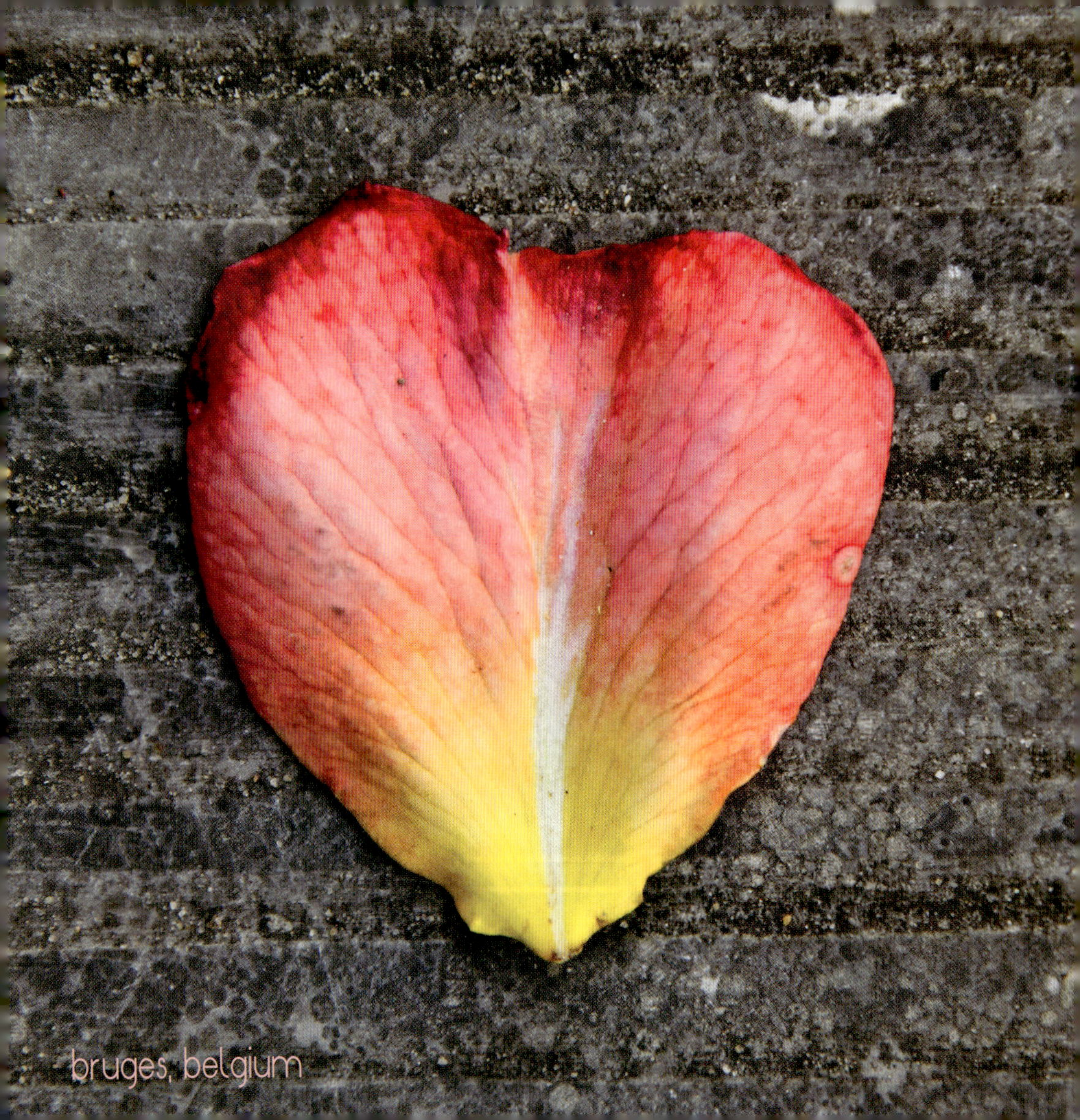
bruges, belgium

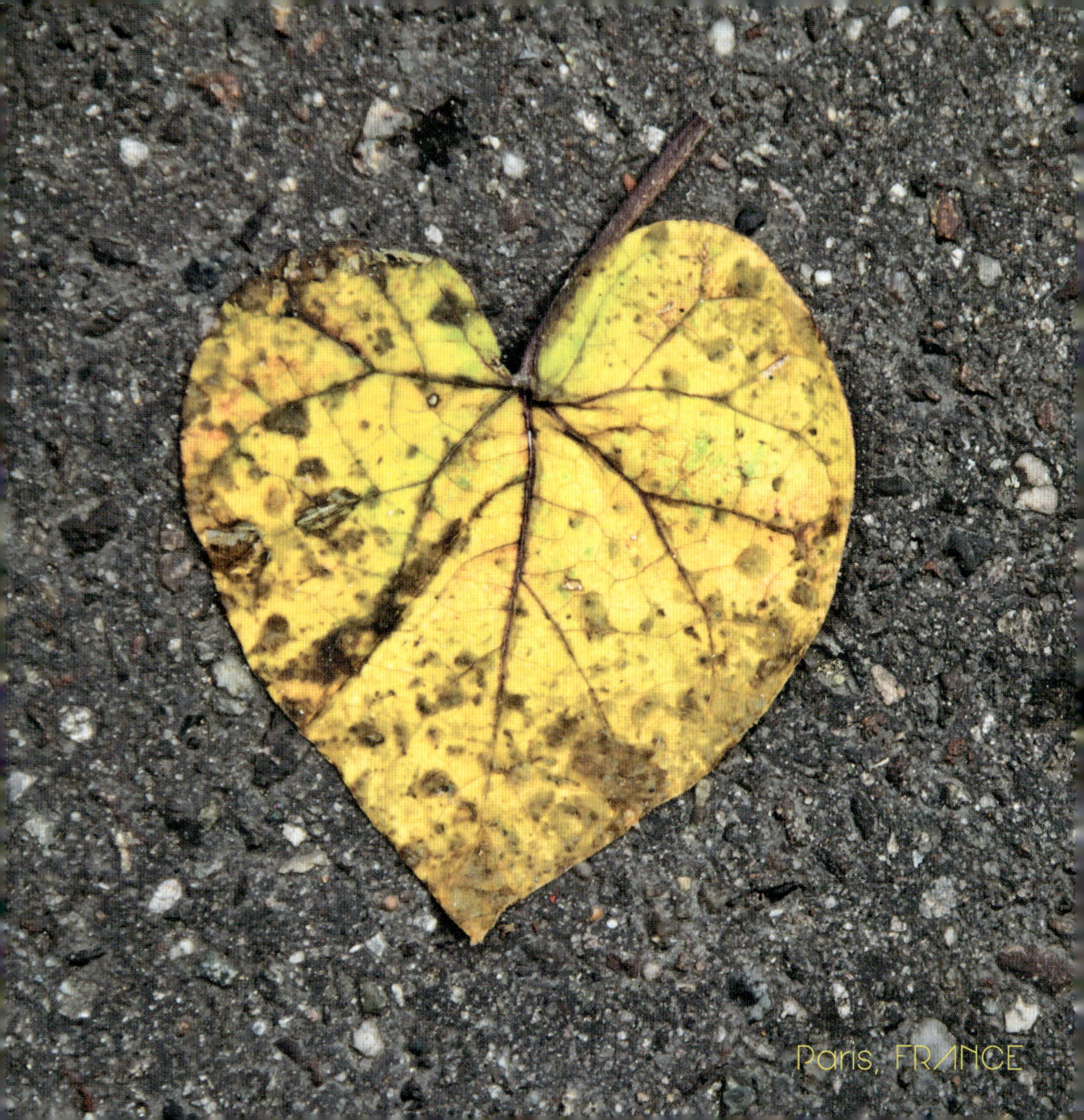
Paris, FRANCE

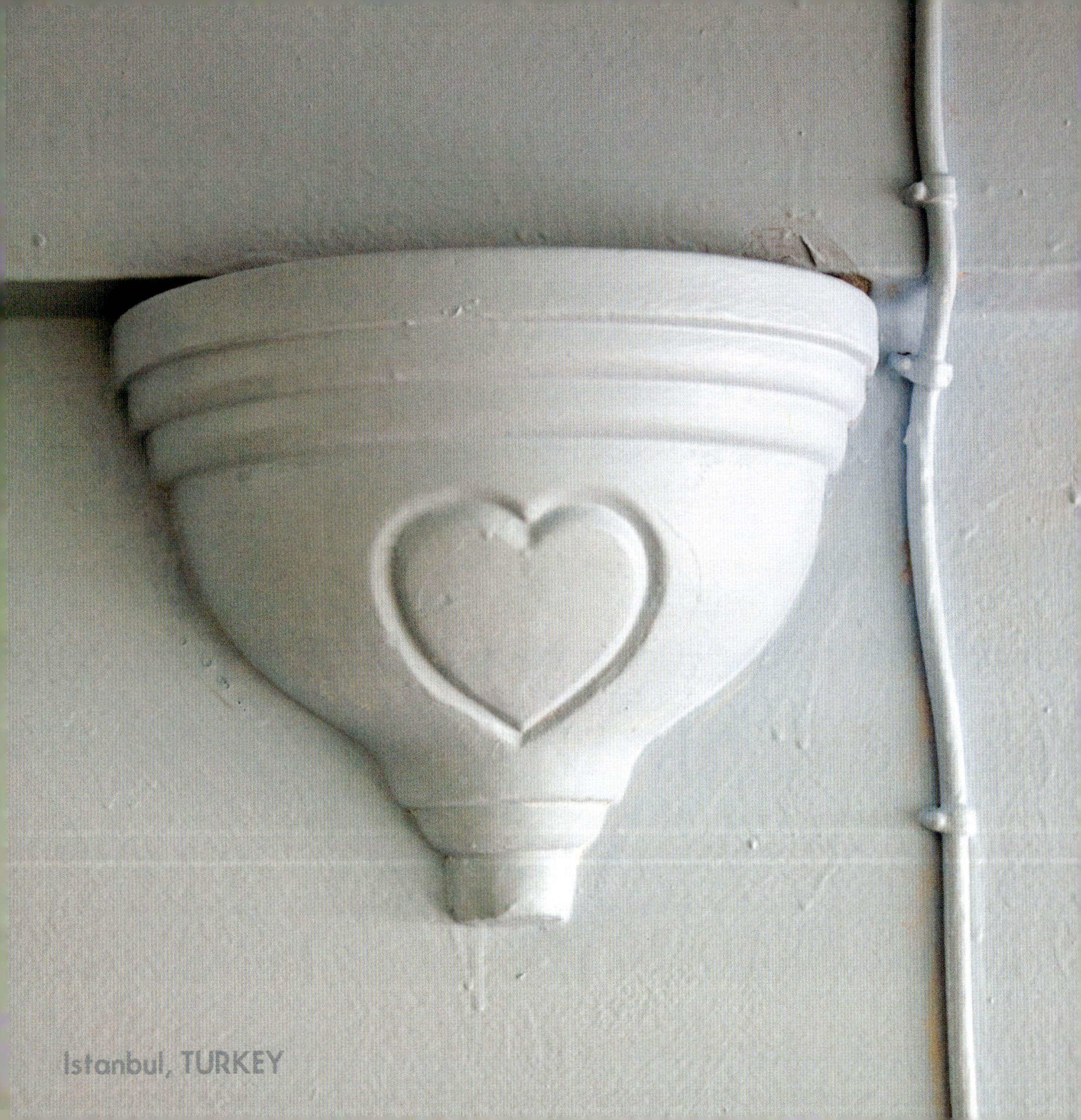
Istanbul, TURKEY

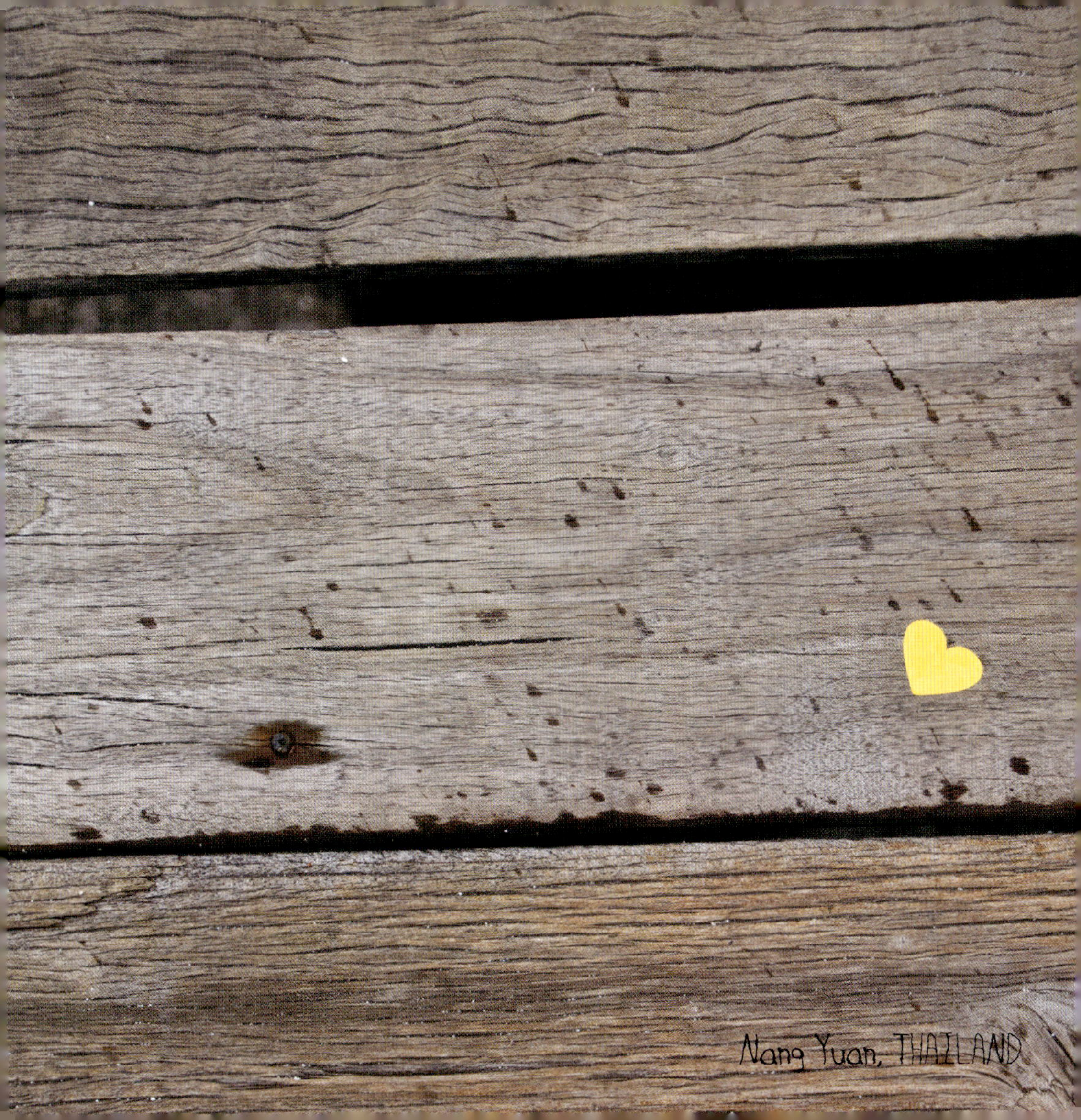
Nang Yuan, THAILAND

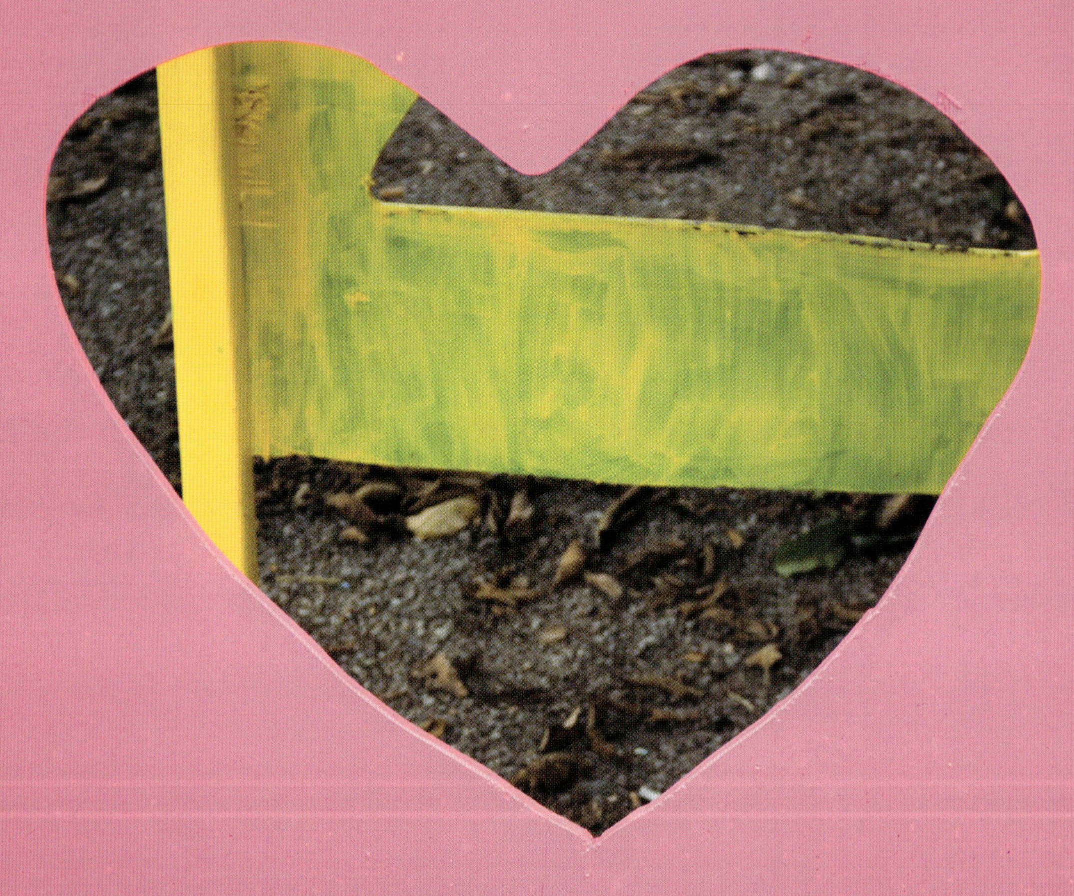
STOCKHOLM SWEDEN

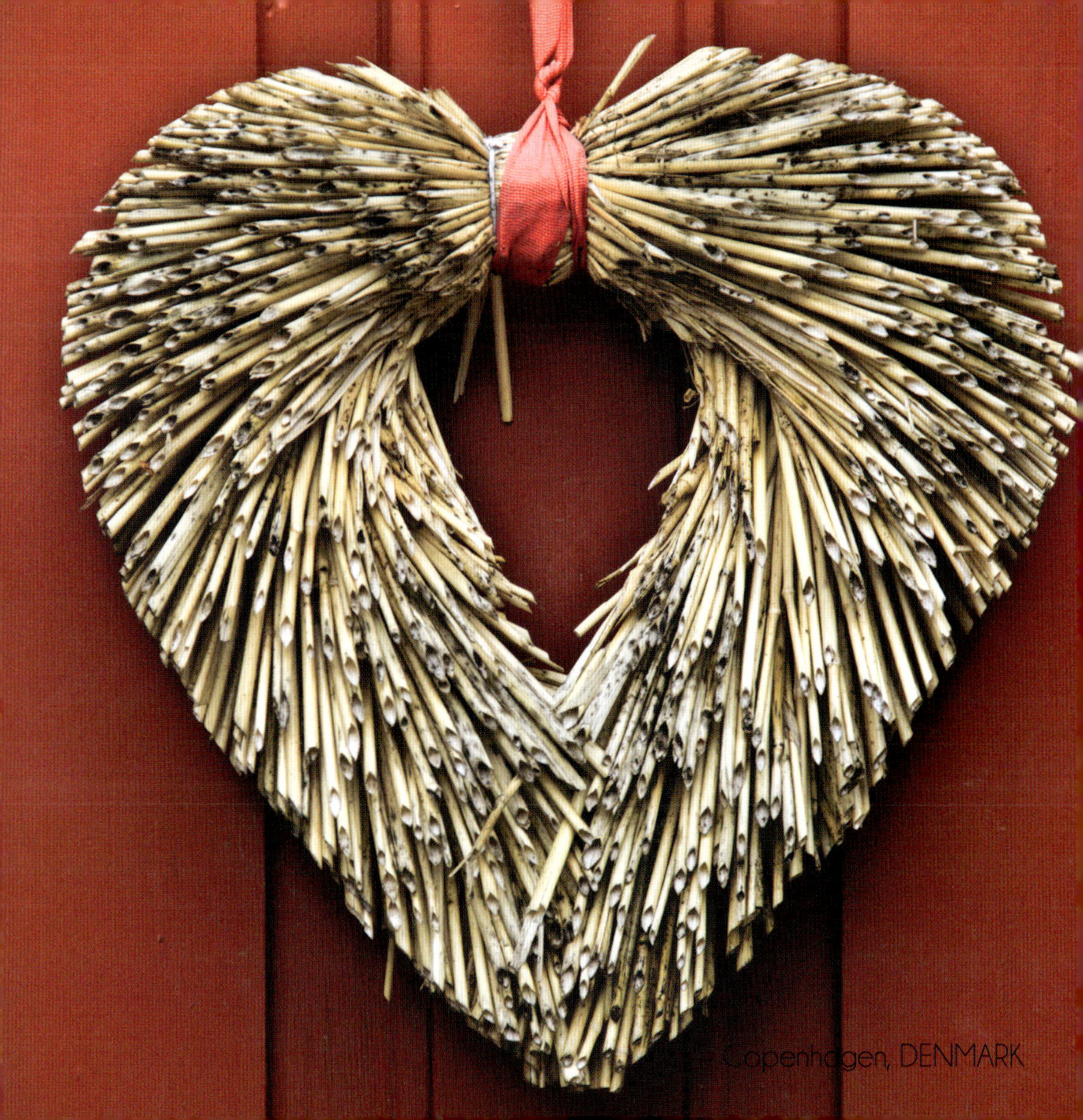
Copenhagen, DENMARK

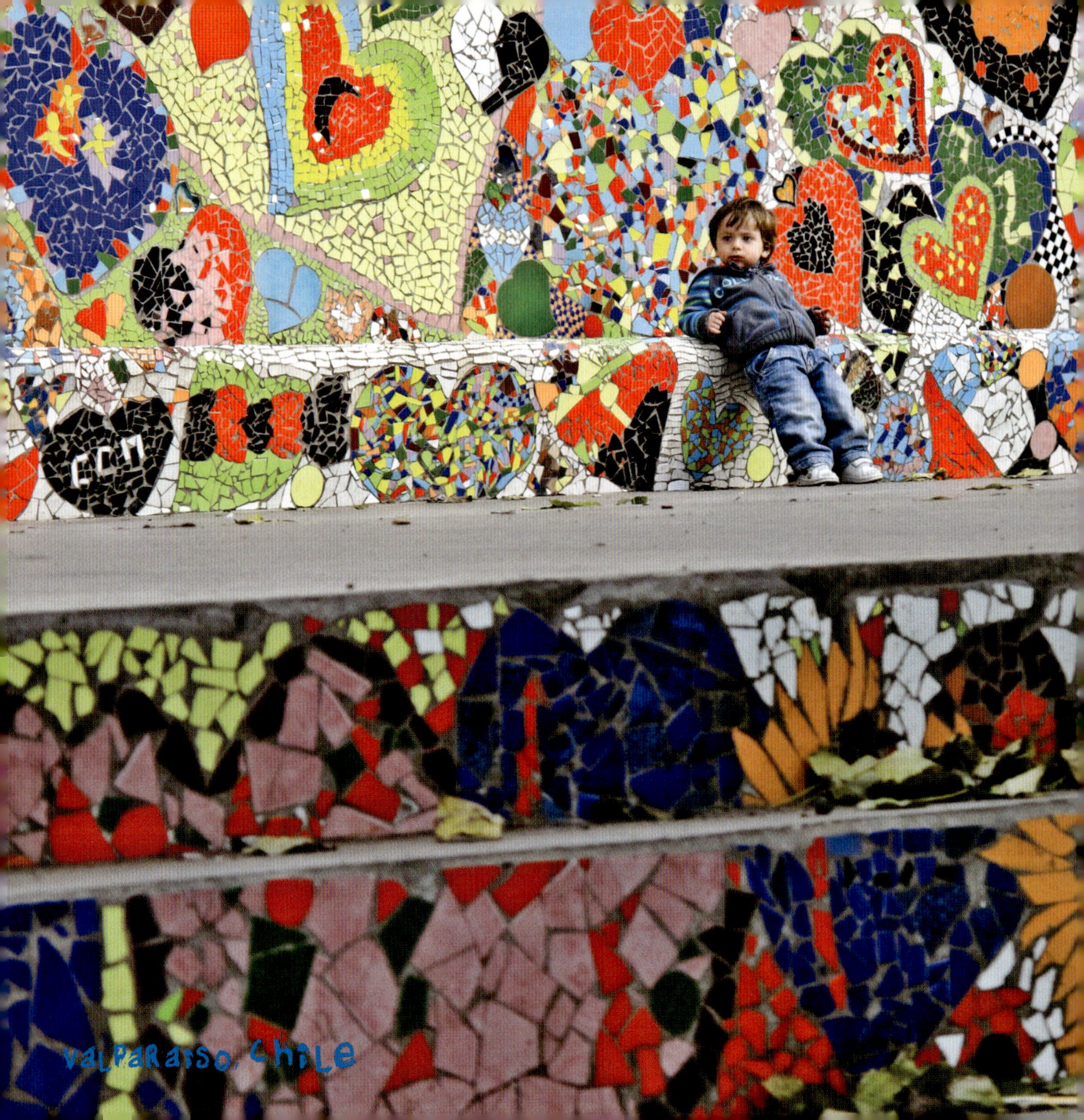
VALPARAISO, CHILE

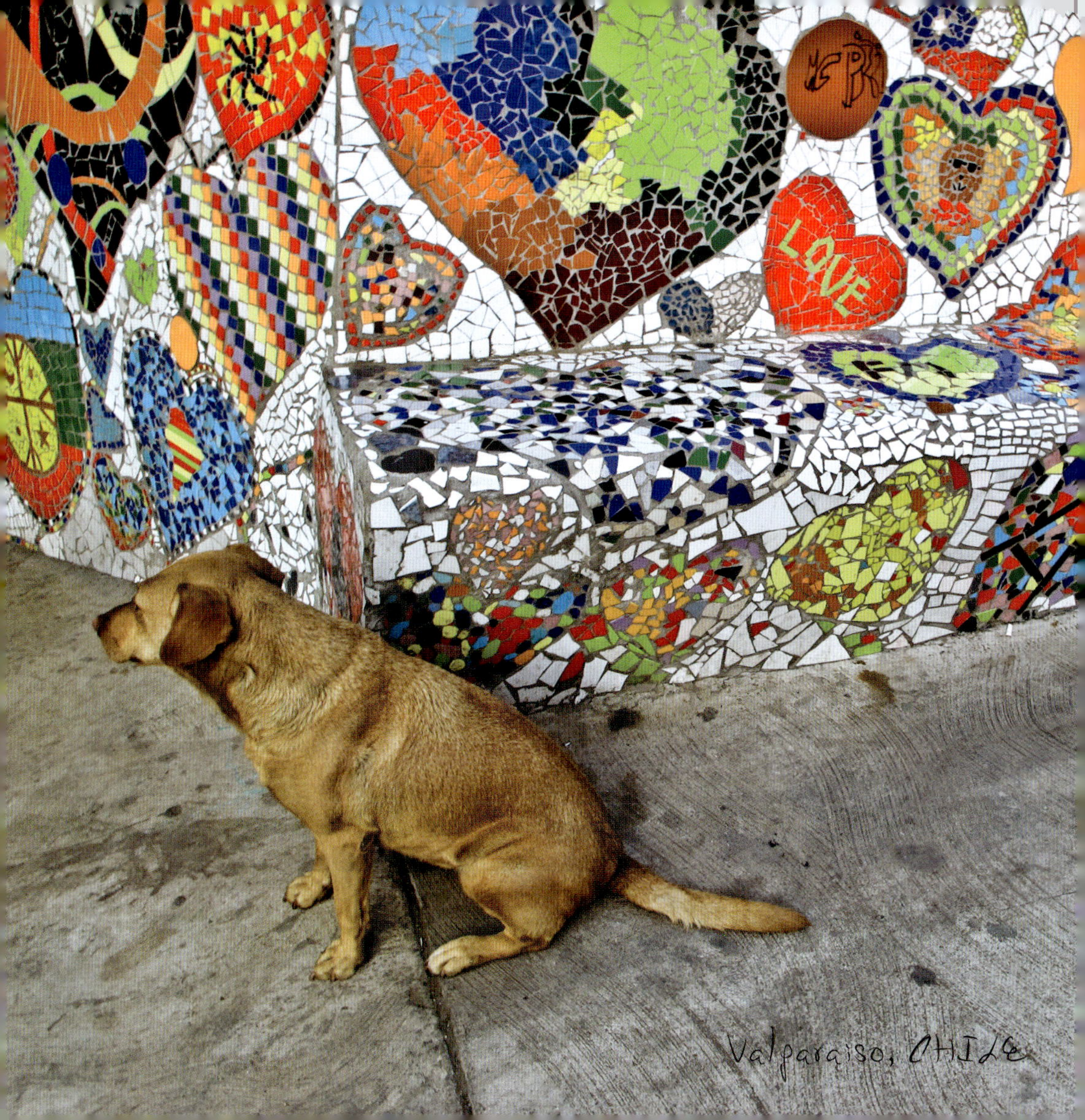
LOVE
Valparaíso, CHILE

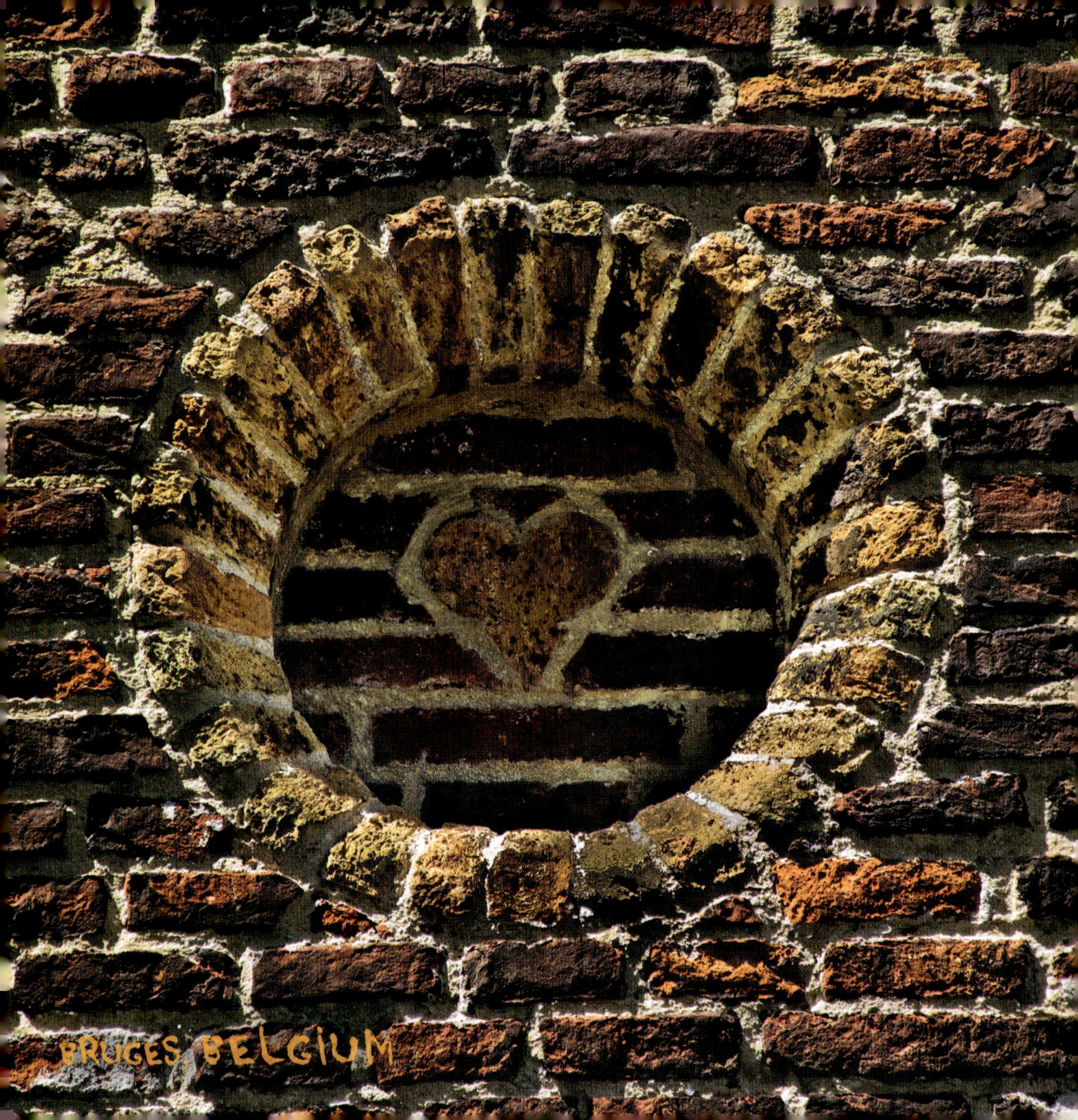
BRUGES, BELGIUM

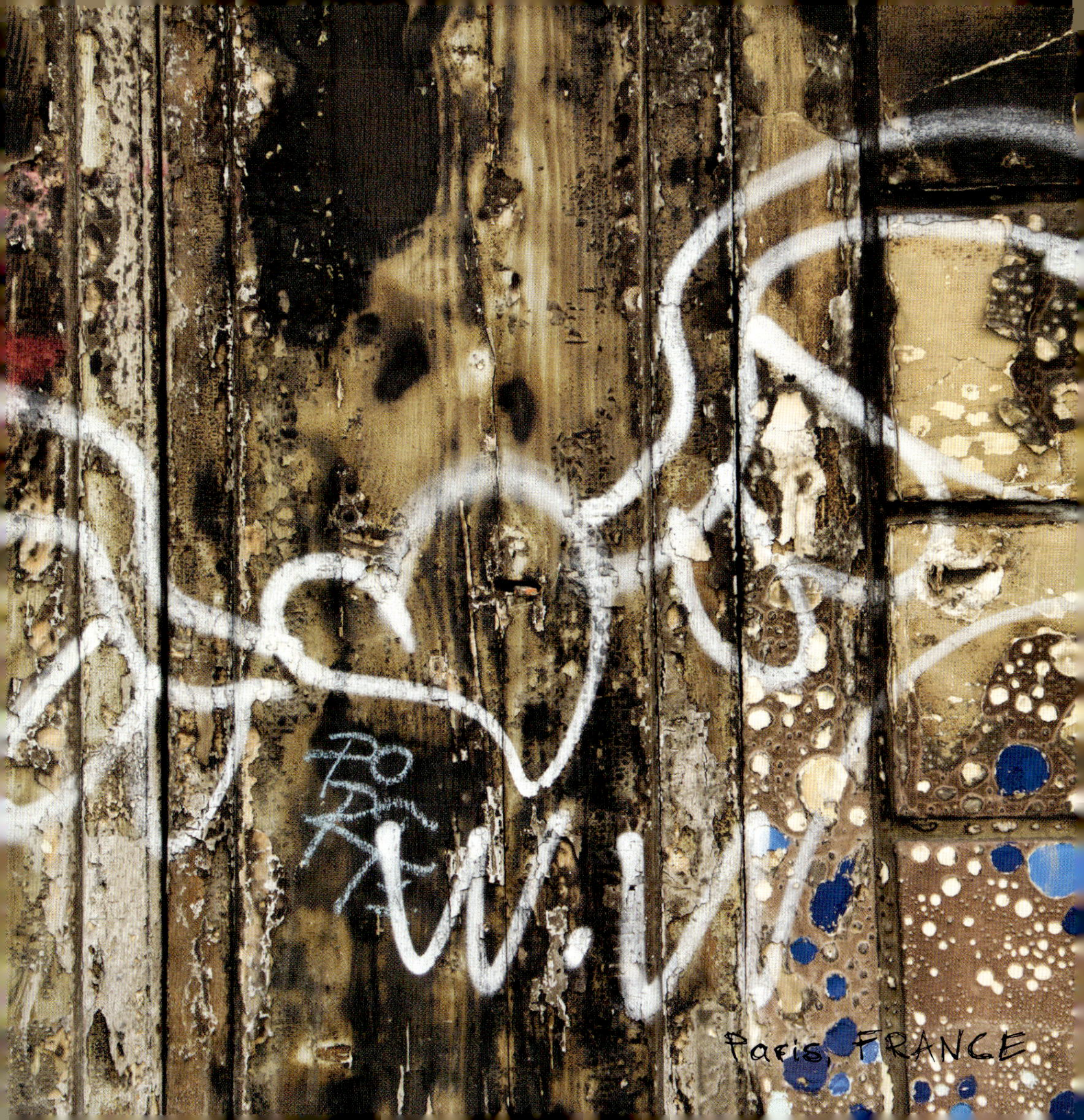
Paris, FRANCE

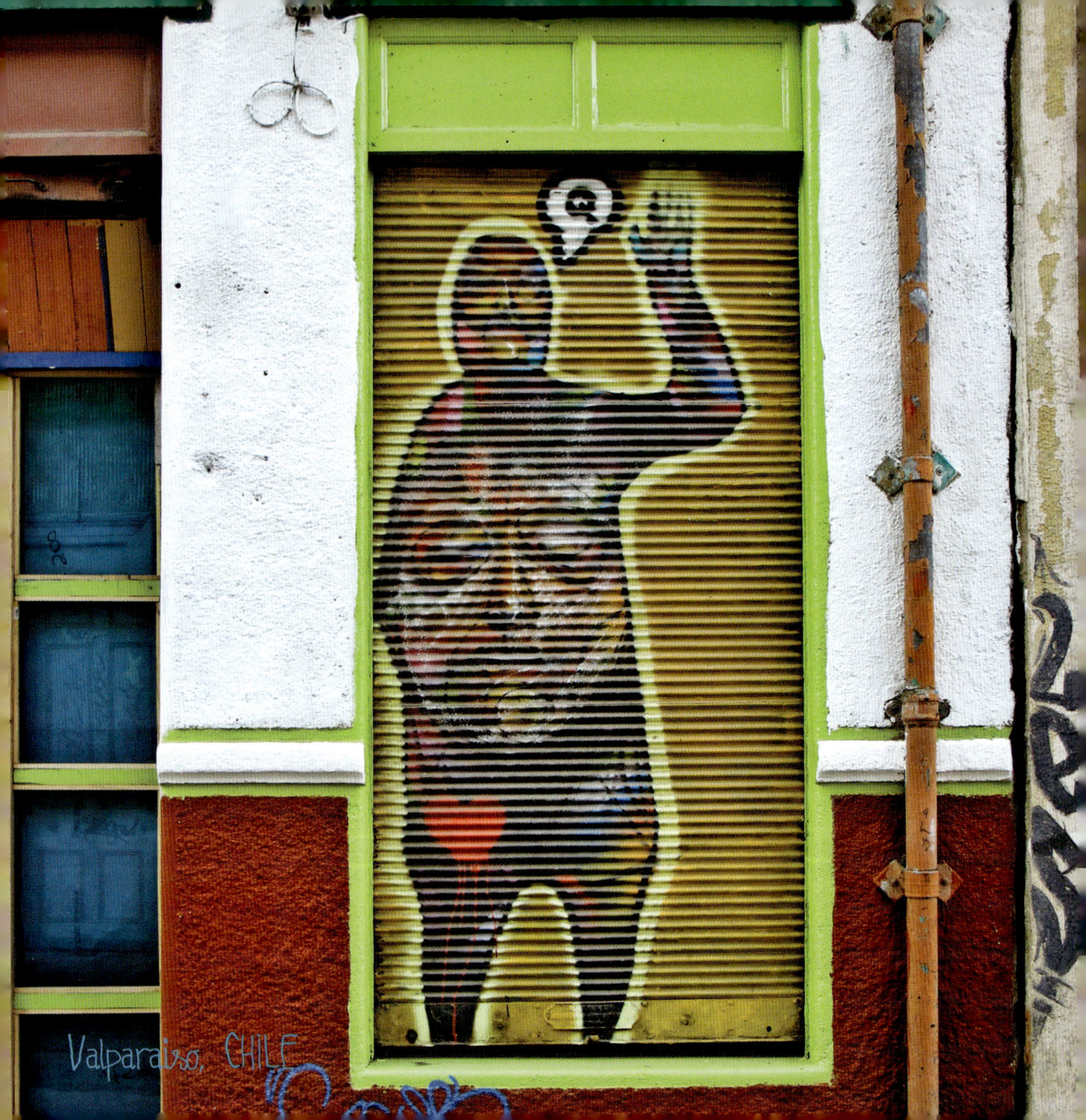

Valparaiso, CHILE

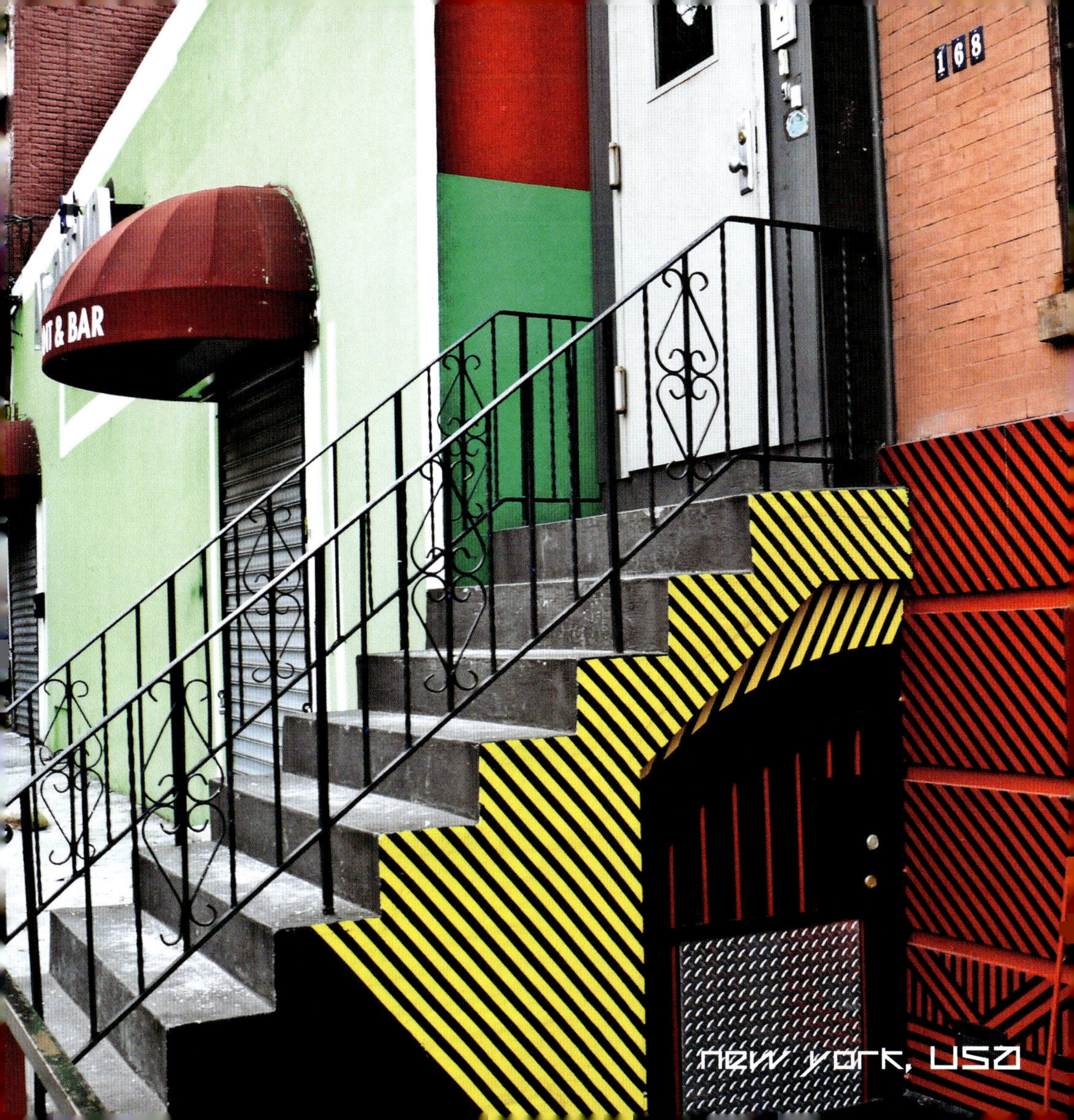
NT & BAR
168
new york, usa

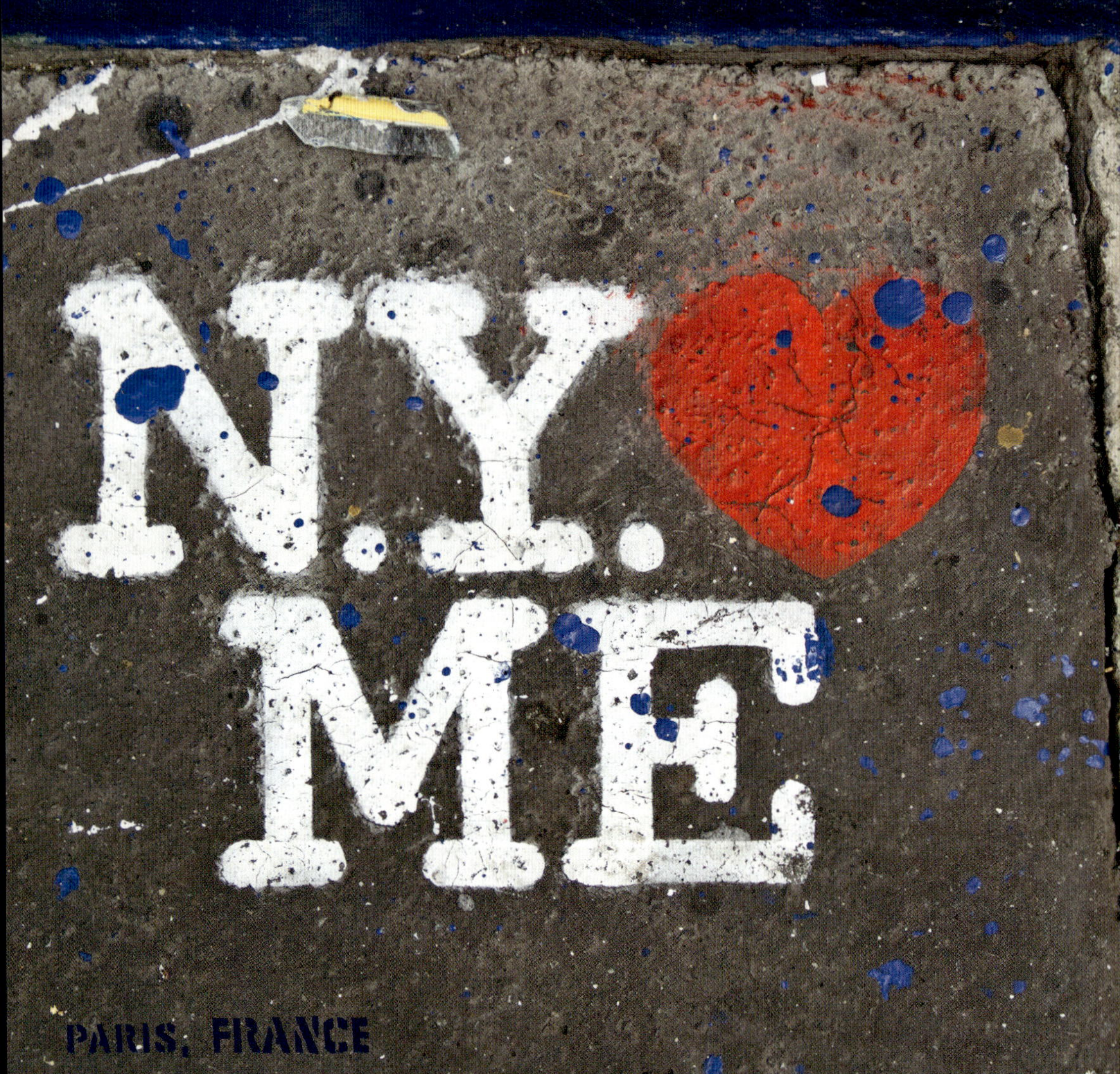

N.Y.
M.E.
PARIS, FRANCE

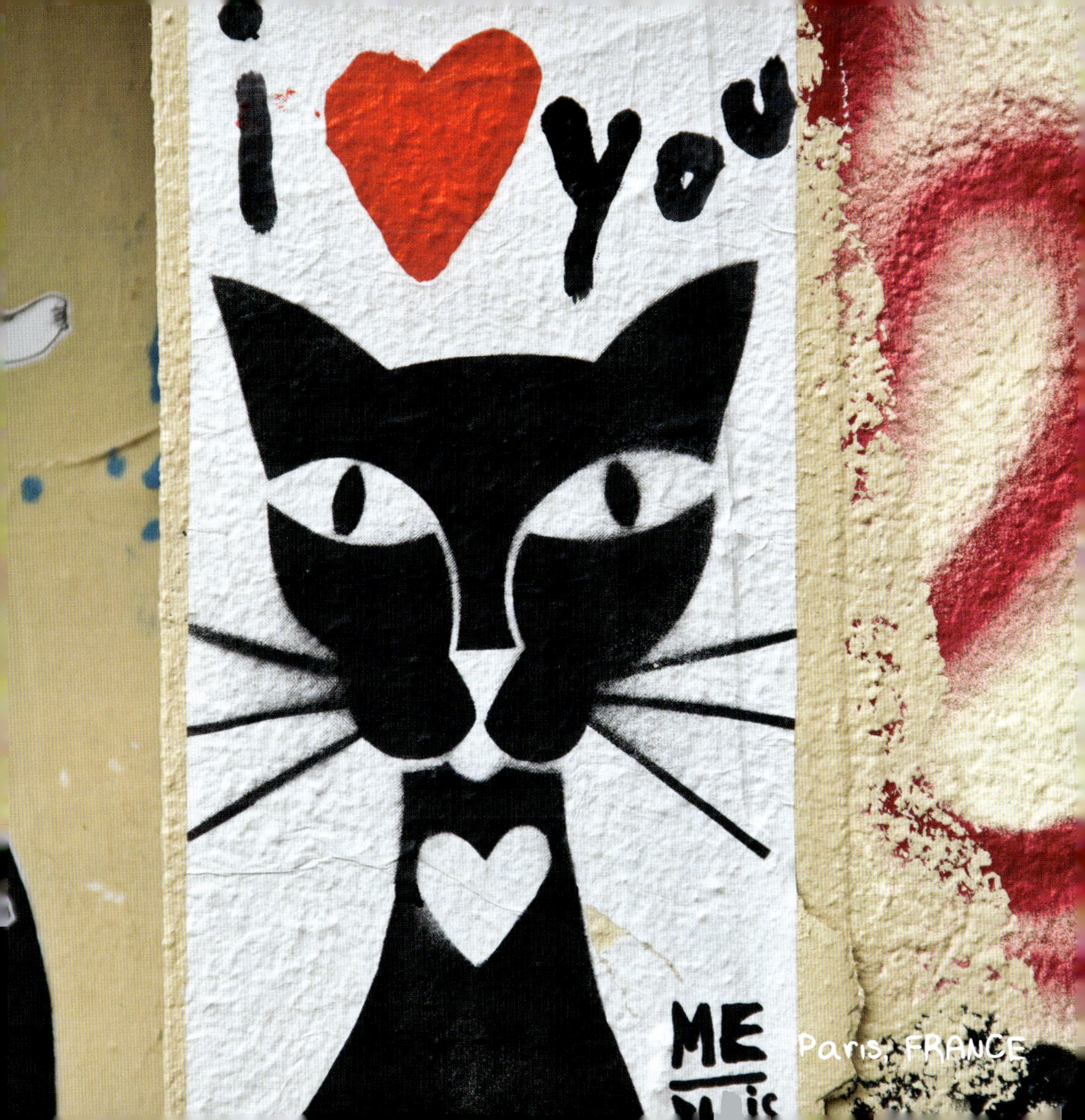

i ♥ YOU
ME
Paris, FRANCE

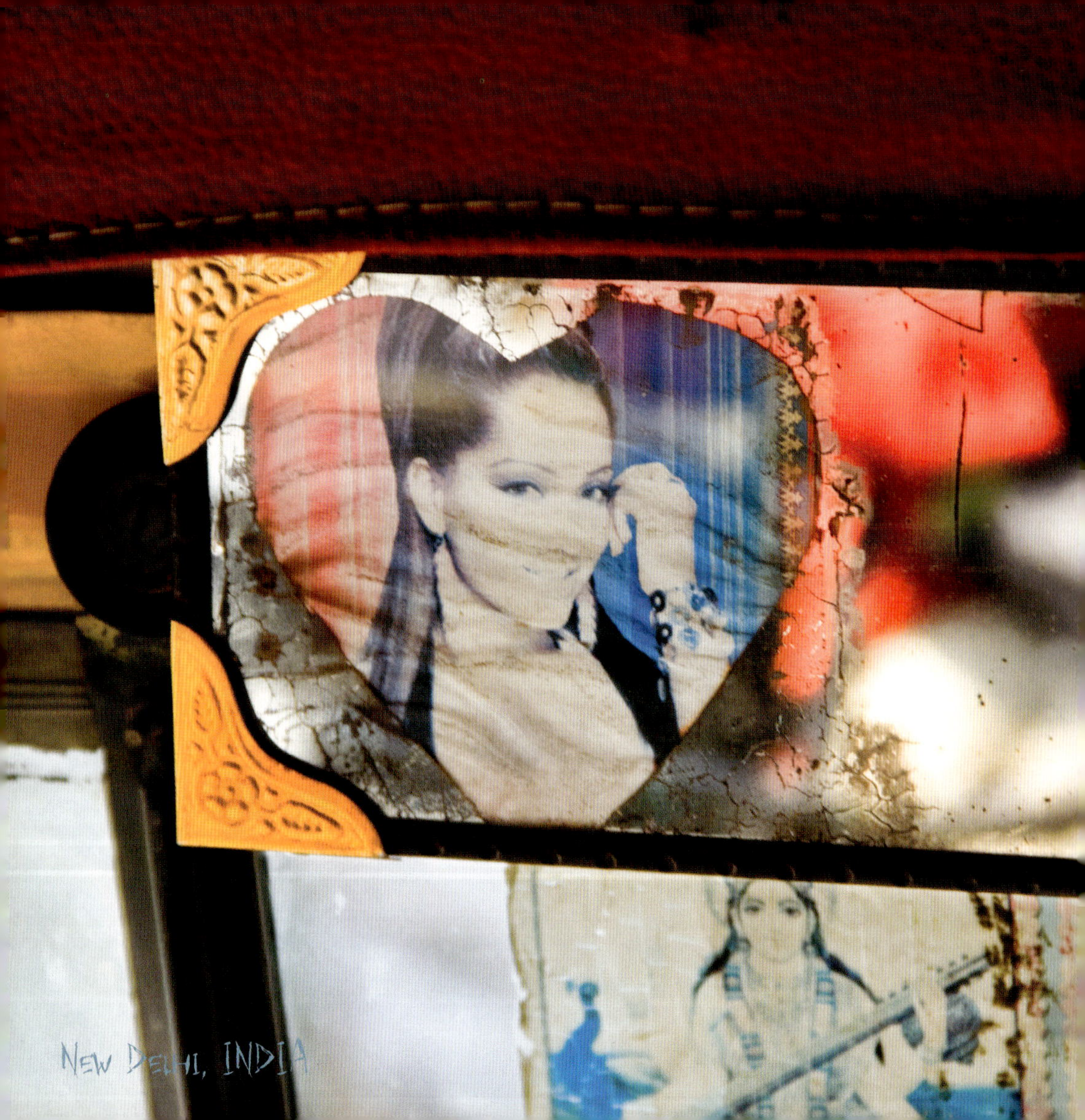
NEW DELHI, INDIA

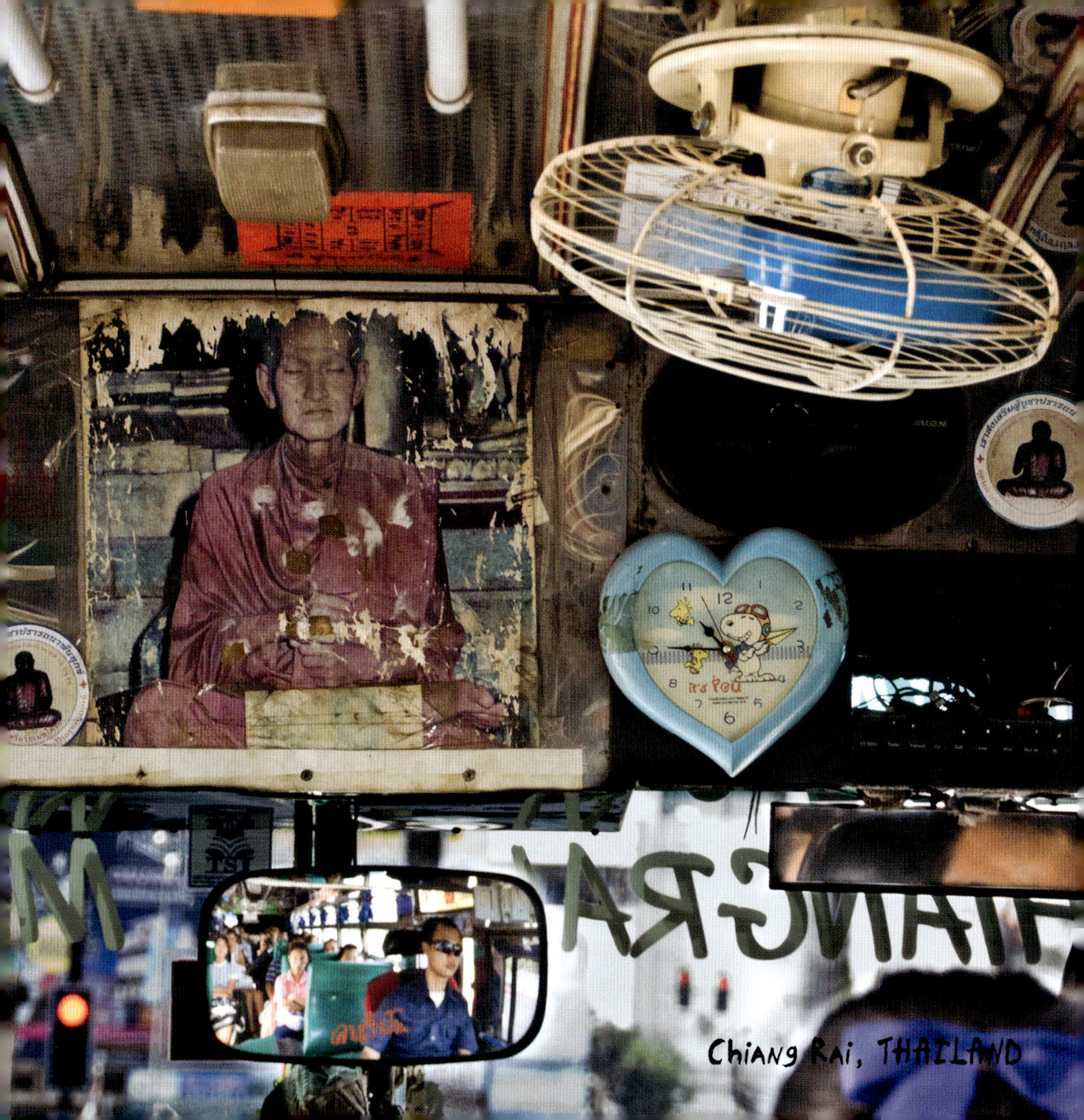

Chiang Rai, THAILAND

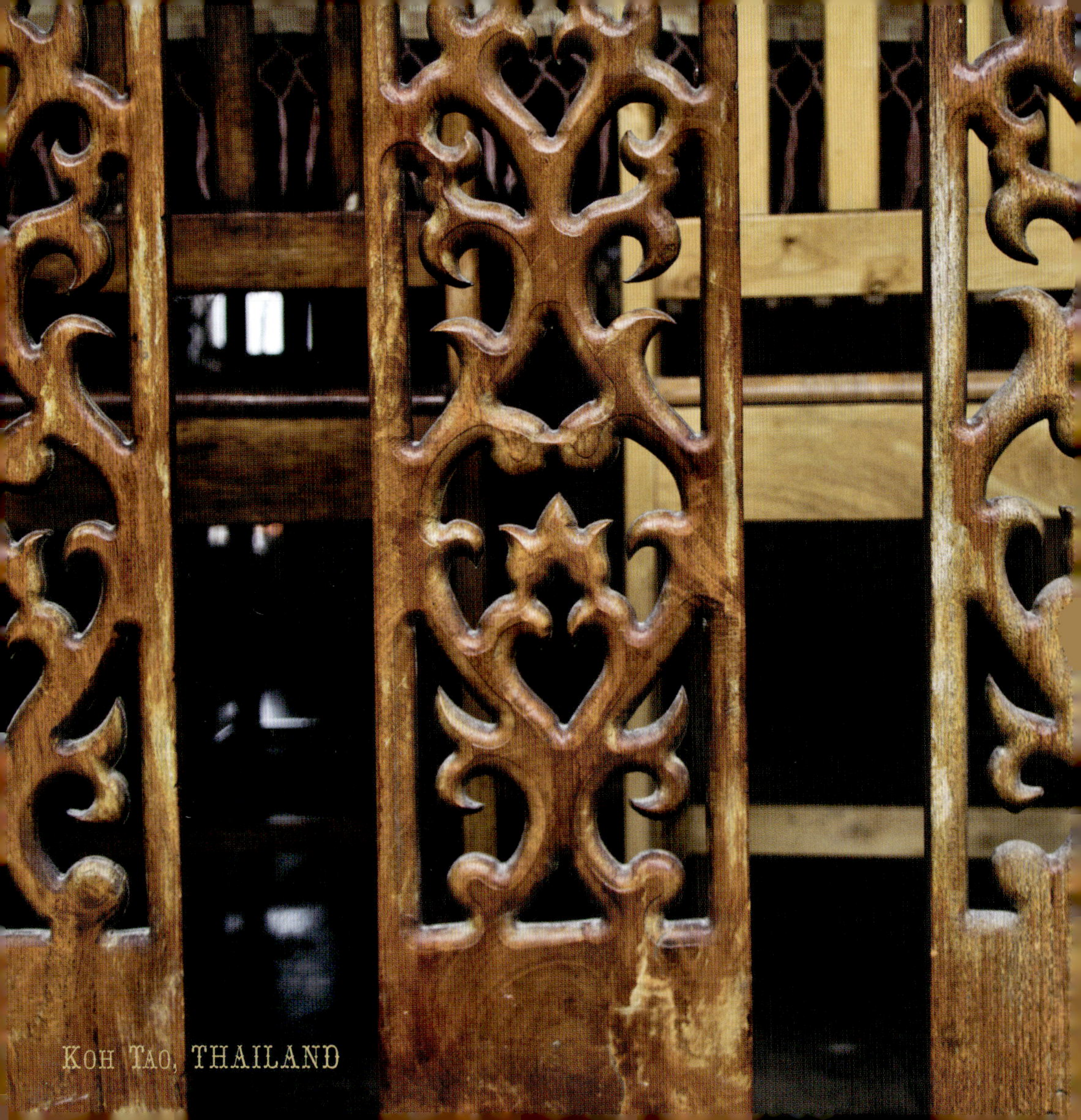
Koh Tao, THAILAND

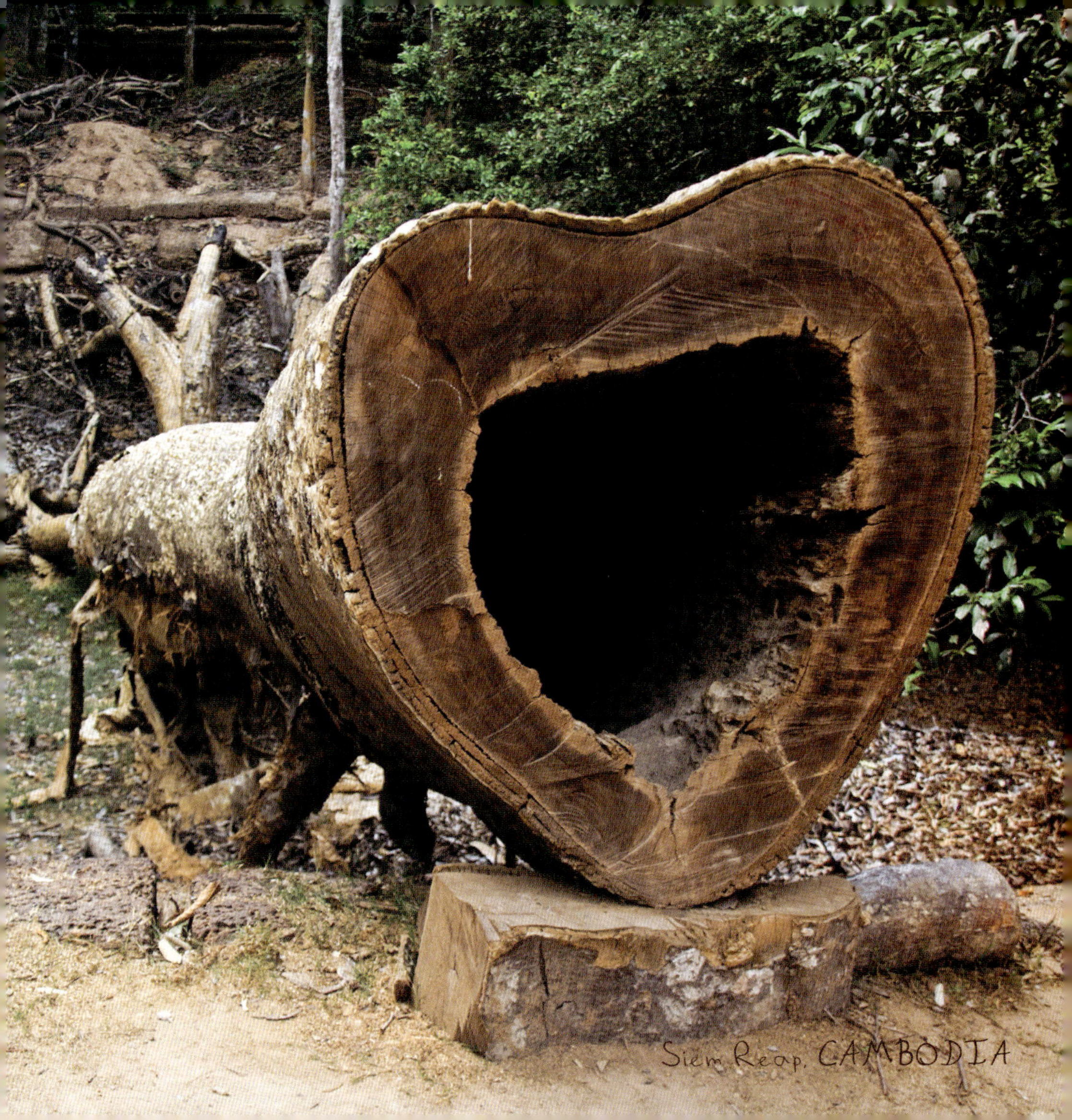

Siem Reap. CAMBODIA

I ♥
ART
Krakow, POLAND

love

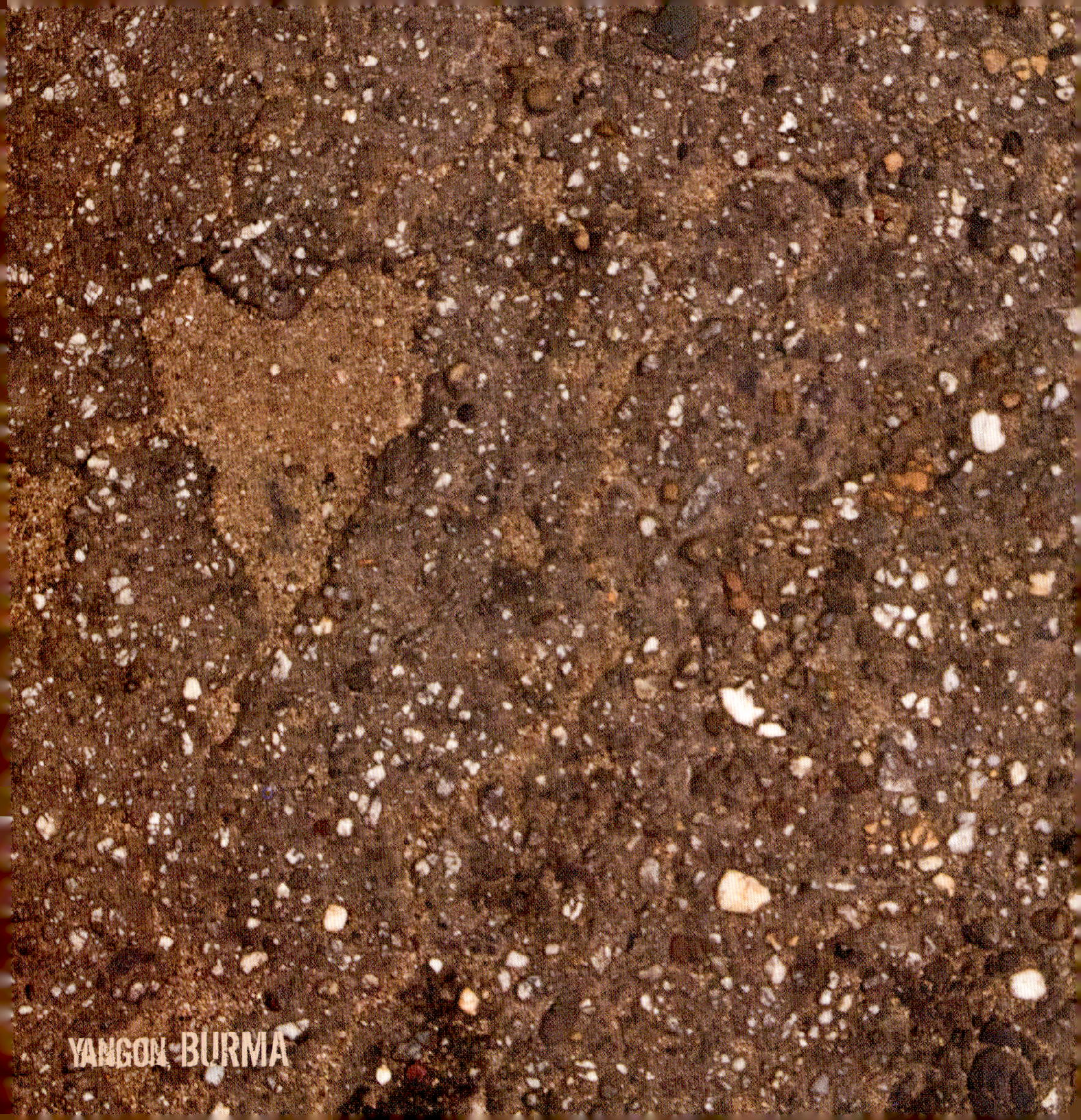
YANGON BURMA

London. ENGLAND

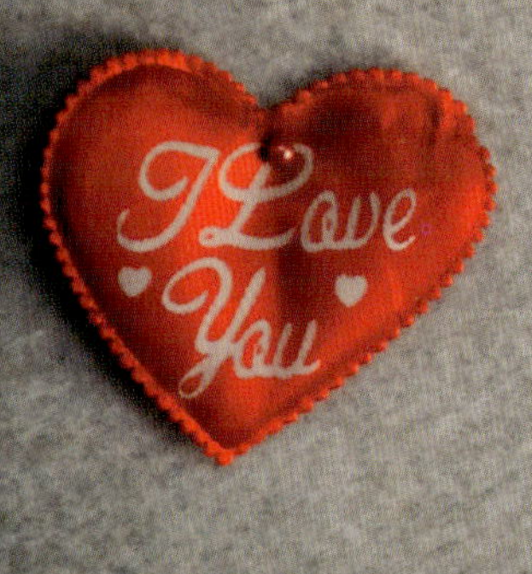

I Love
You

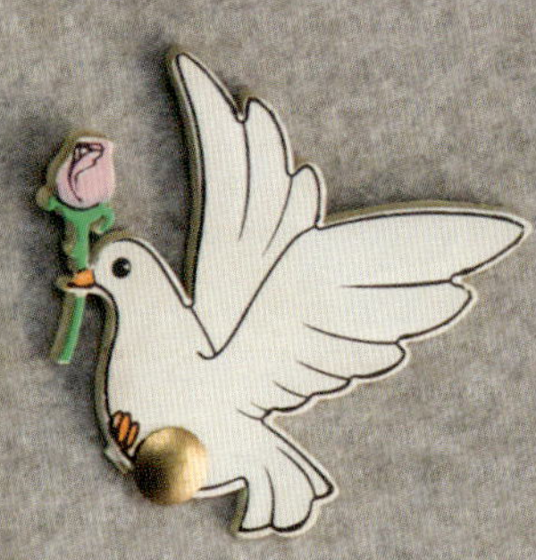

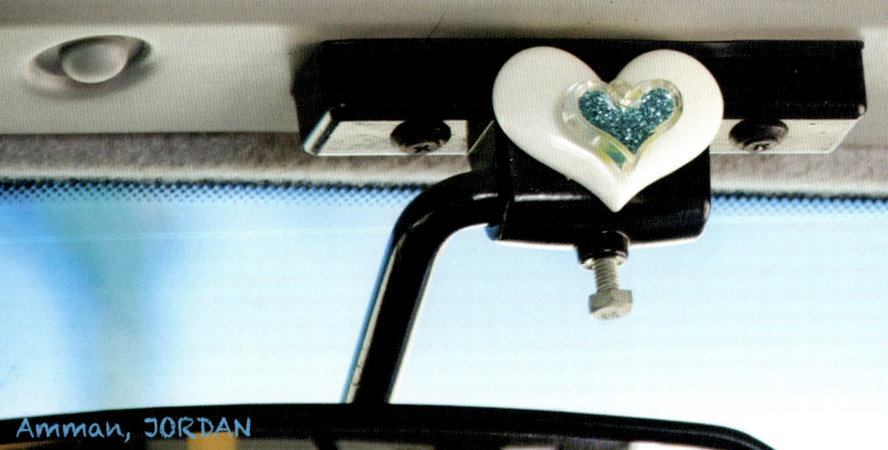

Amman, JORDAN

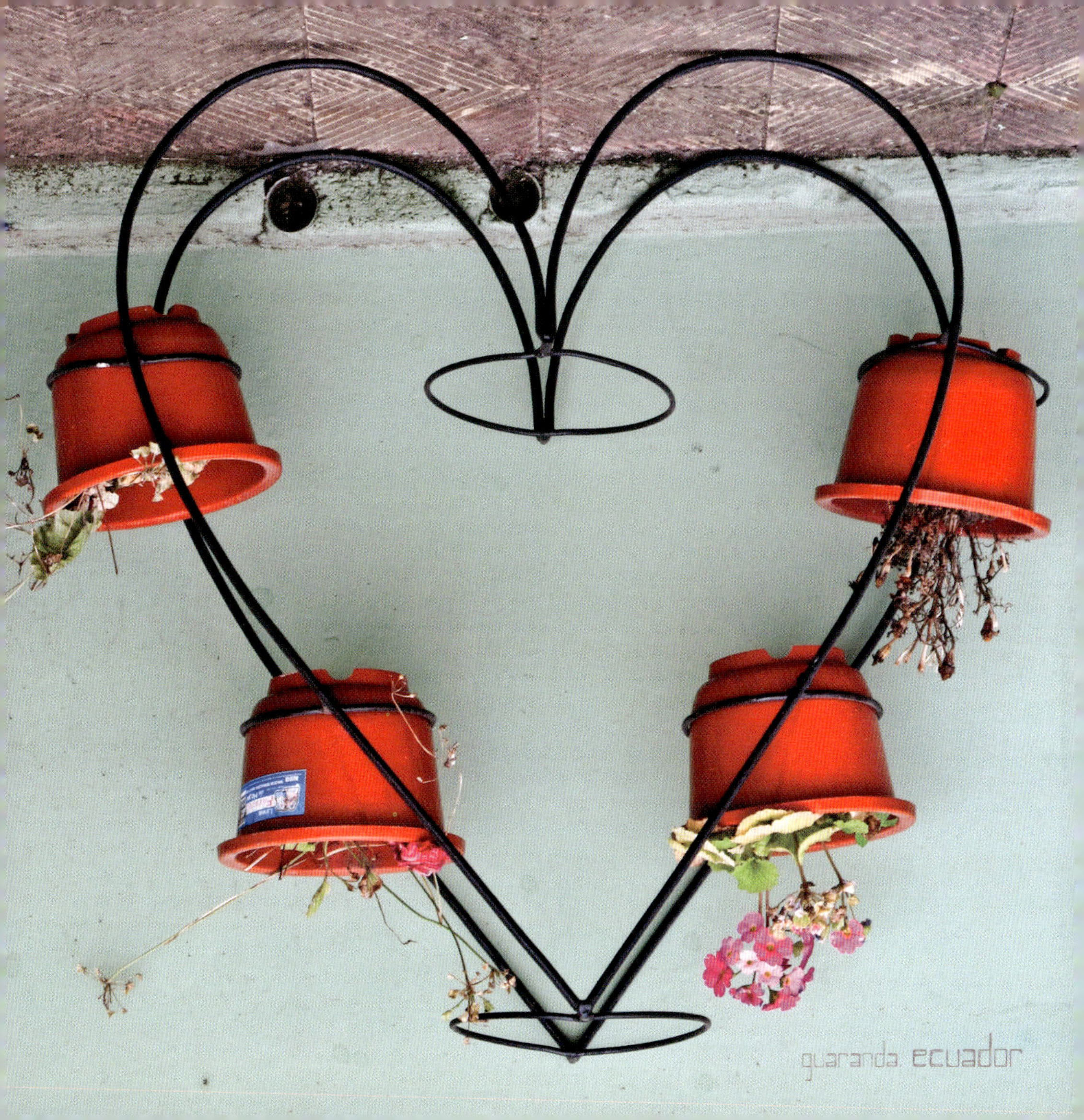
guaranda. ecuador

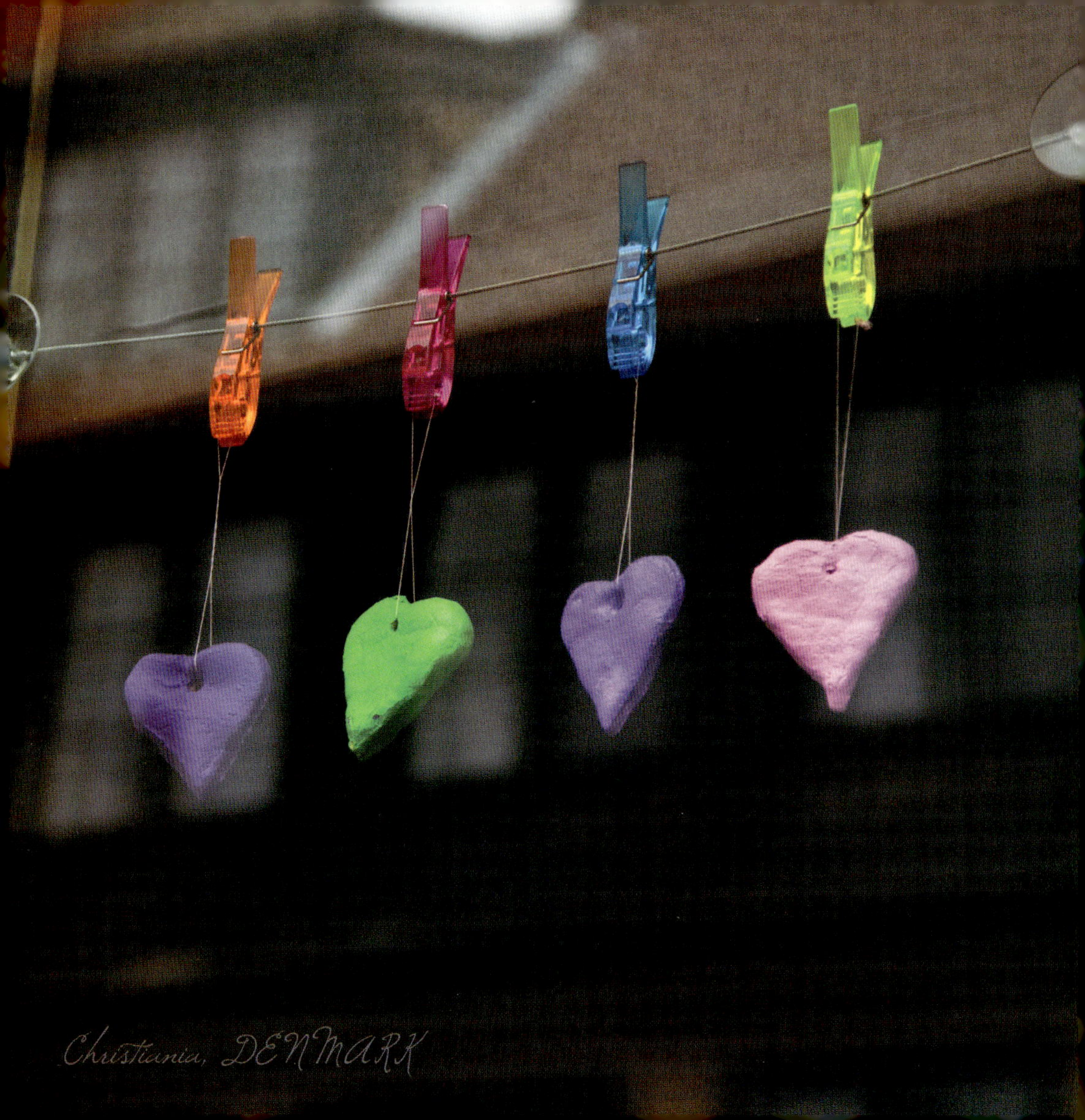
Christiania, DENMARK

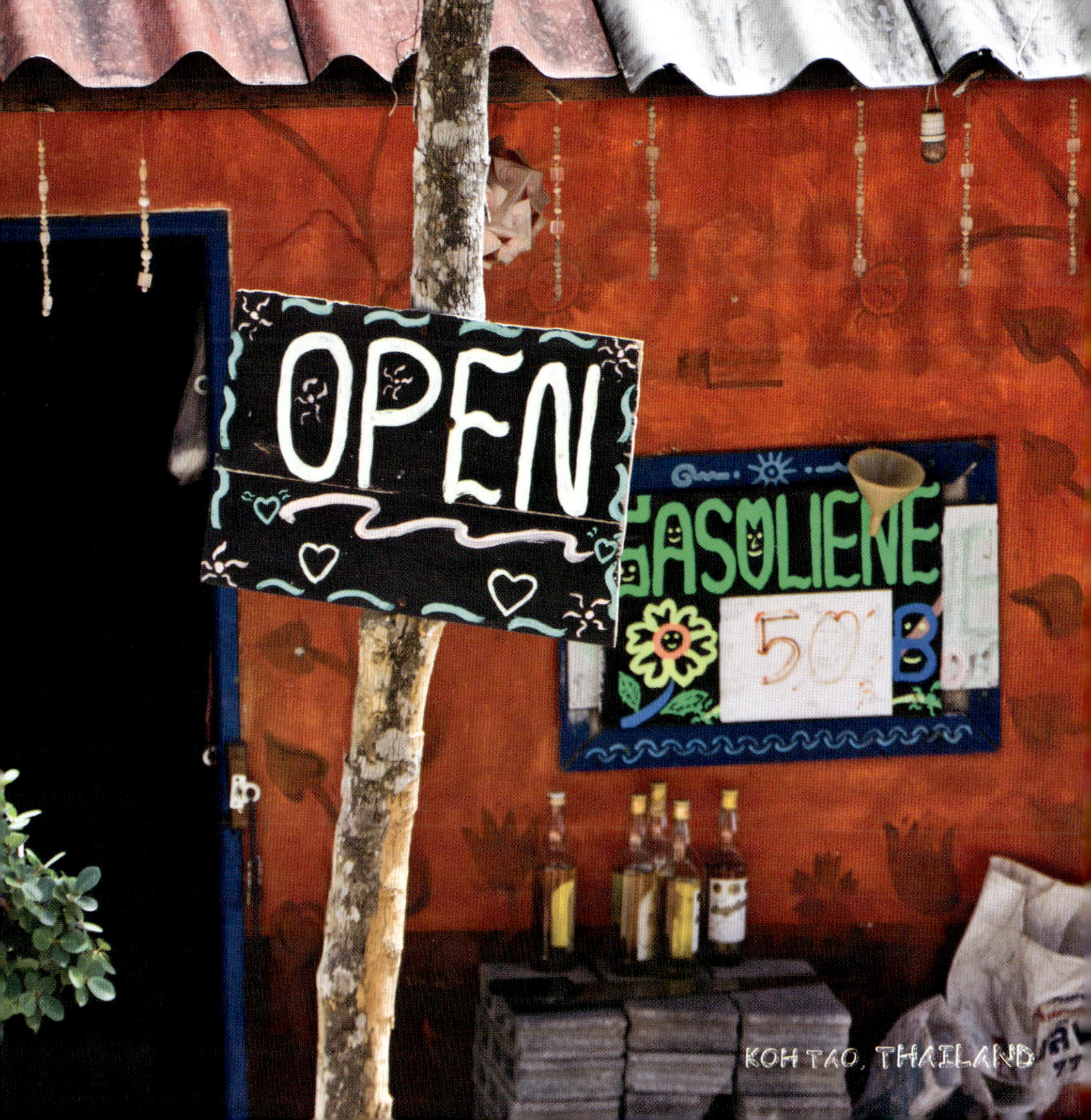
OPEN
GASOLIENE
50 B
KOH TAO, THAILAND

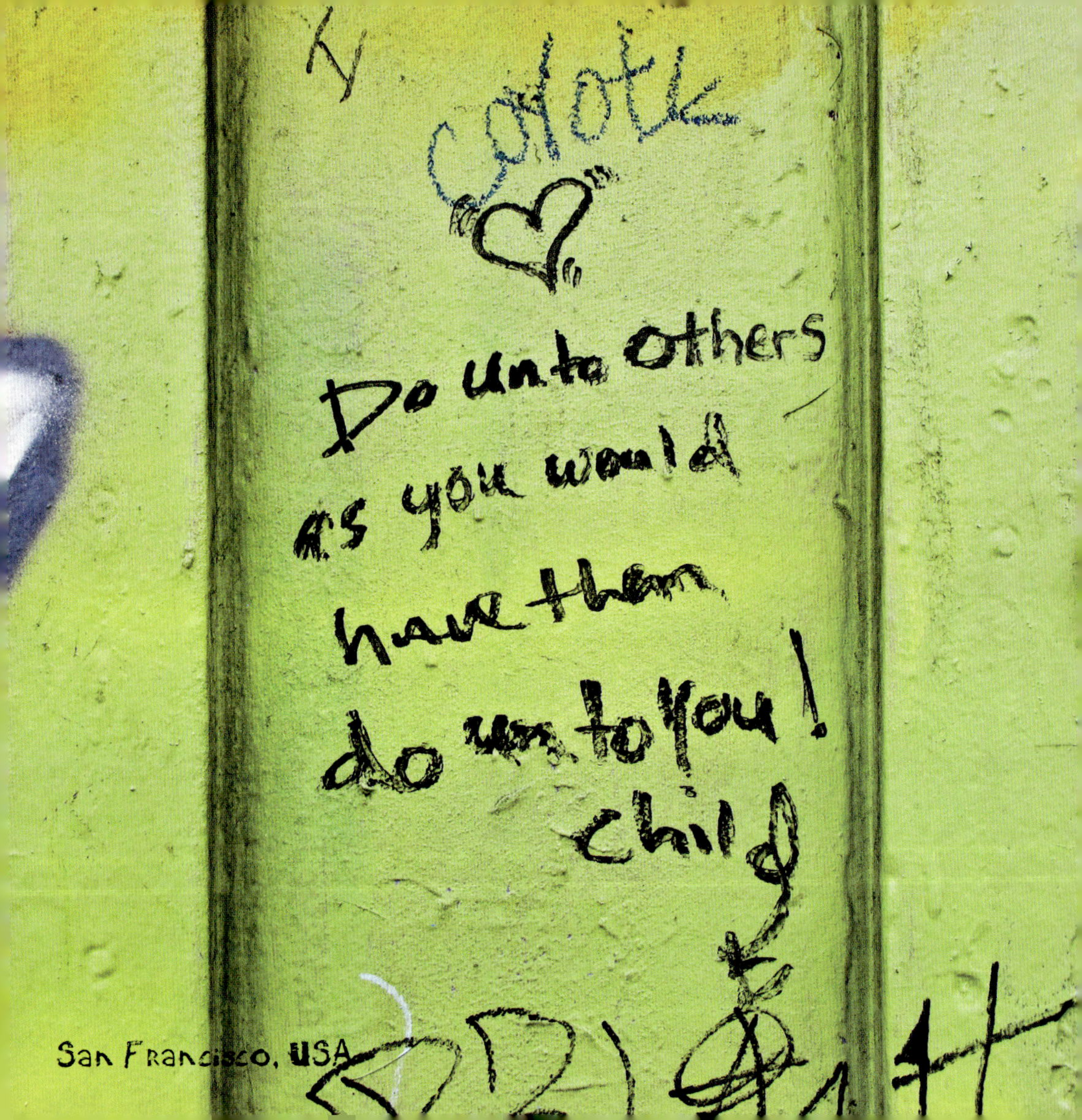

Coyote

Do unto others
as you would
have them
do unto you!
child

San Francisco, USA

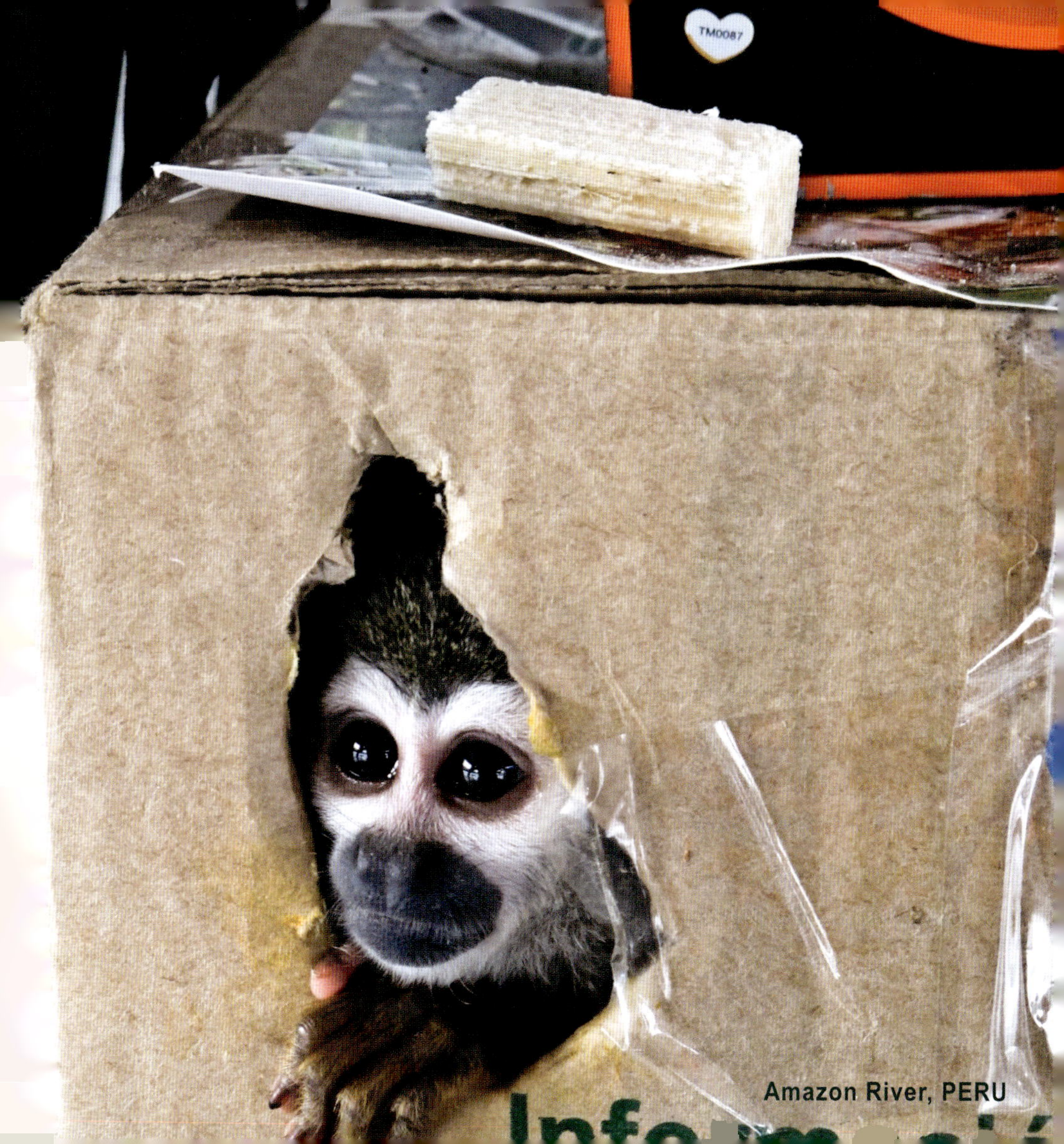
TM0087
Amazon River, PERU

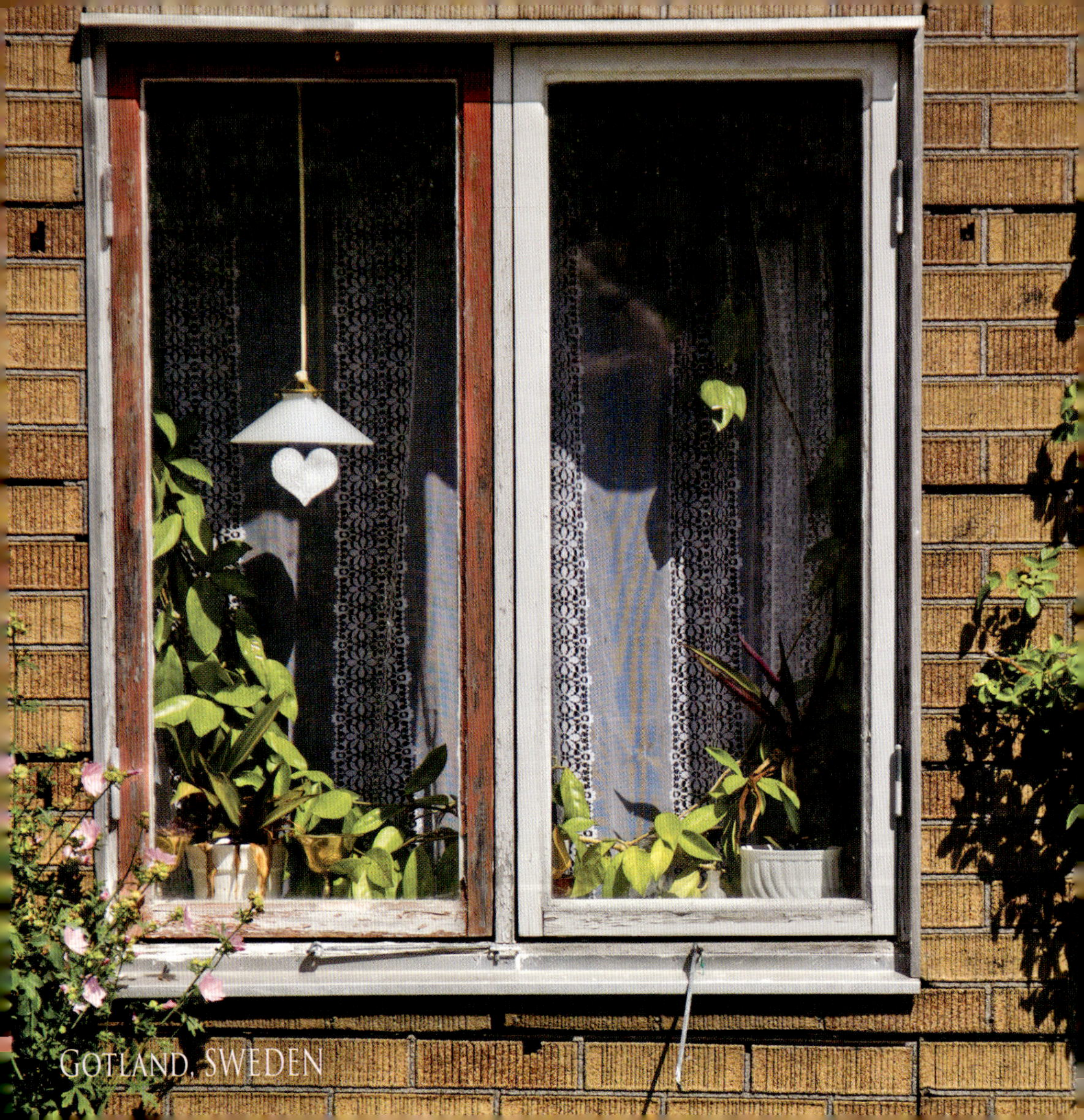

GOTLAND, SWEDEN

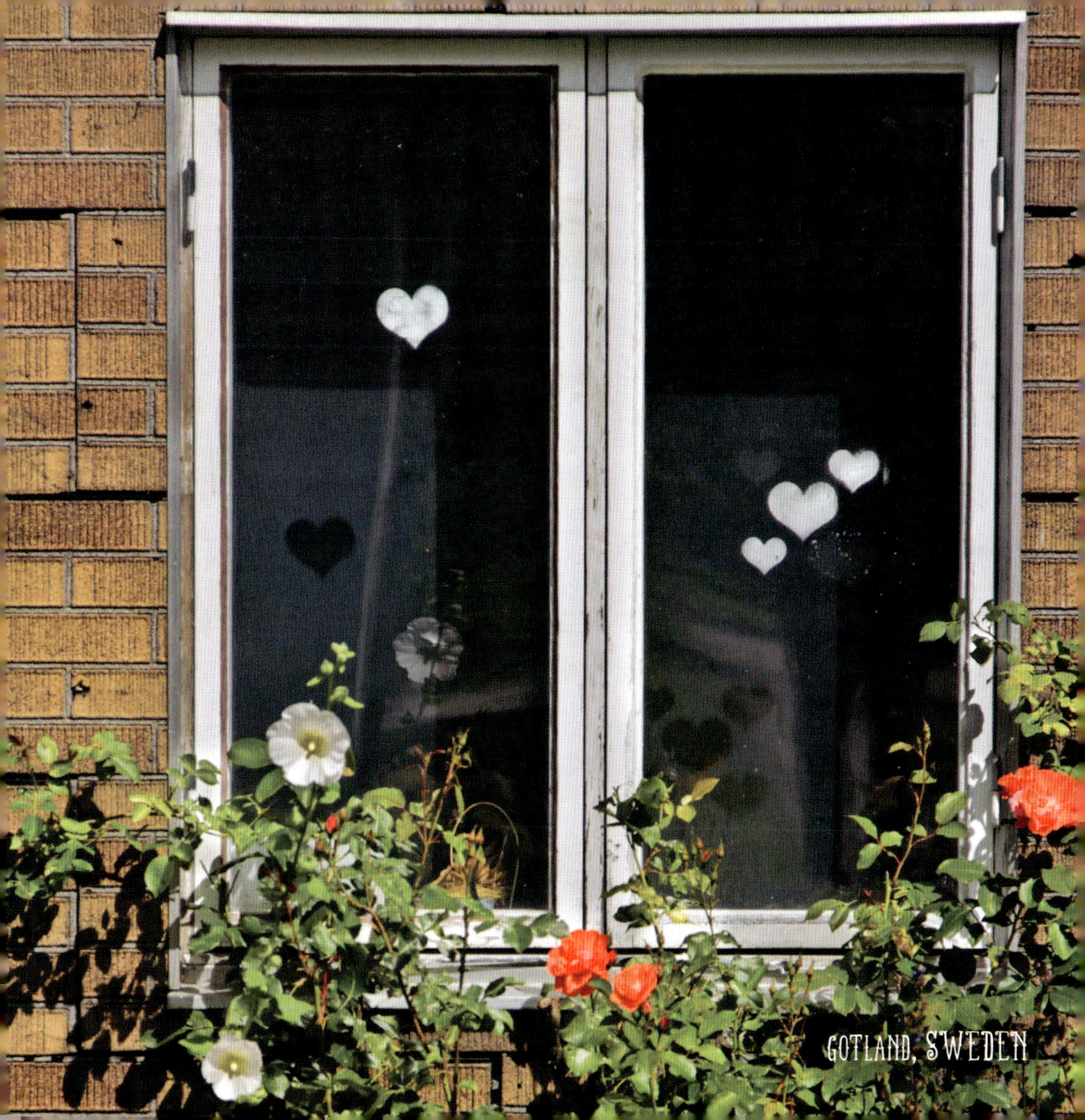
GOTLAND, SWEDEN

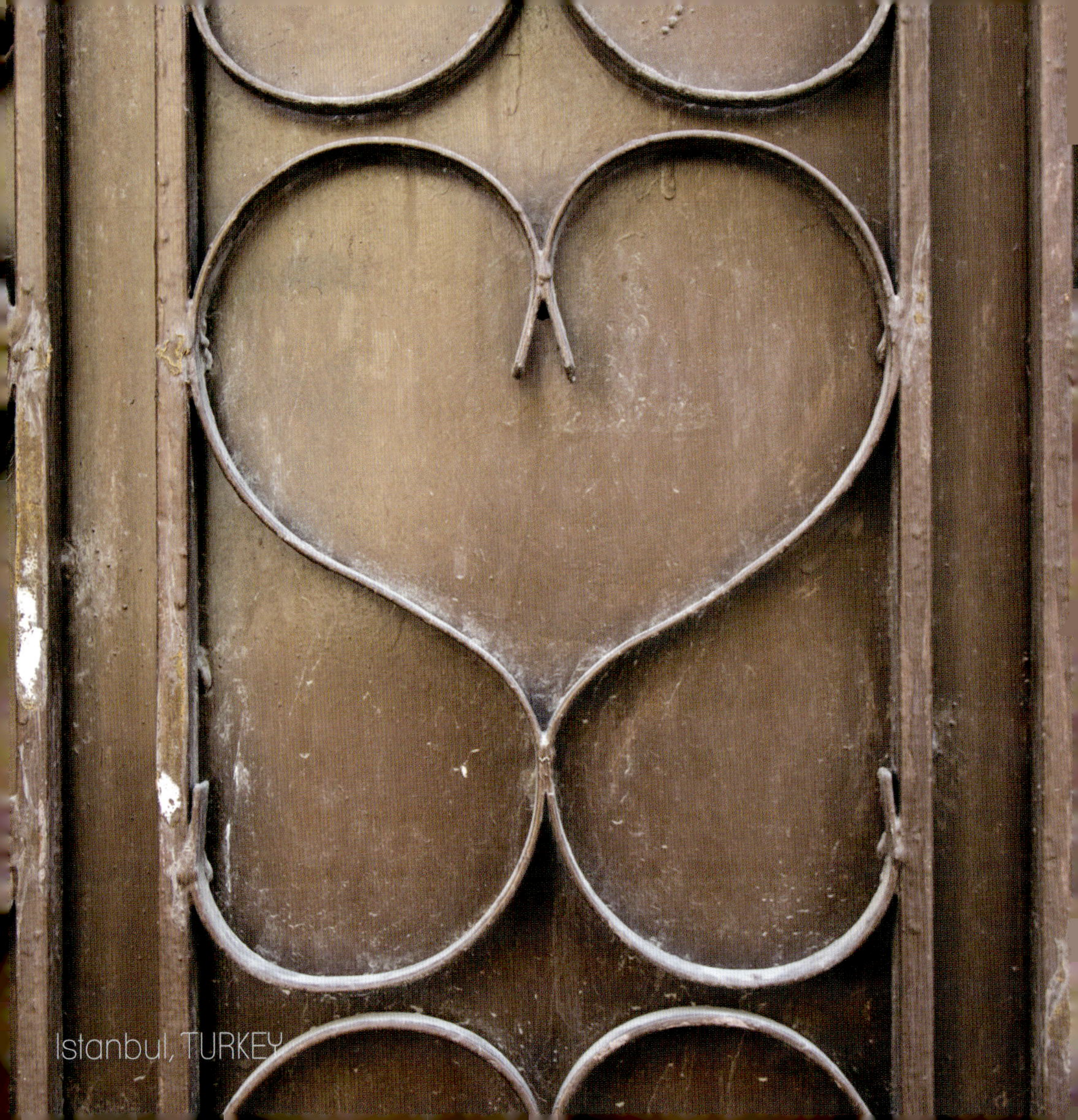

Istanbul, TURKEY

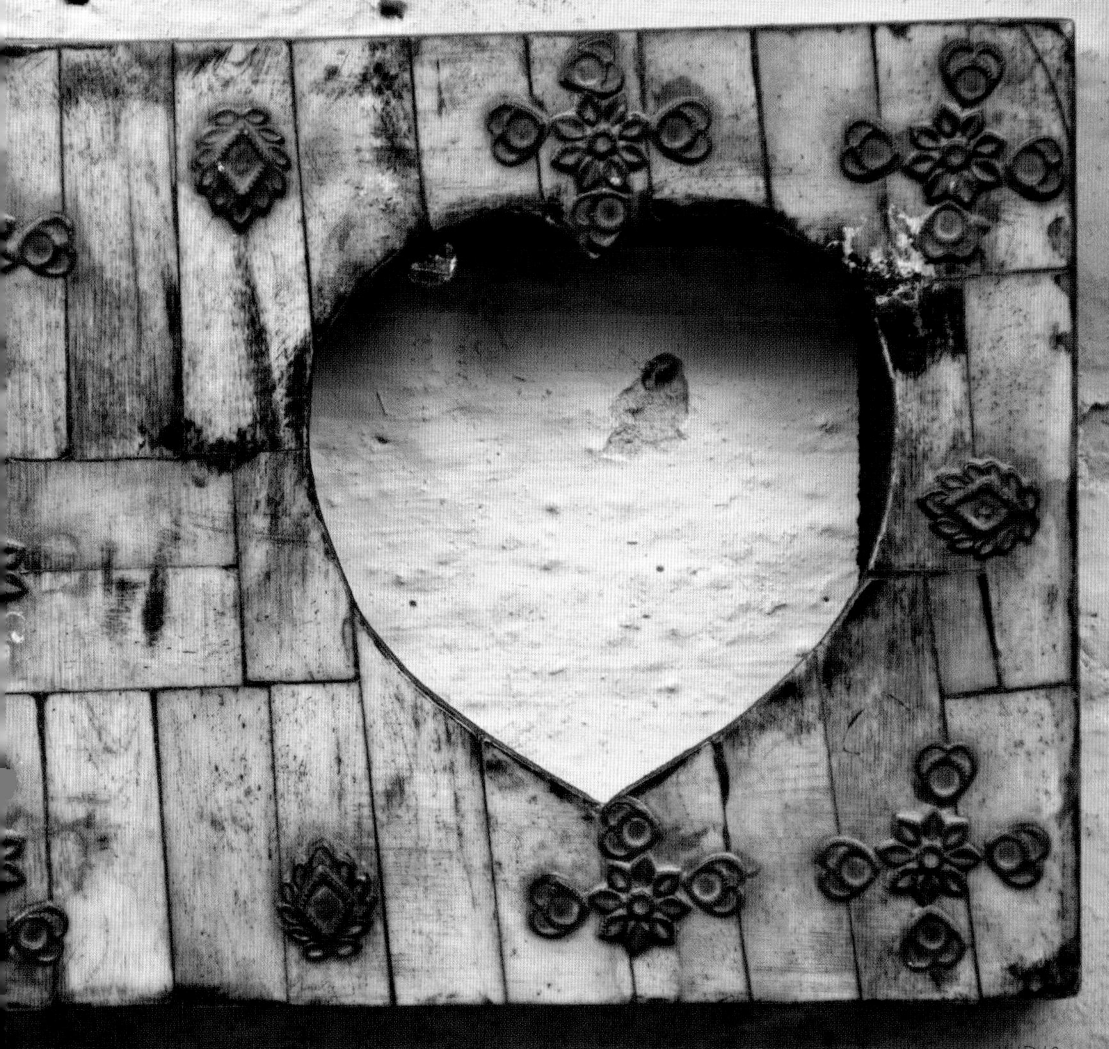

Jaisalmer, INDIA

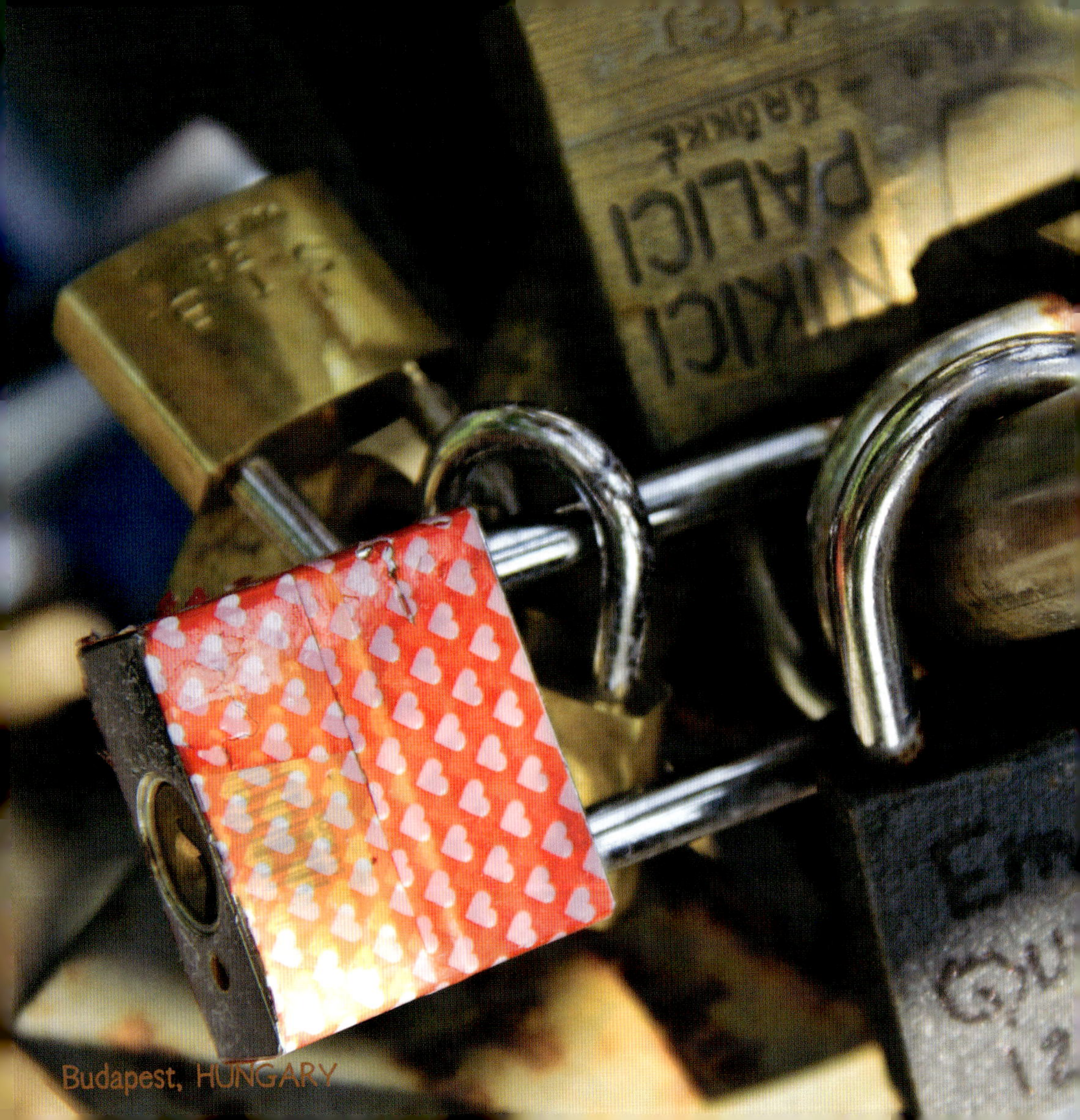

PALICI
NIKICI
Budapest, HUNGARY

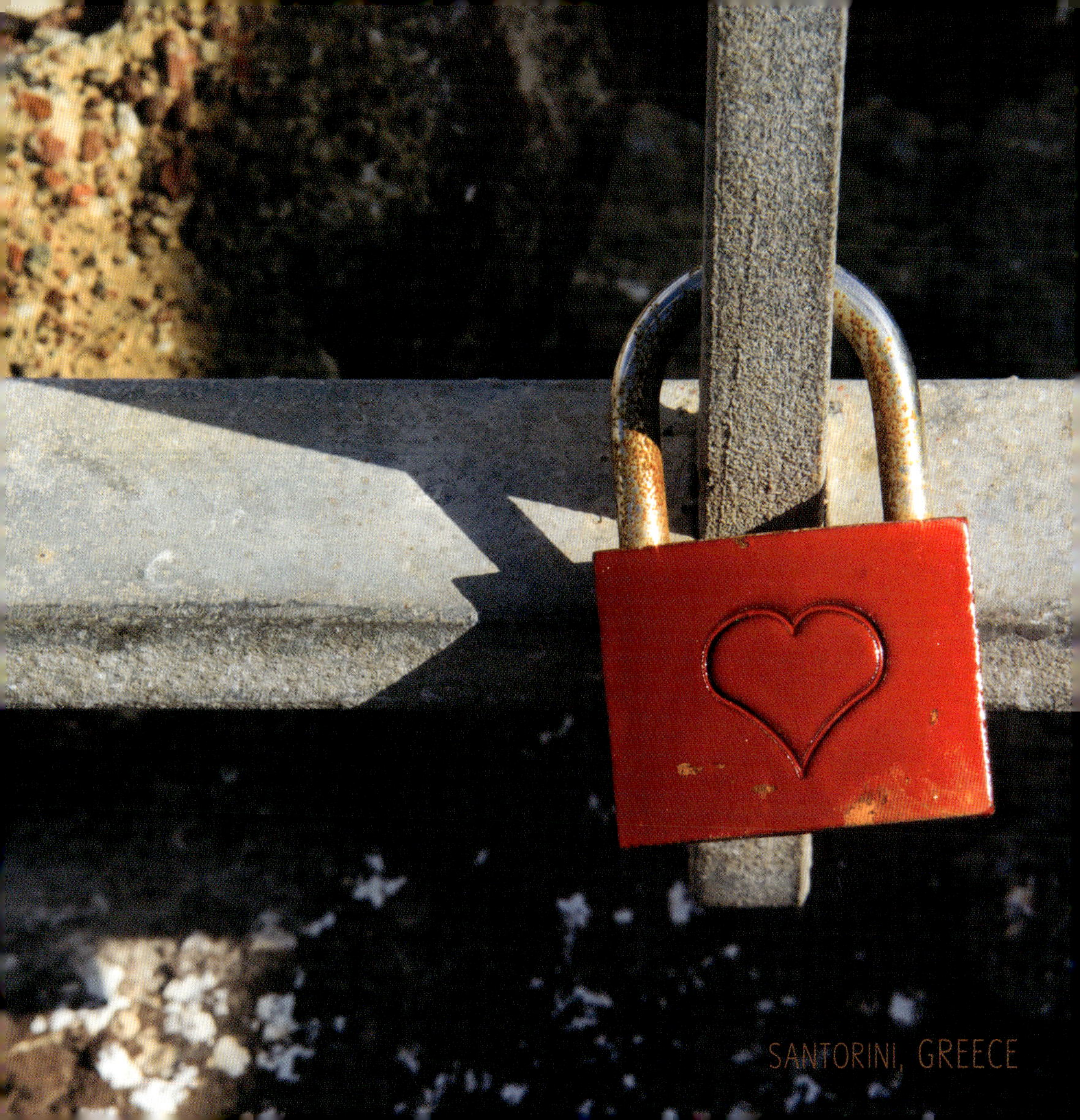
SANTORINI, GREECE

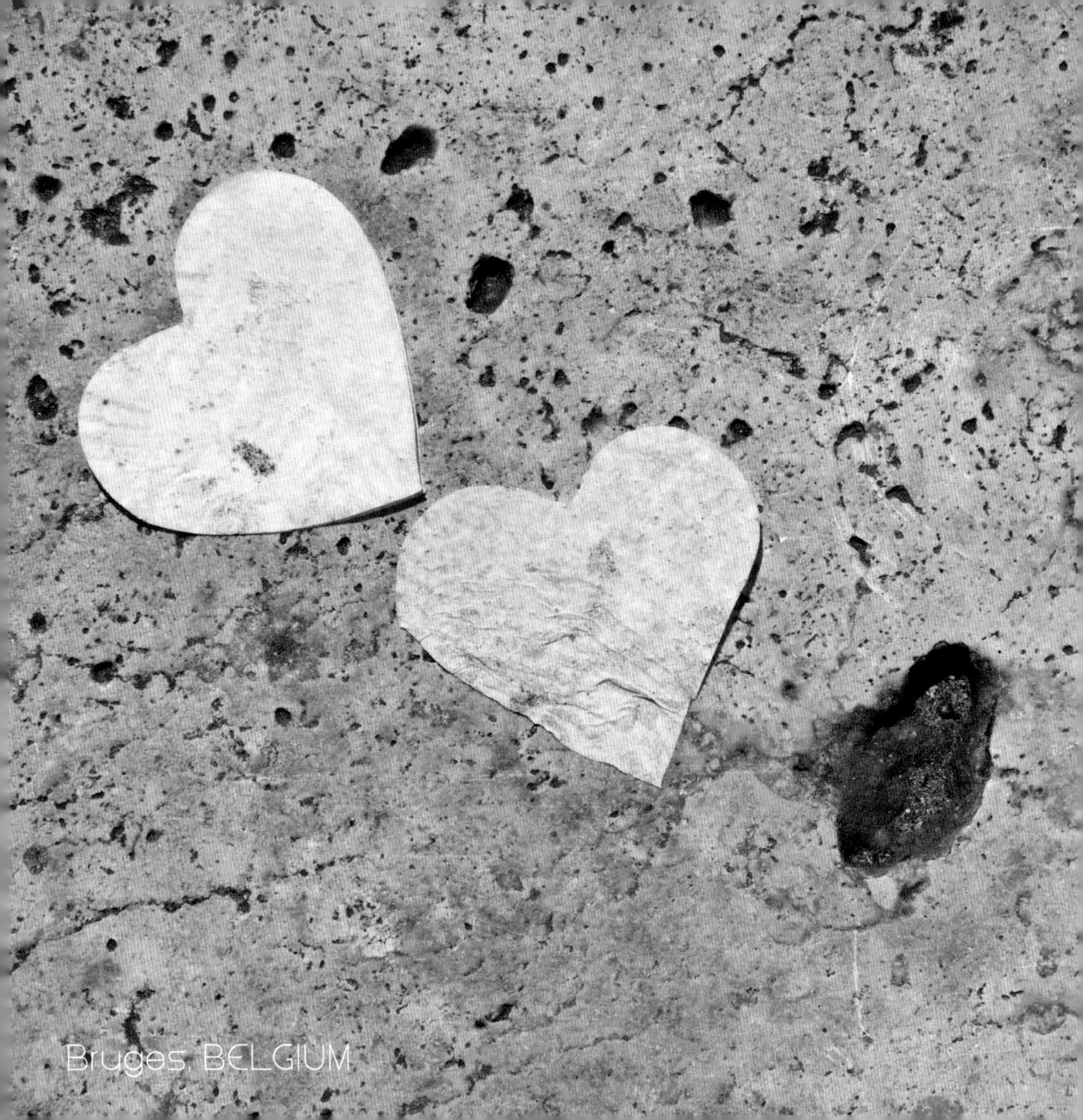

Bruges, BELGIUM

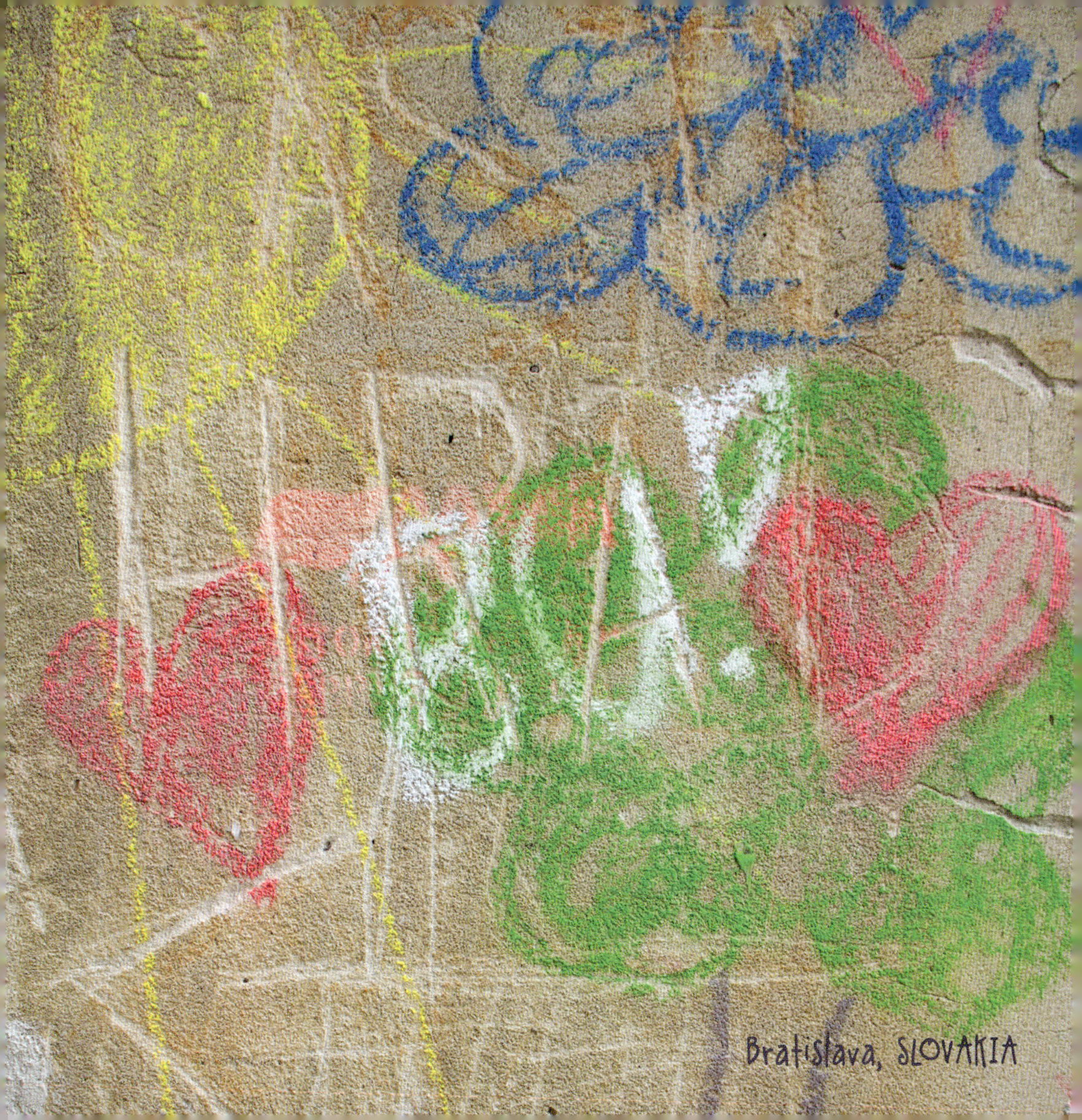

Bratislava, SLOVAKIA

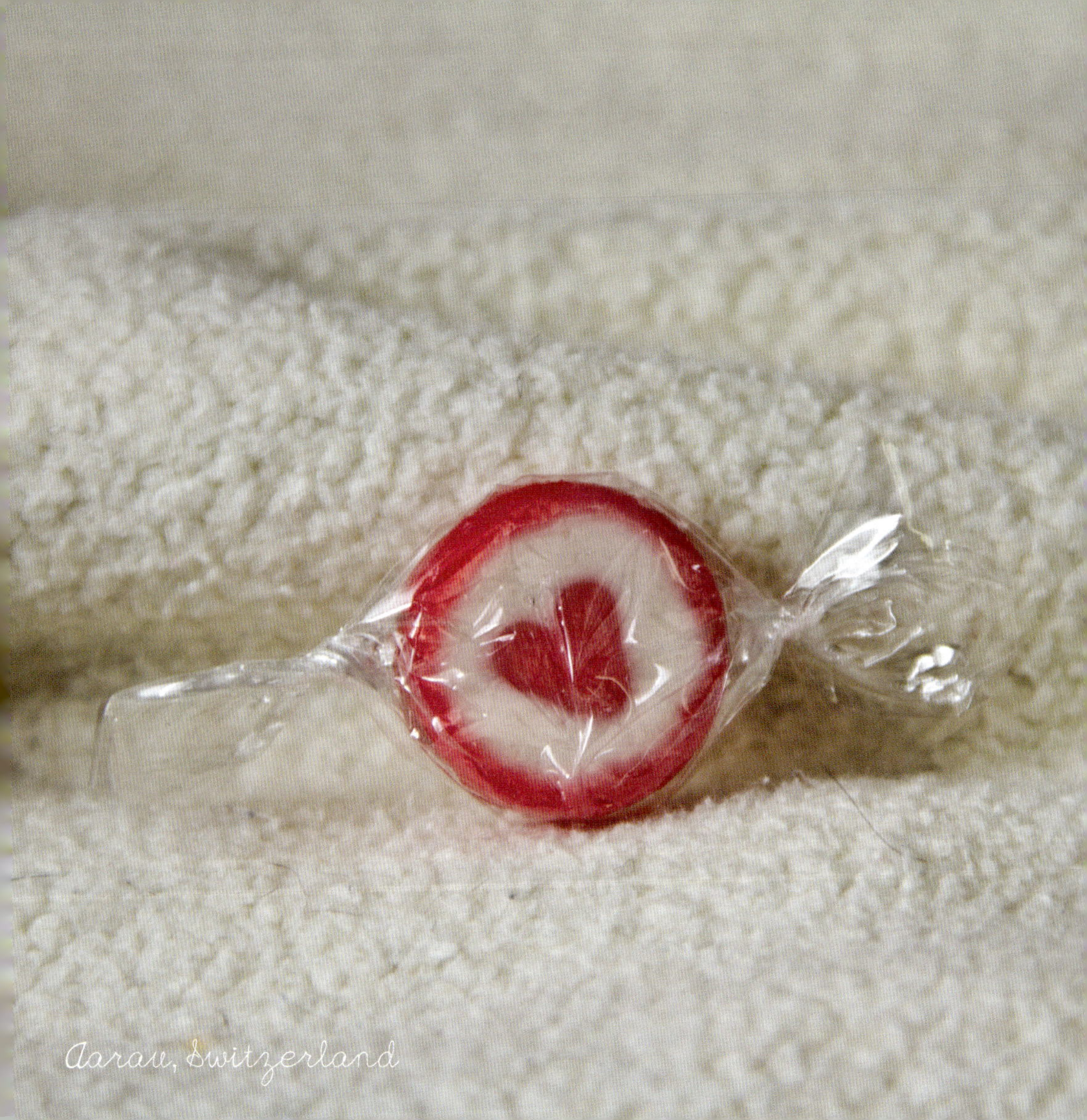

Aarau, Switzerland

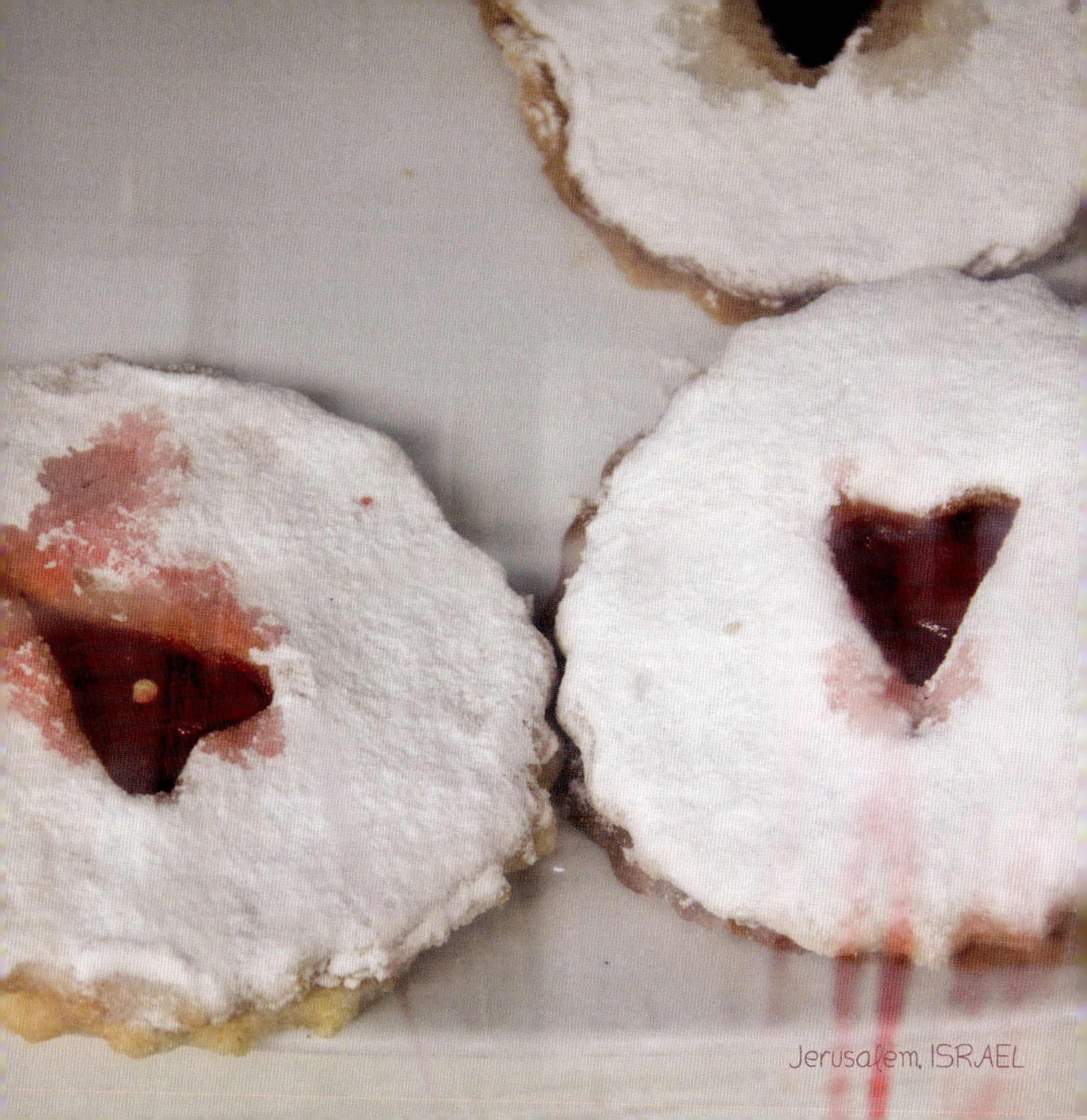
Jerusalem, ISRAEL

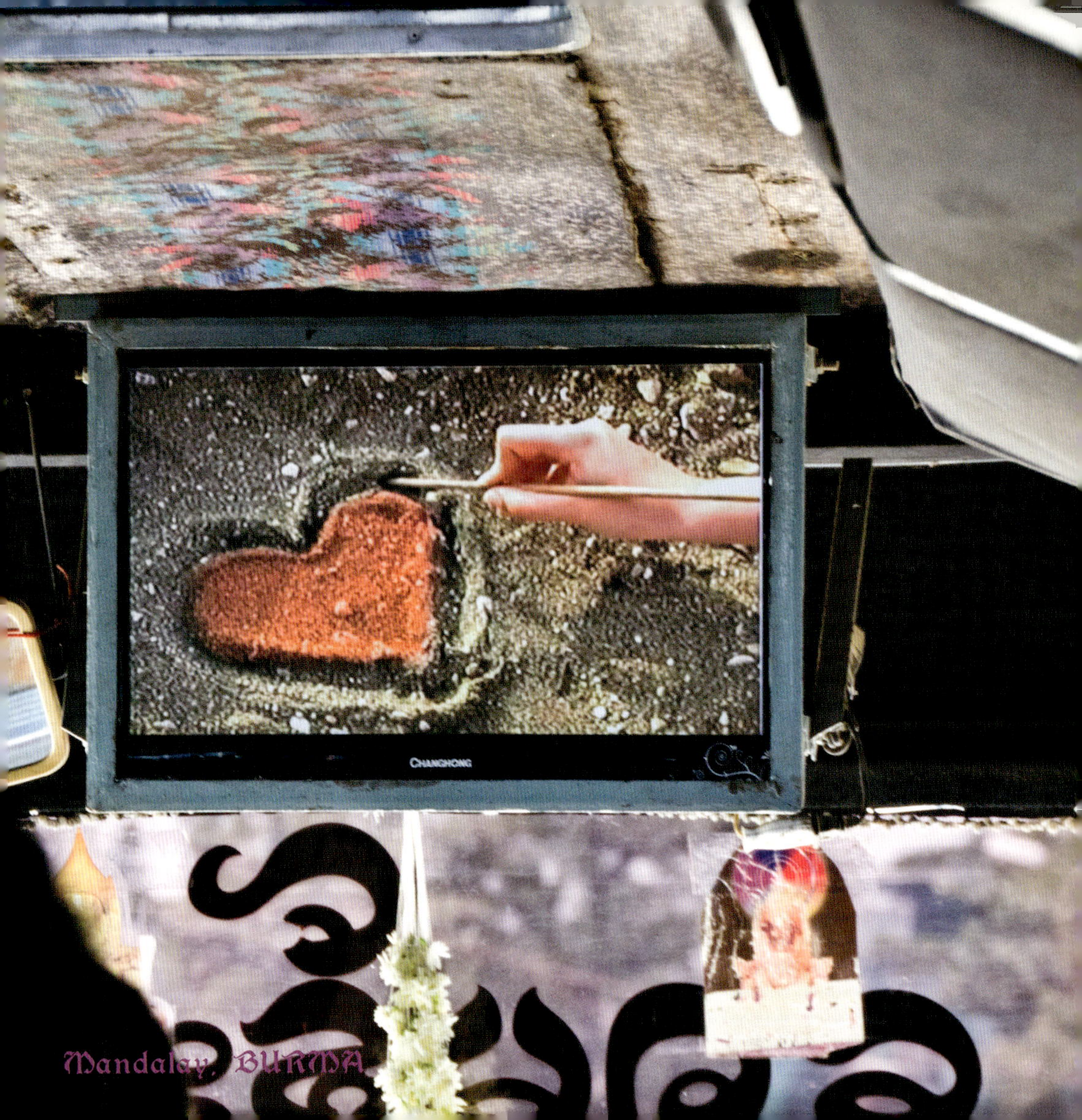
CHANGHONG
Mandalay, BURMA

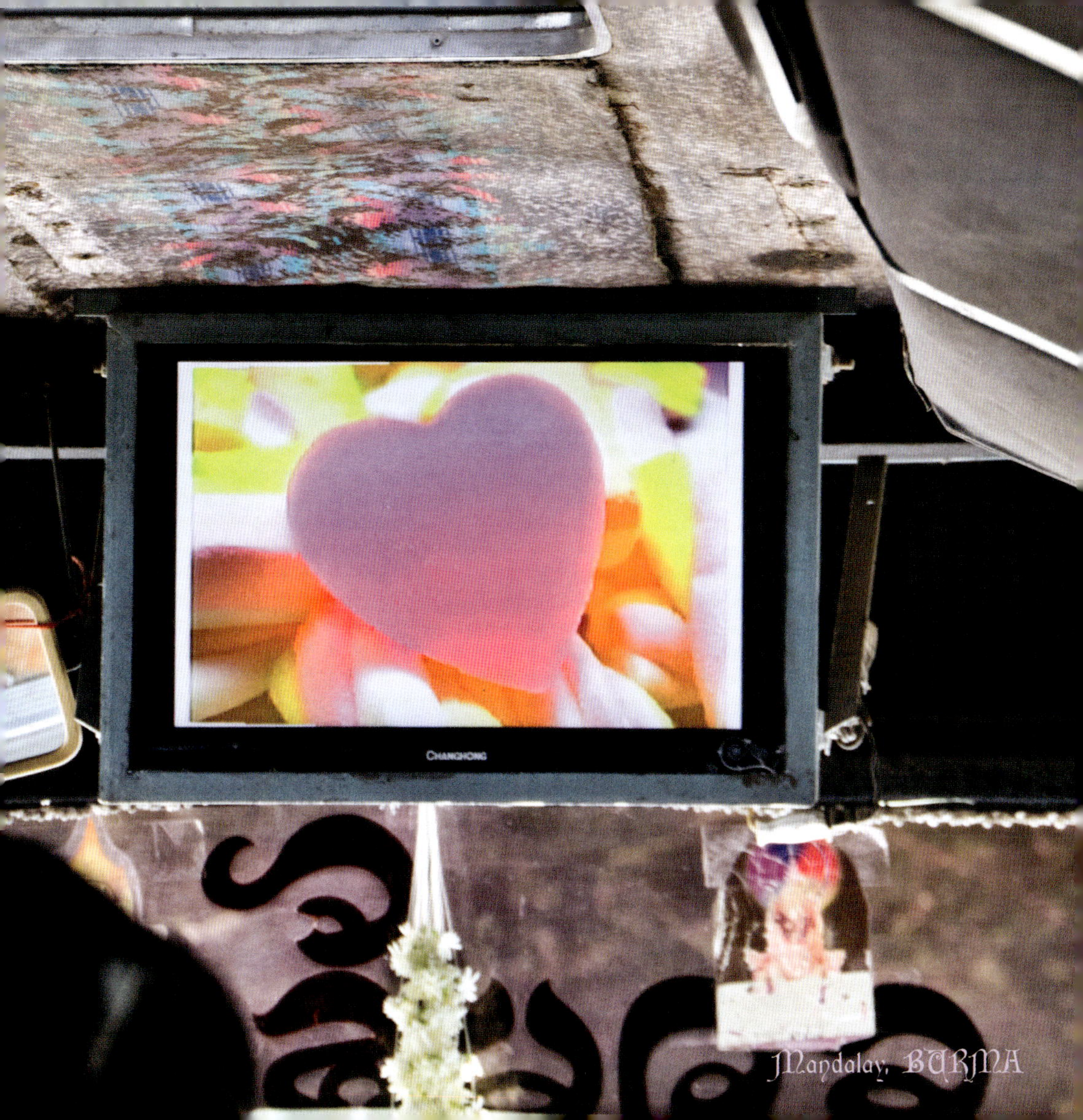
CHANGHONG
Mandalay, BURMA

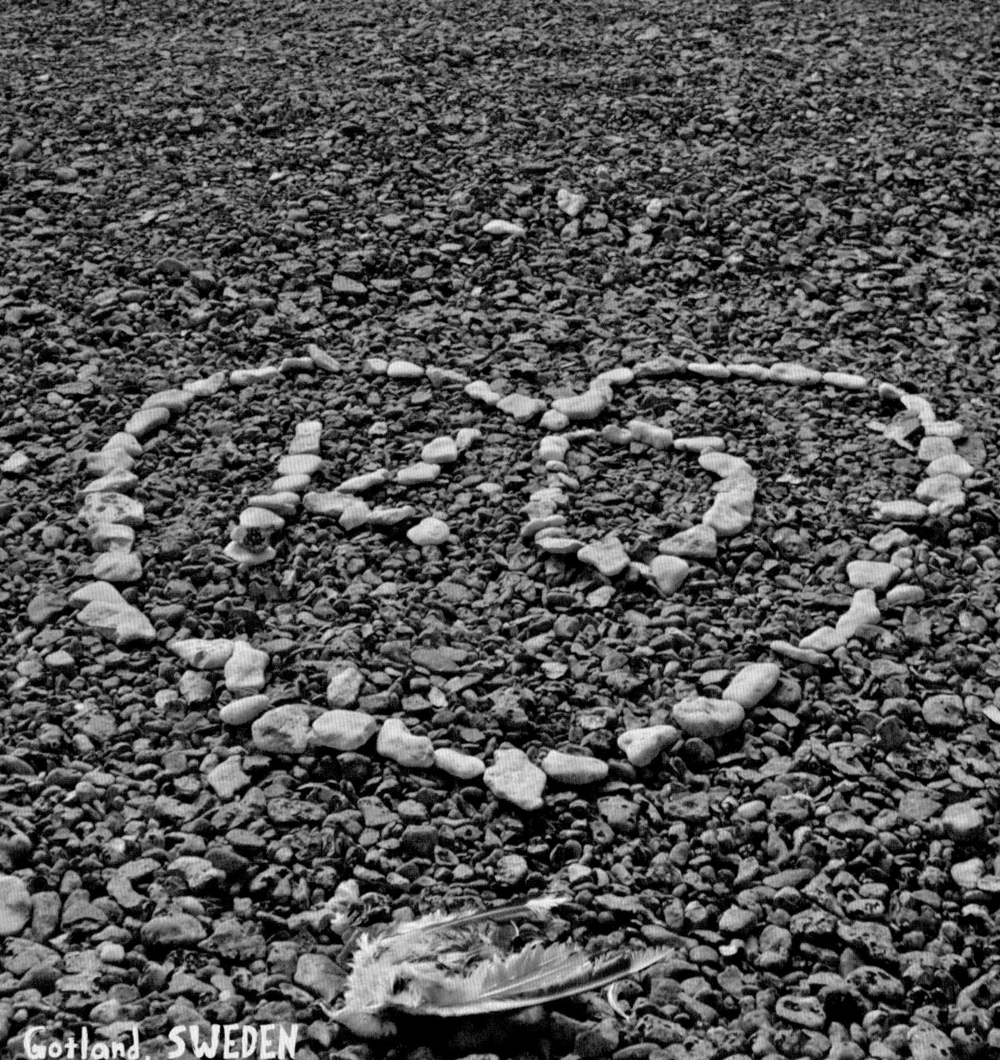
Gotland, SWEDEN

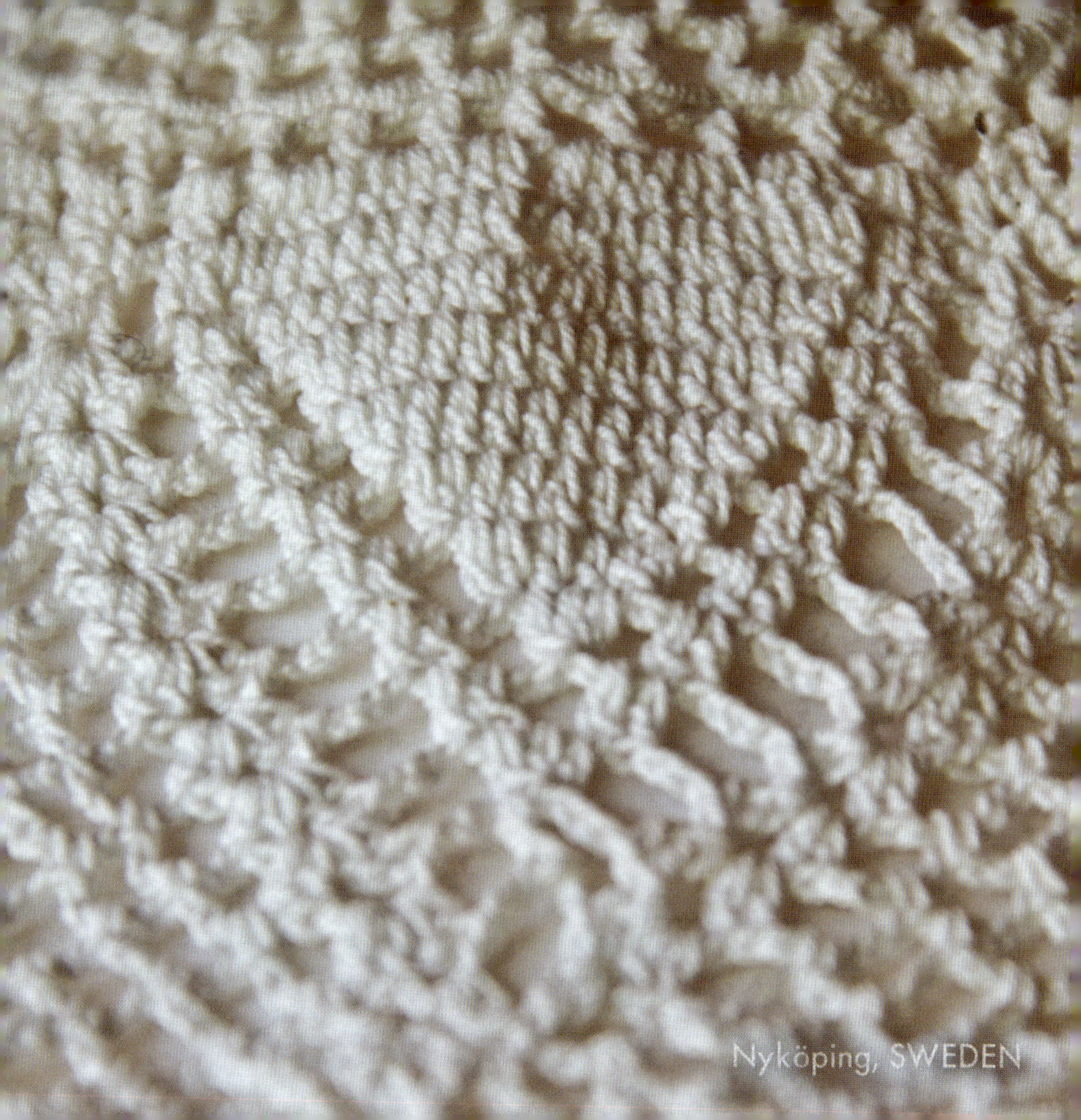
Nyköping, SWEDEN

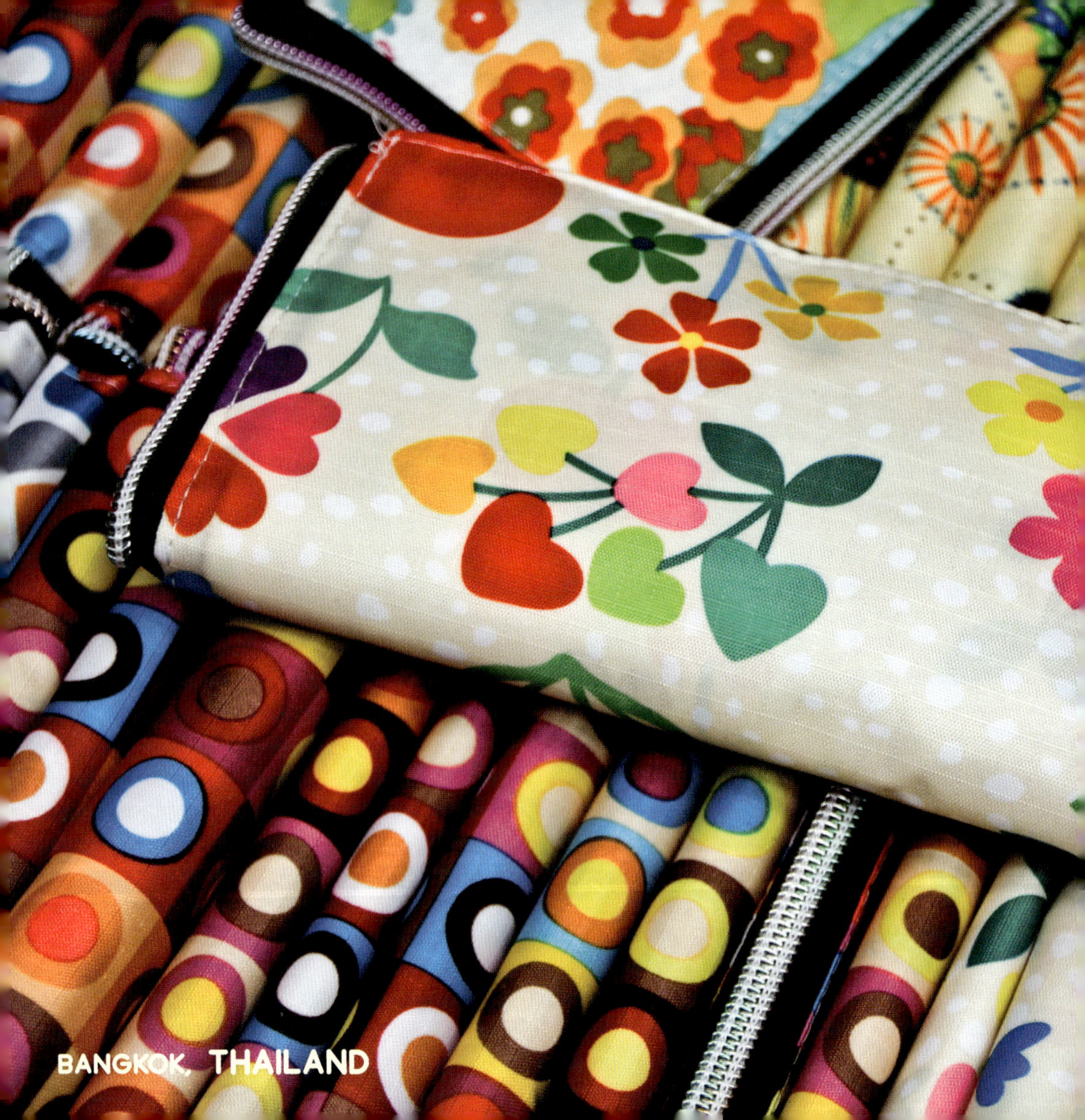
BANGKOK, THAILAND

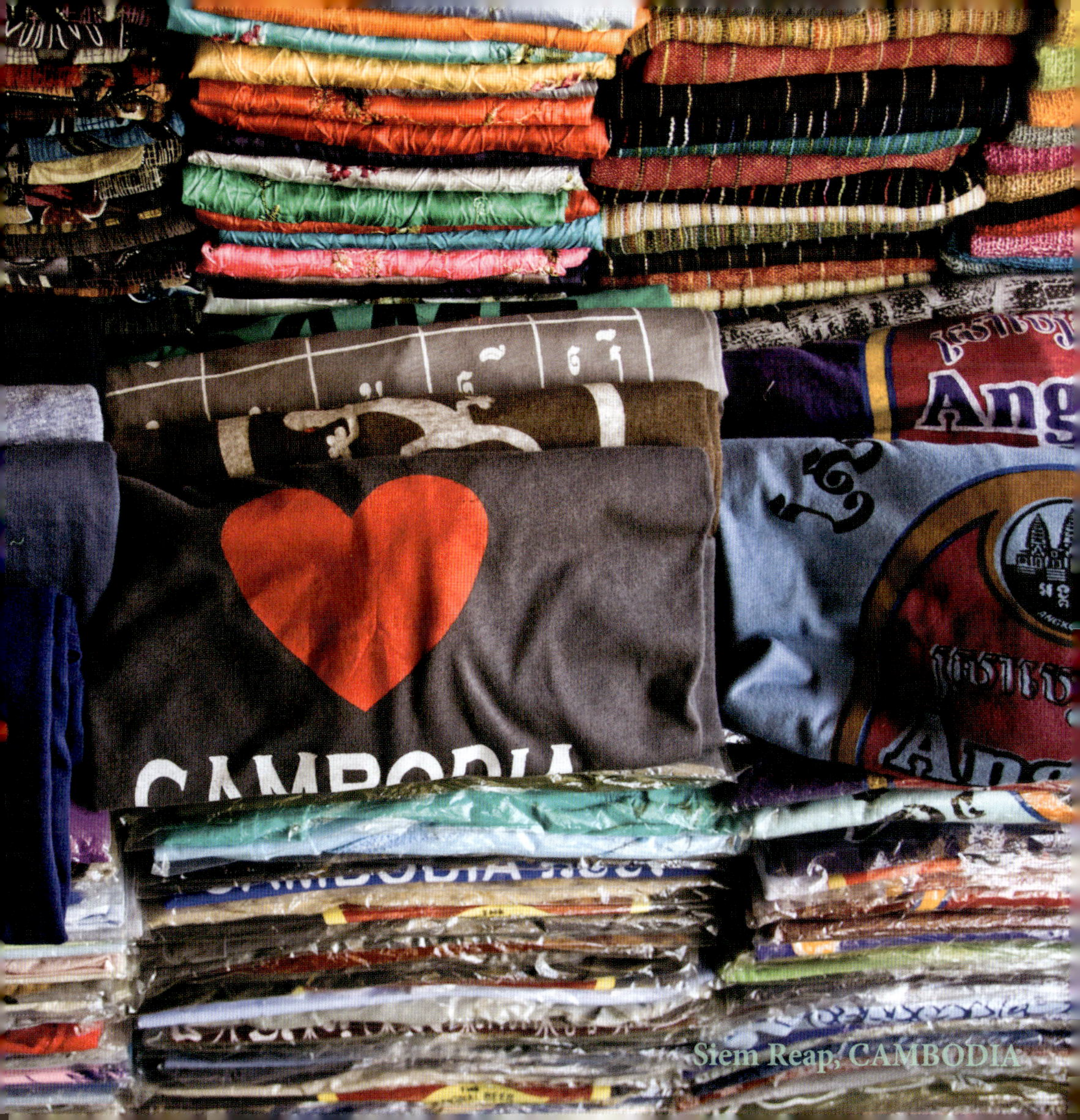
CAMBODIA
Siem Reap, CAMBODIA

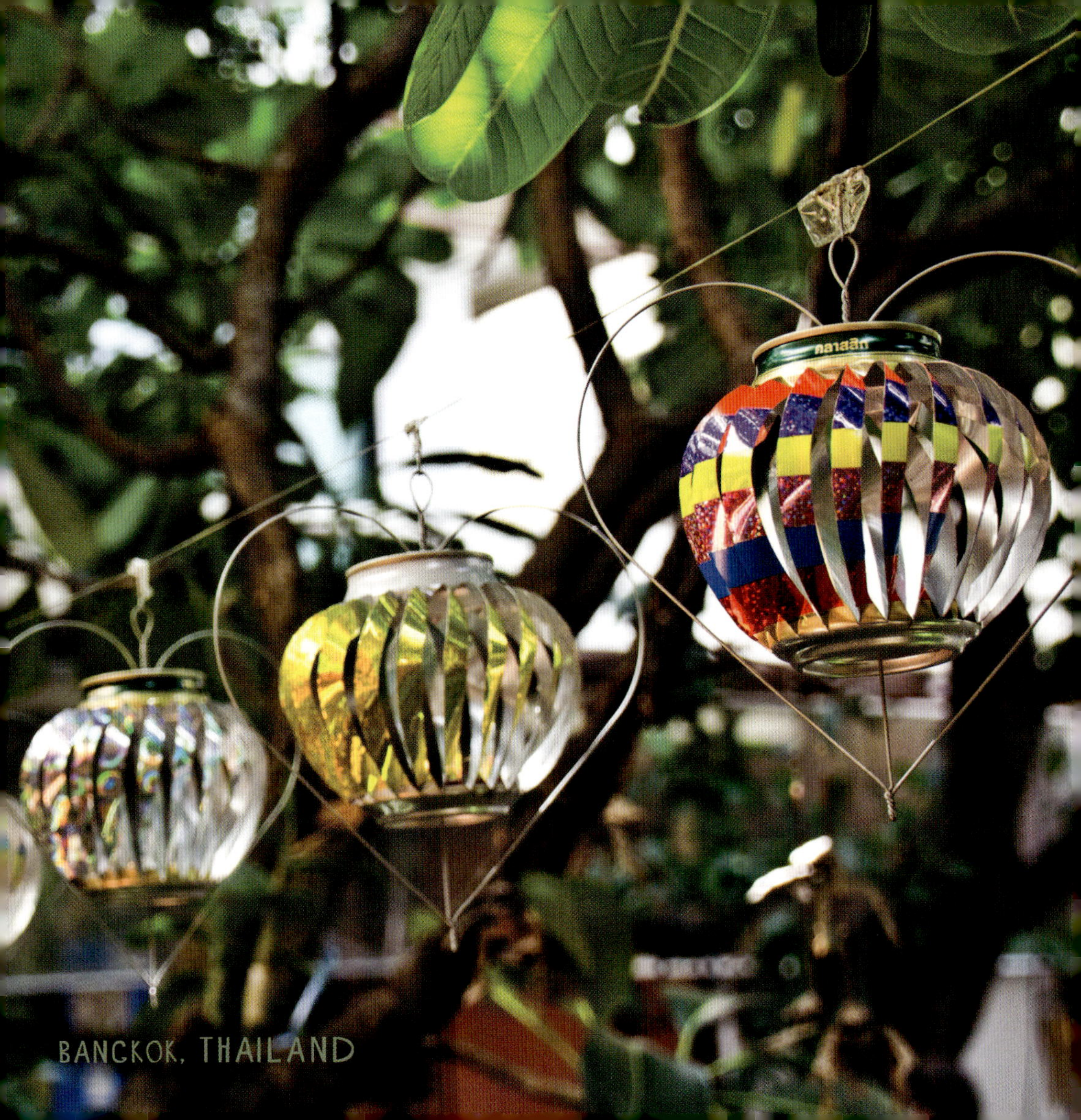
BANGKOK, THAILAND

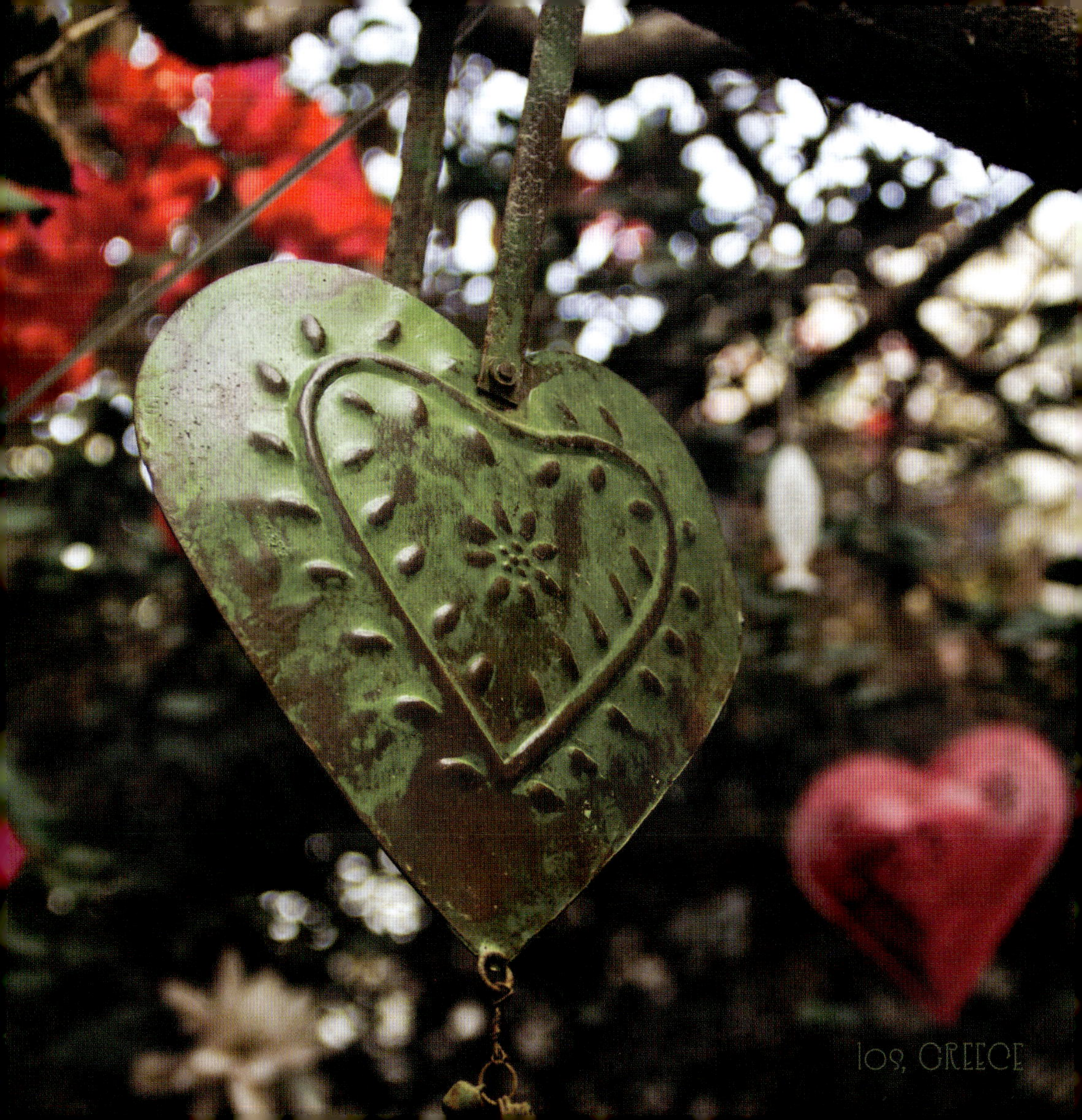
Ios, GREECE

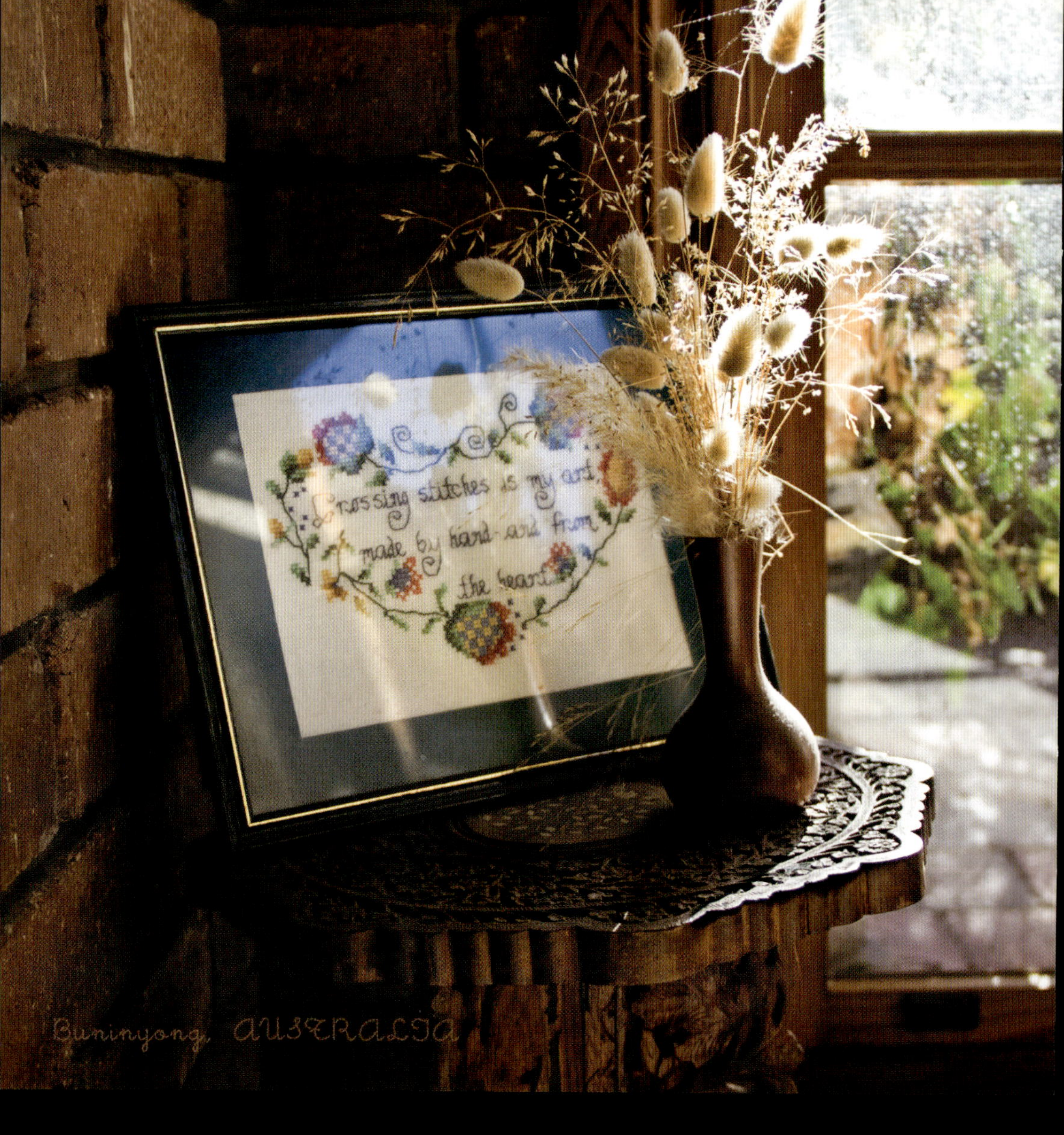

Crossing stitches is my art,
made by hand and from
the heart
Buninyong, AUSTRALIA

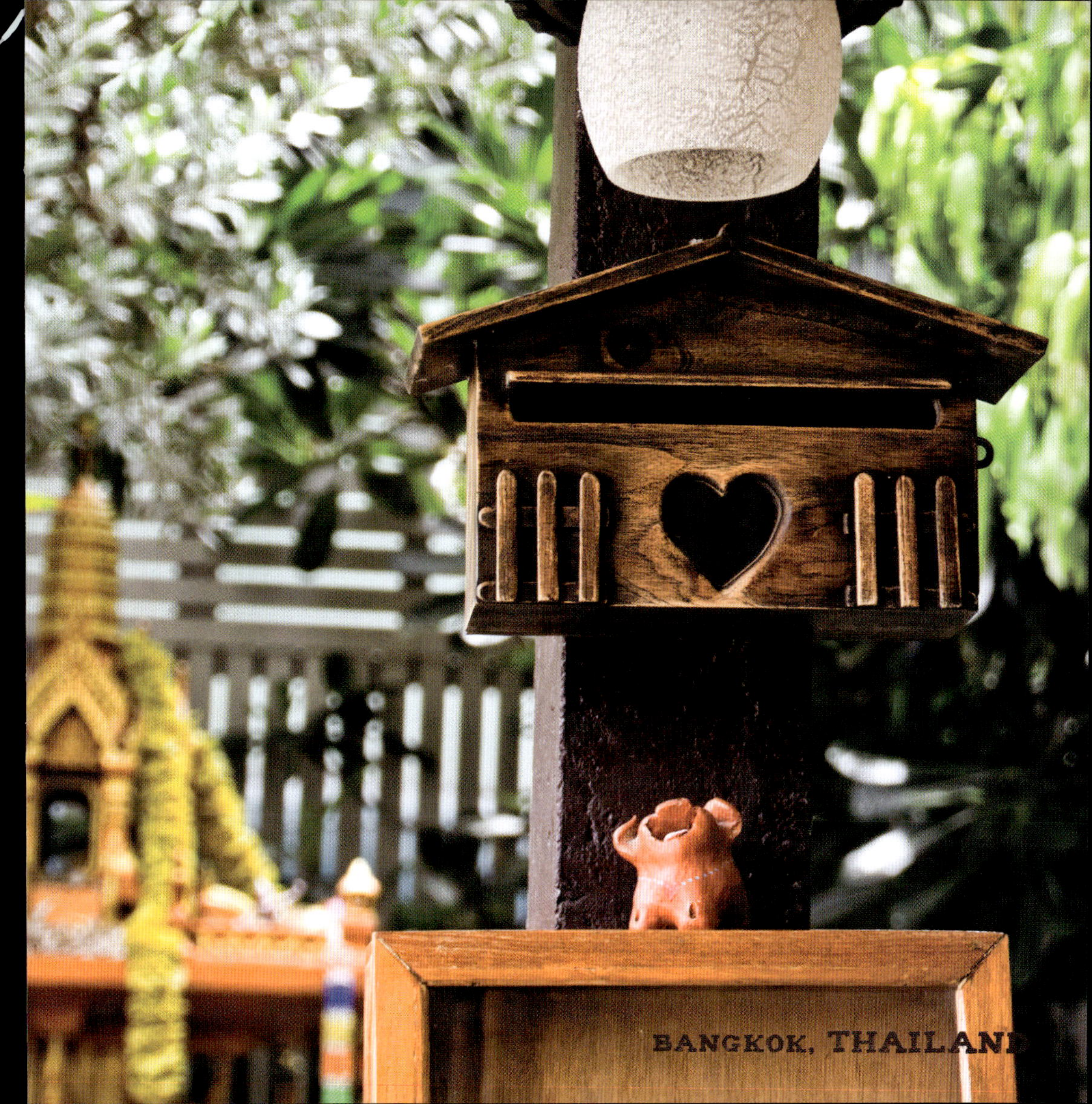

BANGKOK, THAILAND

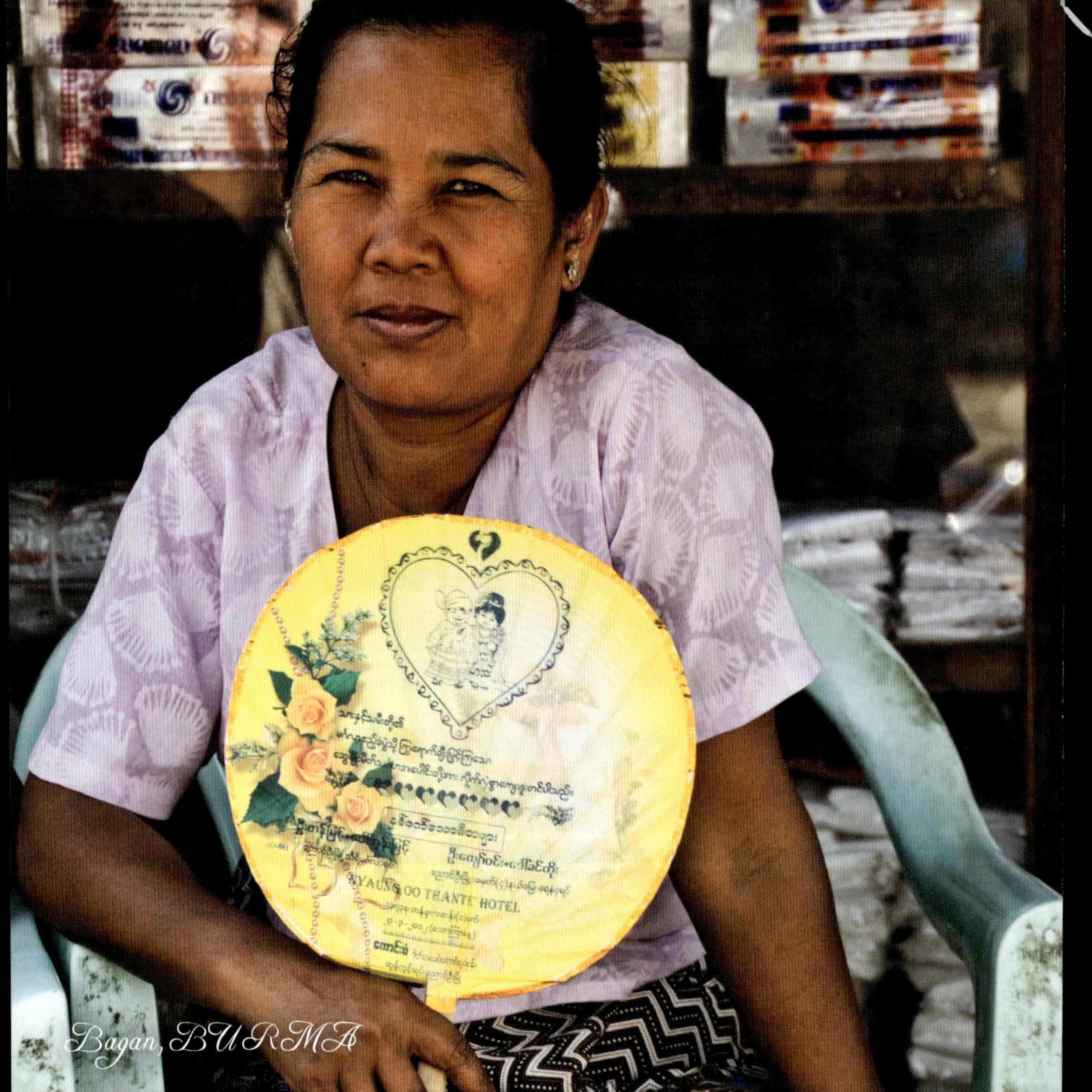
NYAUNG OO THANTE HOTEL
Bagan, BURMA

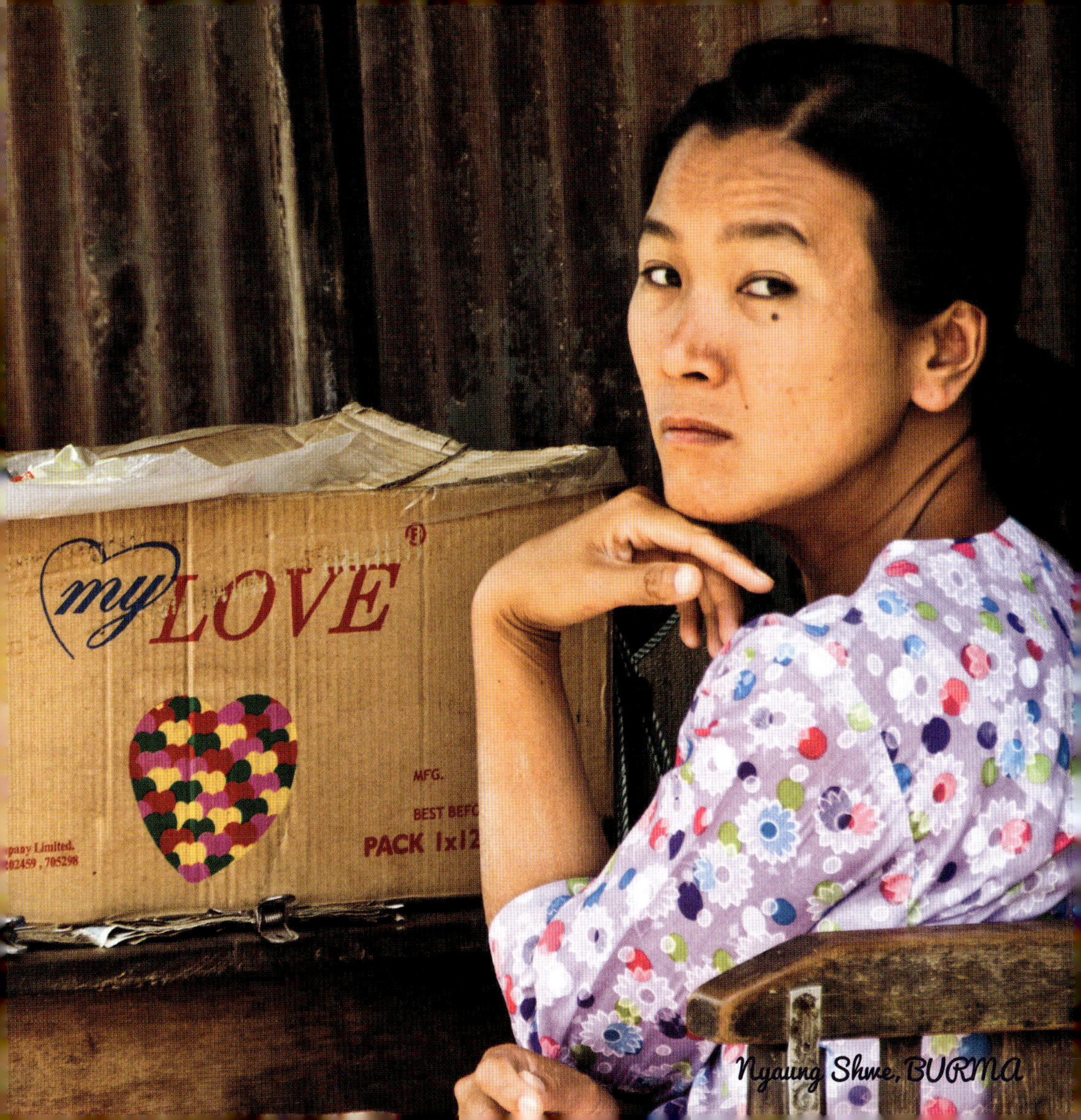
my LOVE
MFG.
BEST BEFO
PACK 1x12
pany Limited.
02459 , 705298
Nyaung Shwe, BURMA

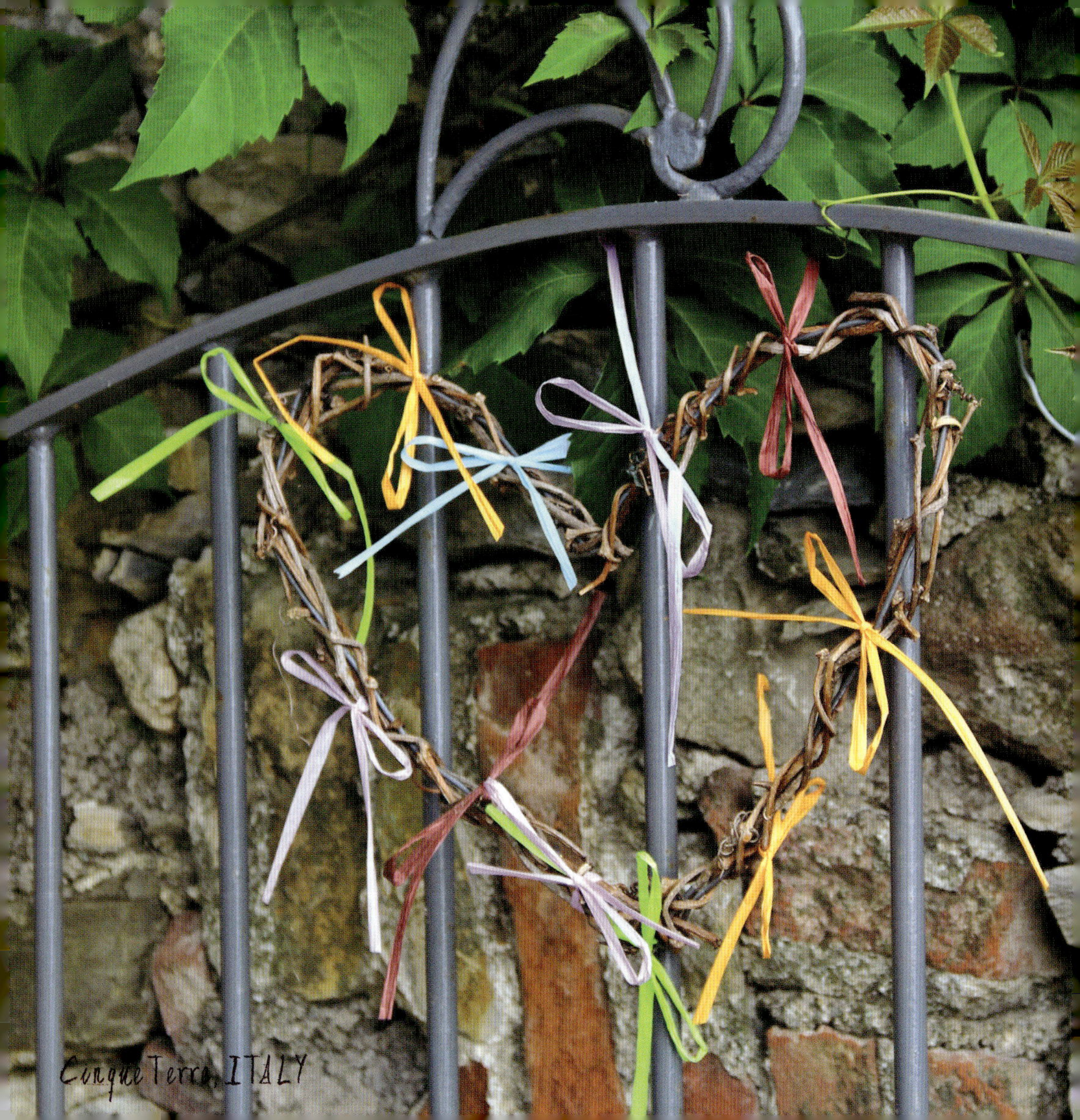

Cinque Terra, ITALY

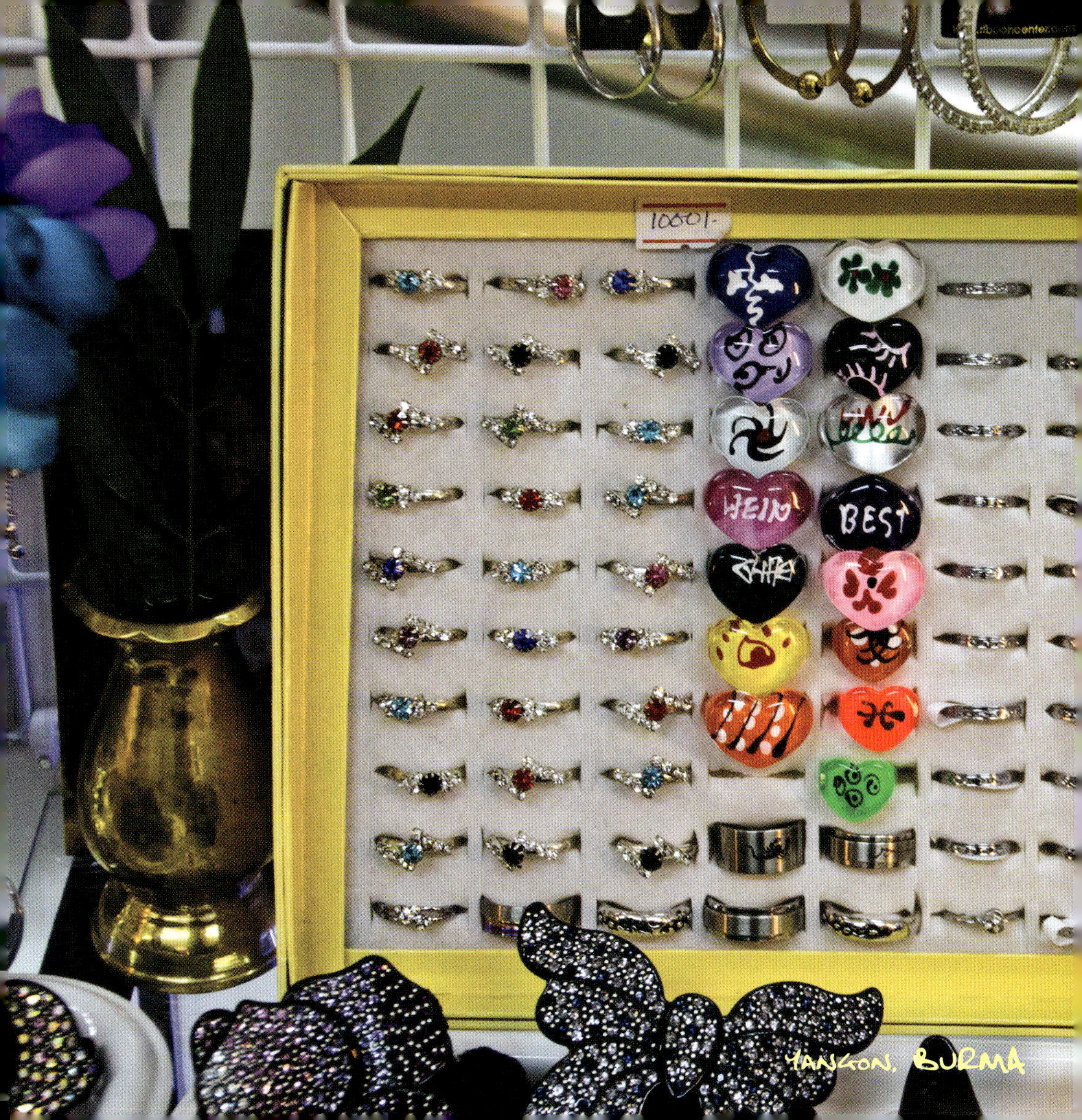

10001-
BEST
YANGON, BURMA

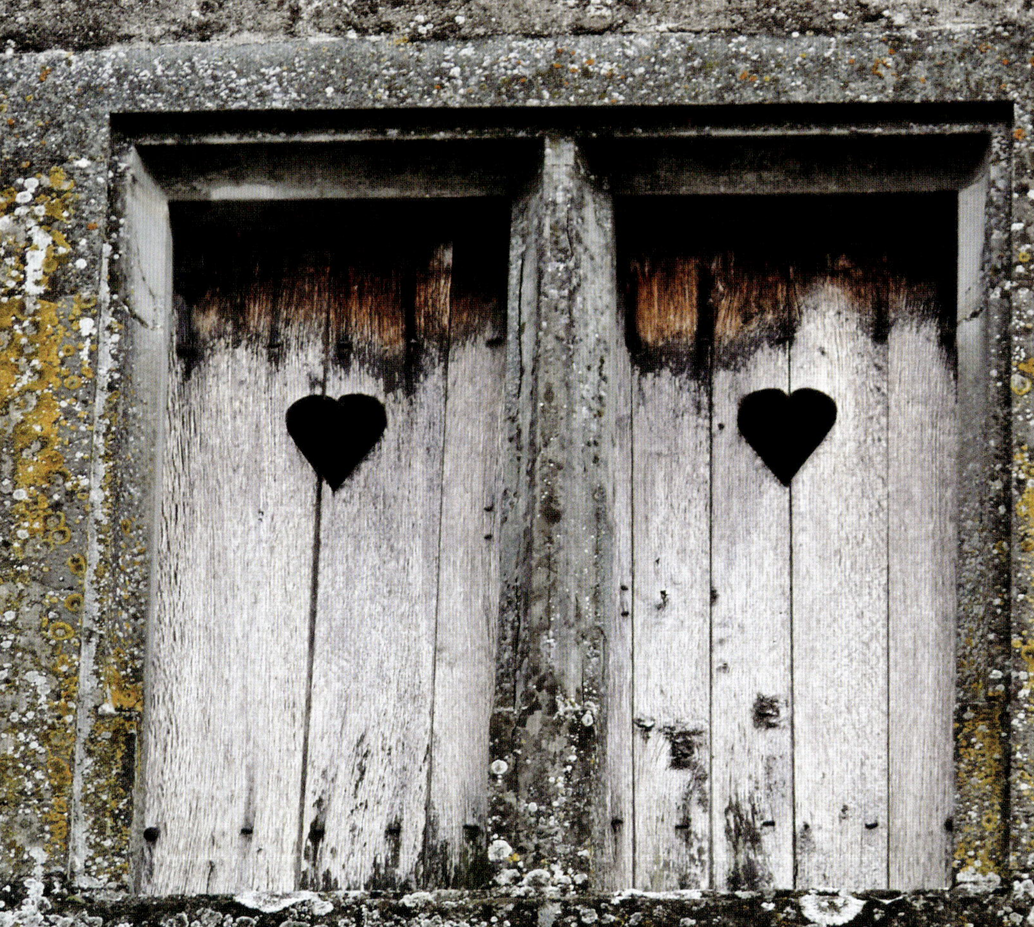
stein am rhein, switzerland

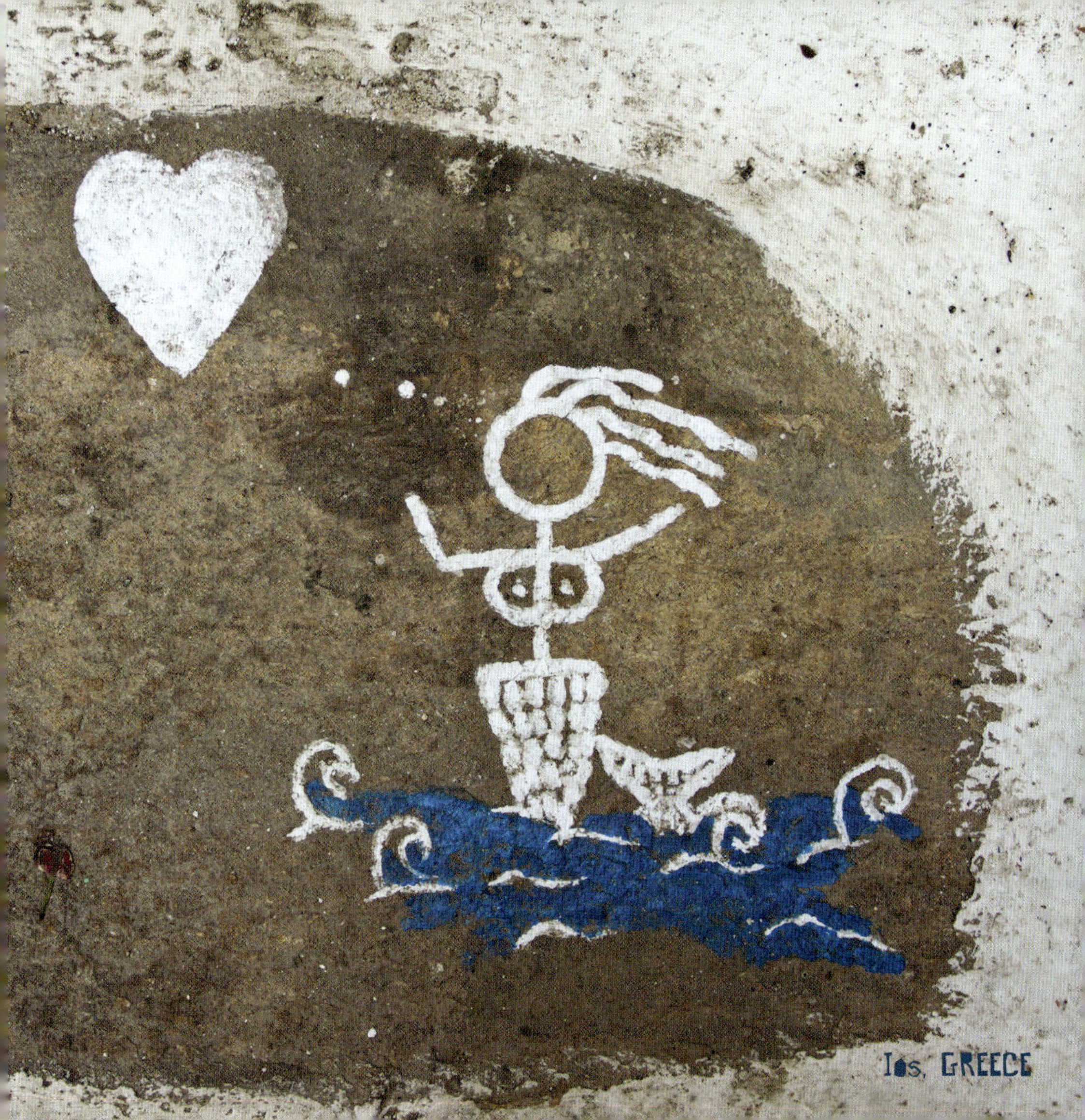

Ios, GREECE

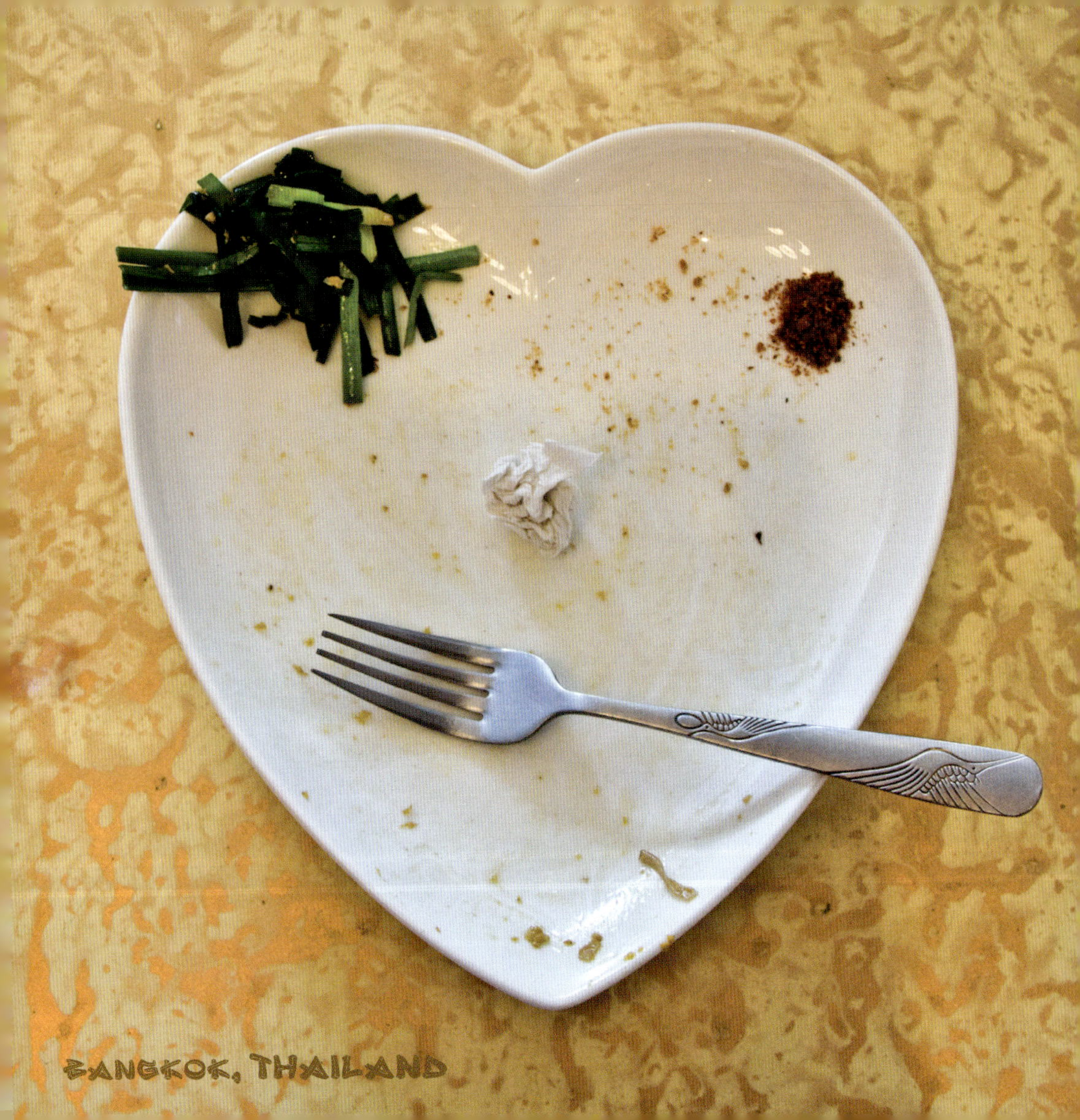
BANGKOK, THAILAND

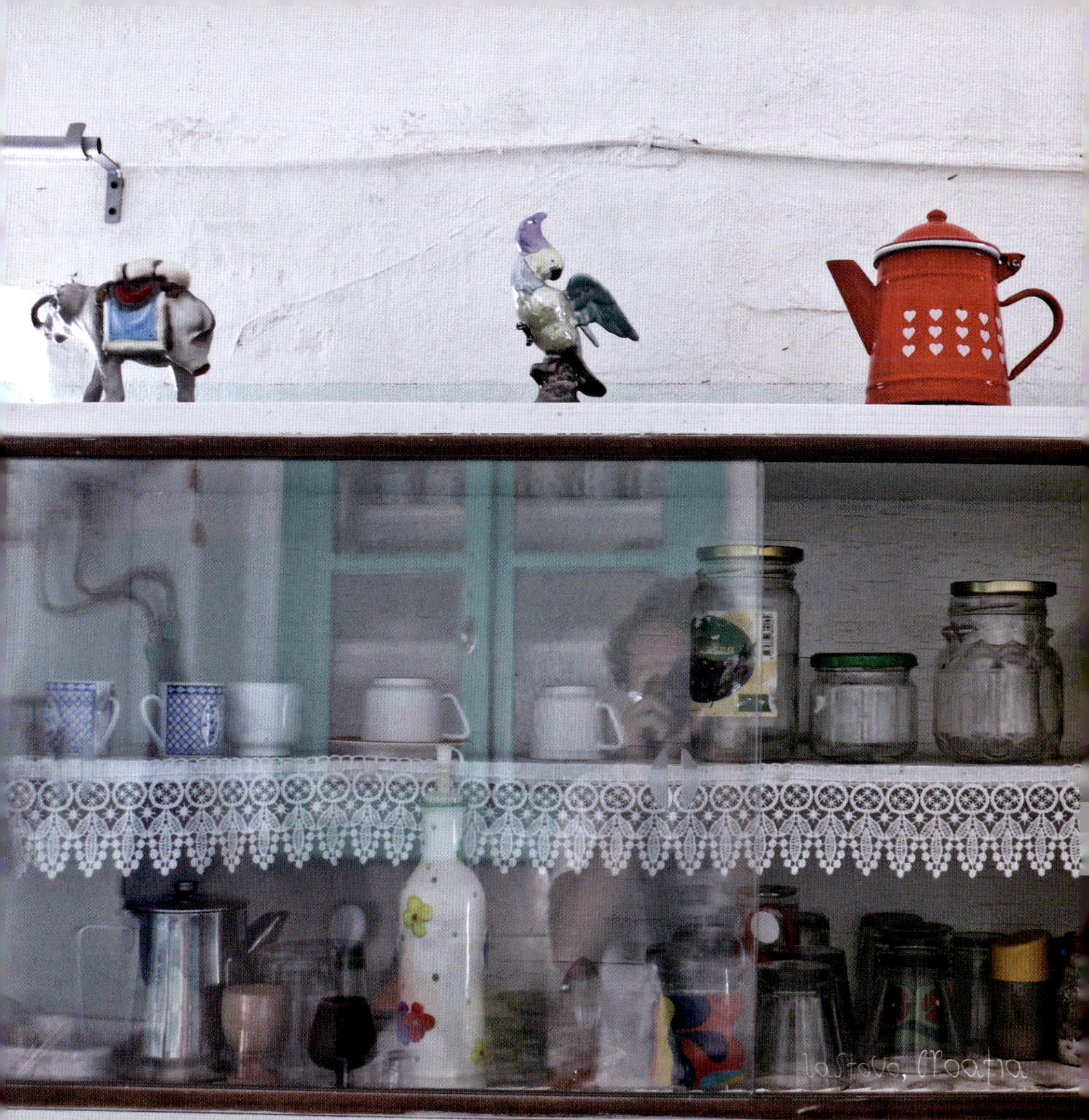

Lastovo, Croatia

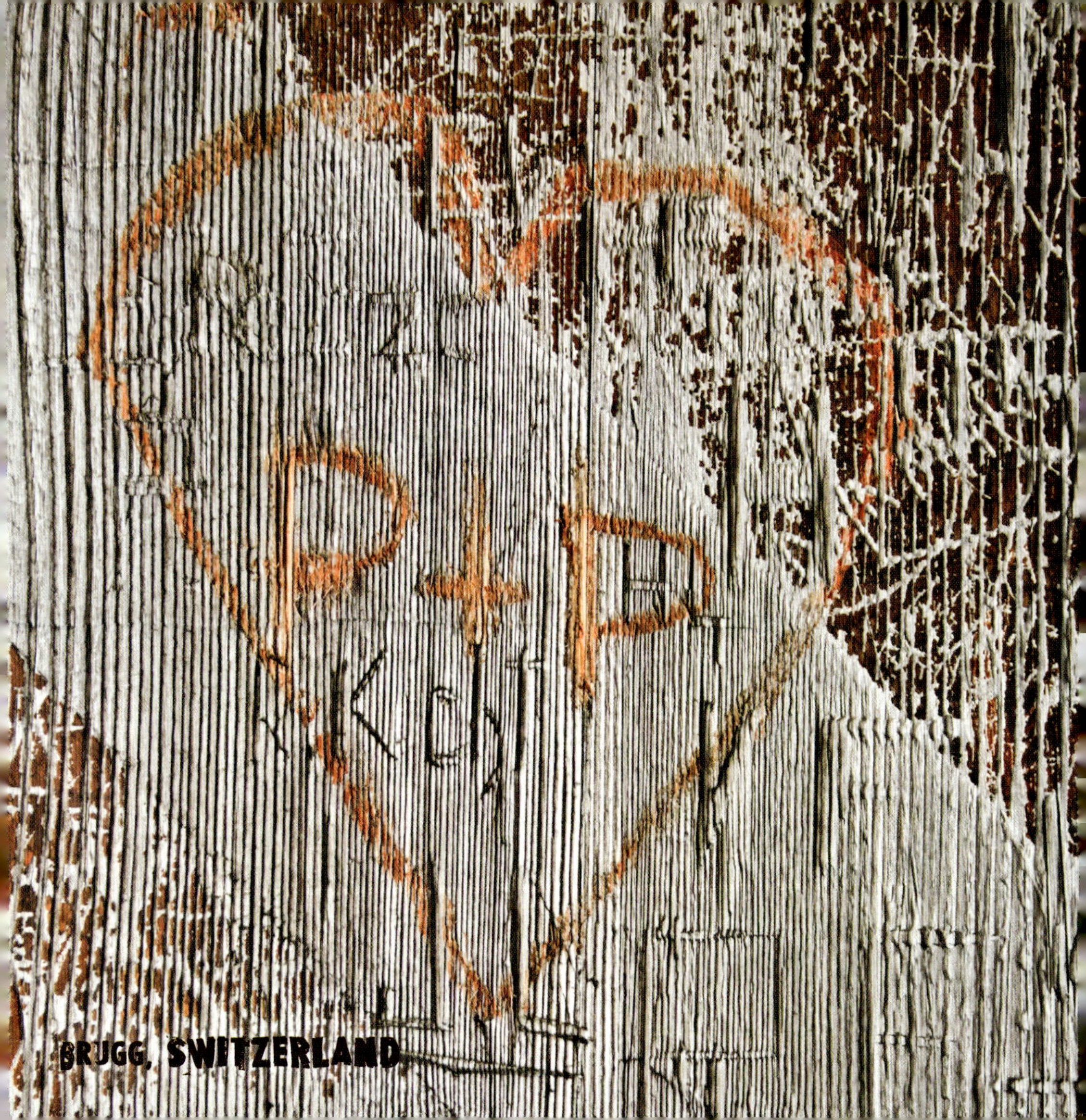
BRUGG, SWITZERLAND

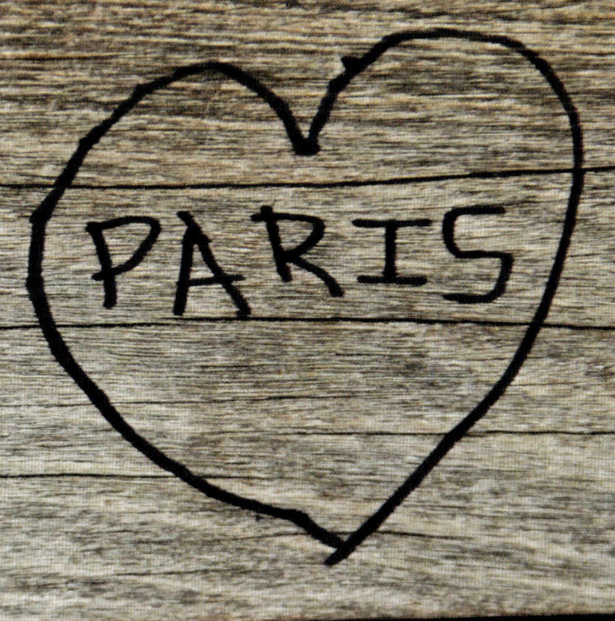

Paris, FRANCE

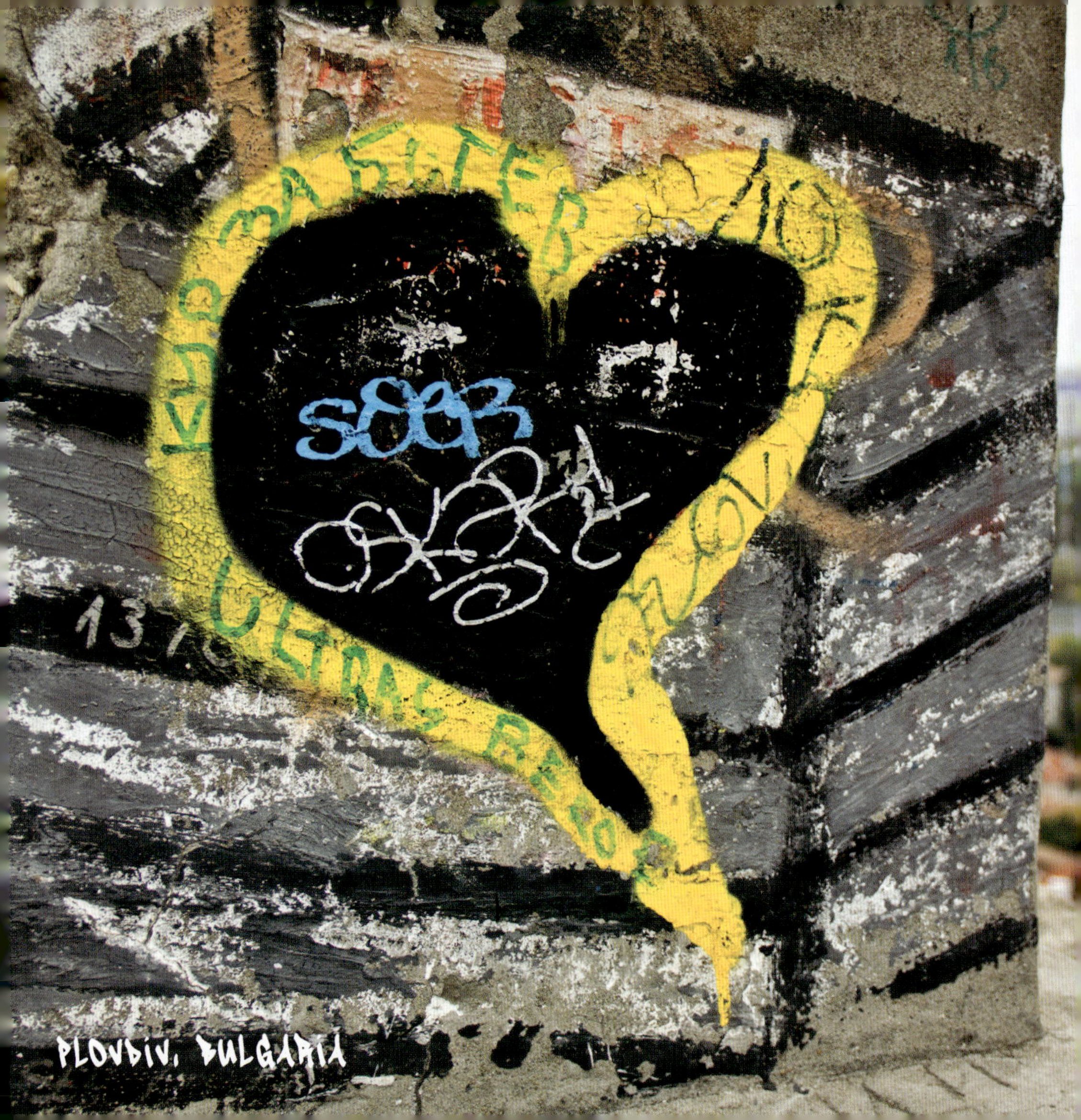

PLOVDIV, BULGARIA

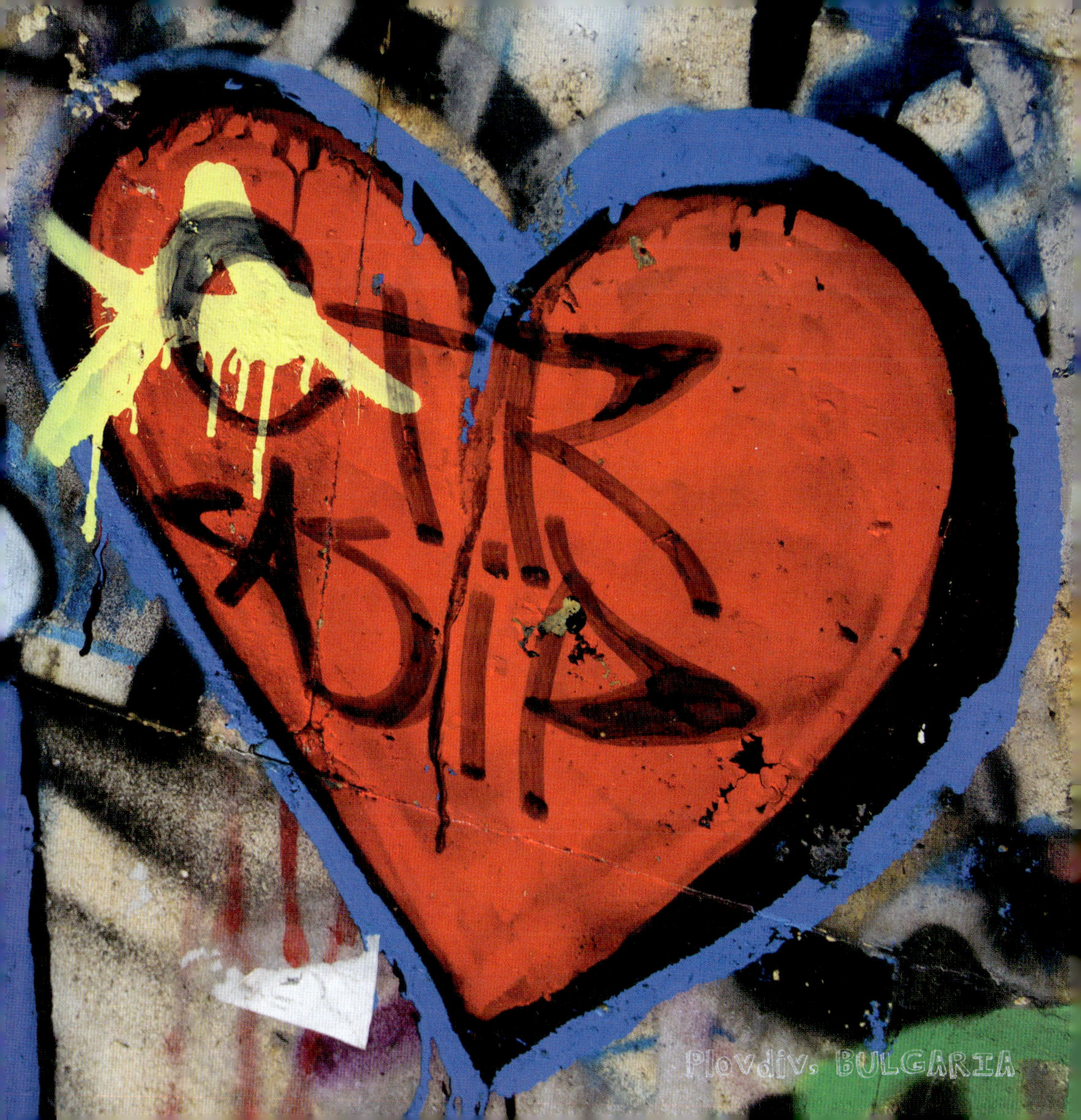
Plovdiv, BULGARIA

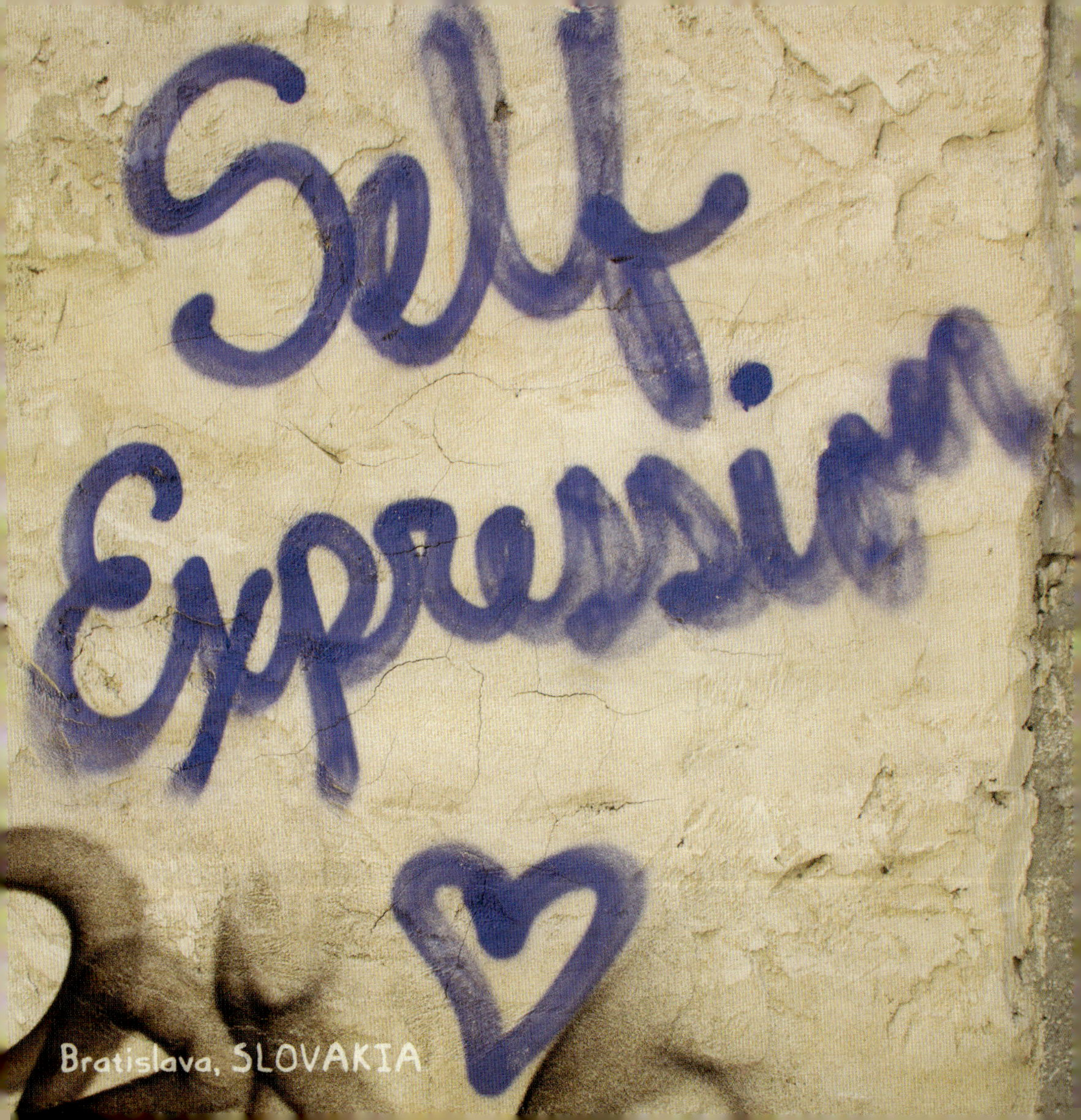
Self
Expression
Bratislava, SLOVAKIA

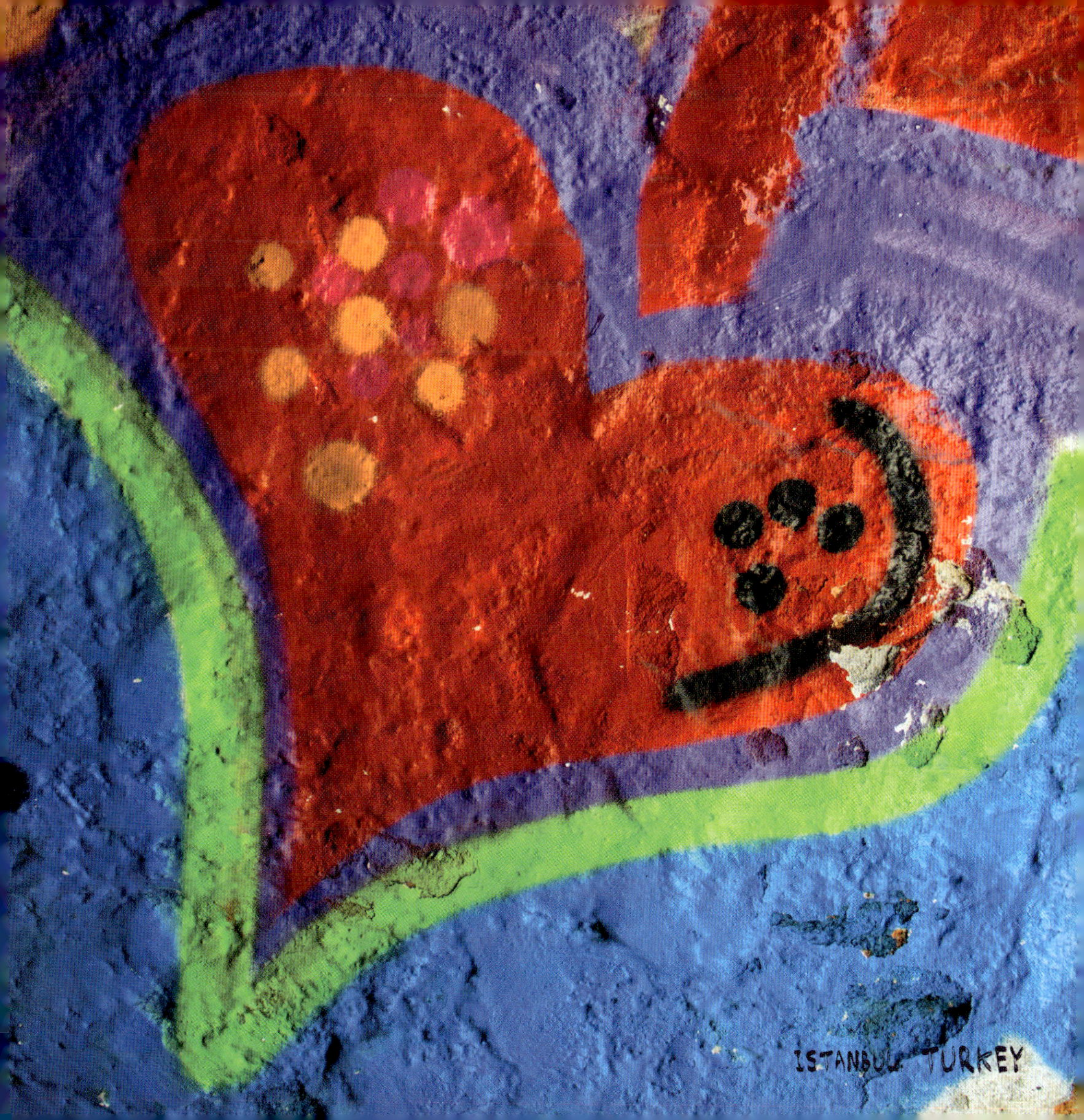
ISTANBUL TURKEY

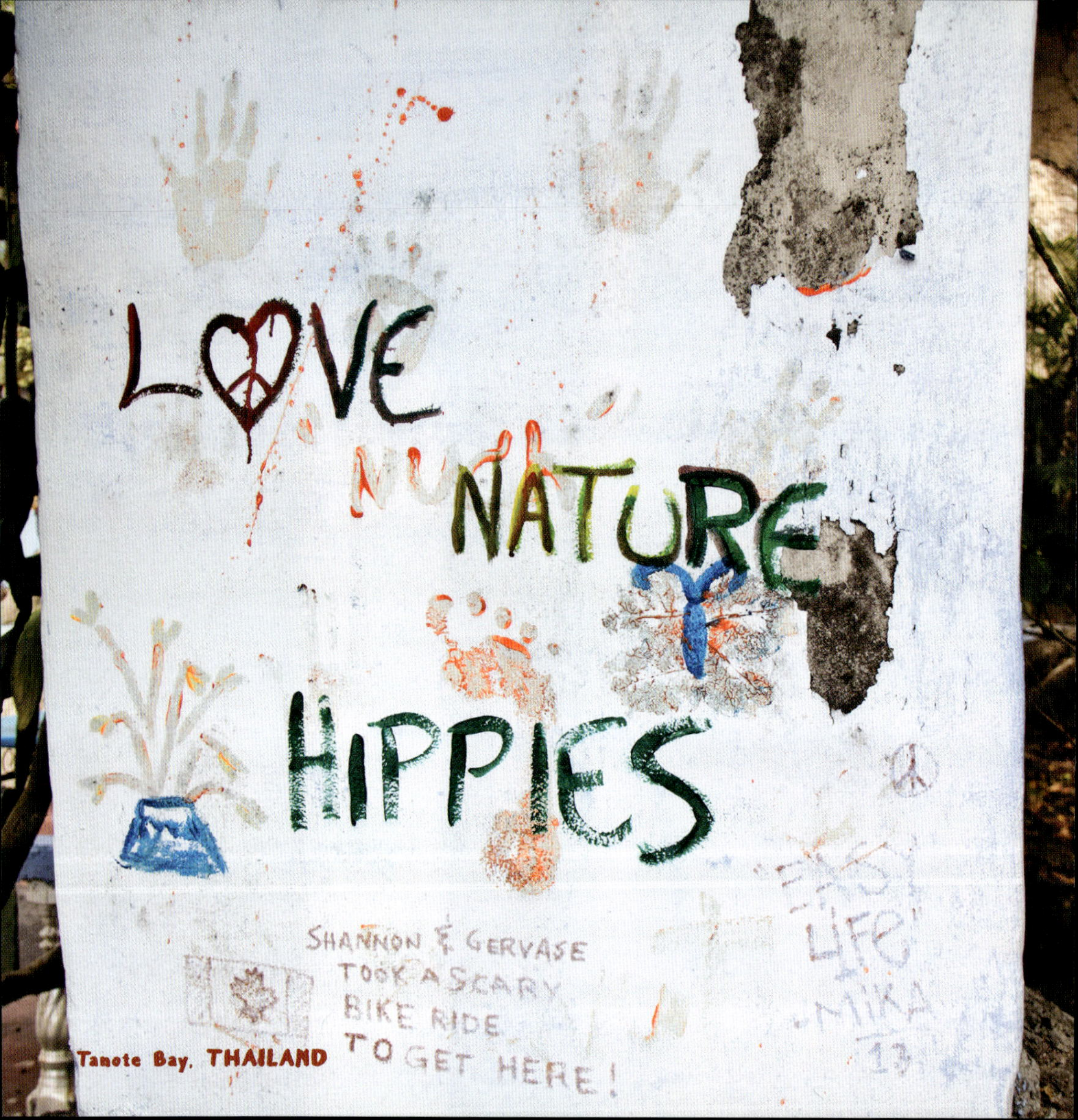

LOVE
NATURE
HIPPIES
SHANNON & GERVASE
TOOK A SCARY
BIKE RIDE
TO GET HERE!
Tanote Bay, THAILAND

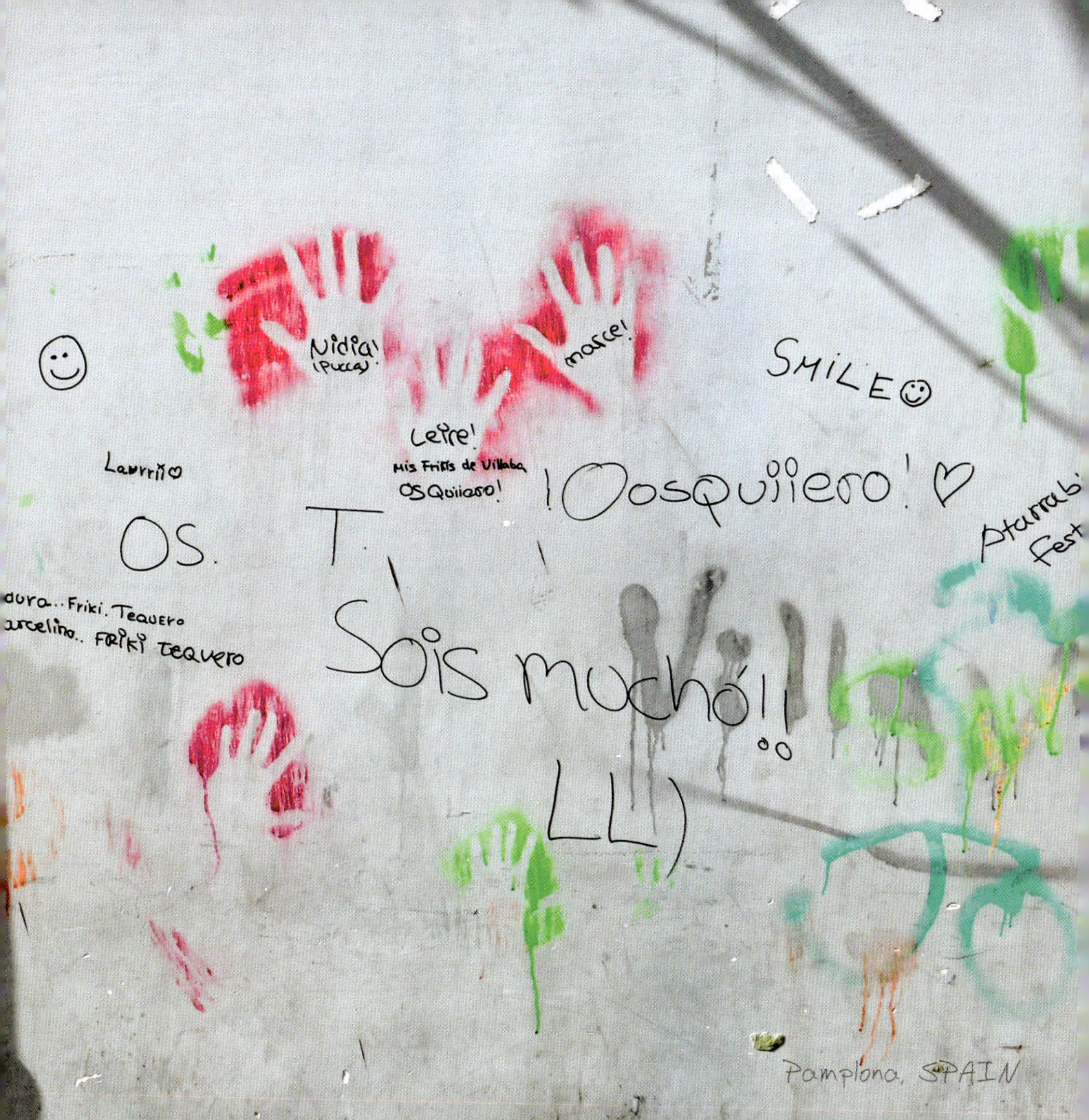
Nidia!
(Pucca)
marcel
SMILE☺
Leire!
Mis Frikis de Villaba
OS Quiiero!
!Oosquiiero!♡
Laurrii♡
Pturrab'
Fest
OS.
T.
Sois mucho!!
LL)
oura..Friki.Tequero
arcelina..Friki Tequero
Pamplona, SPAIN

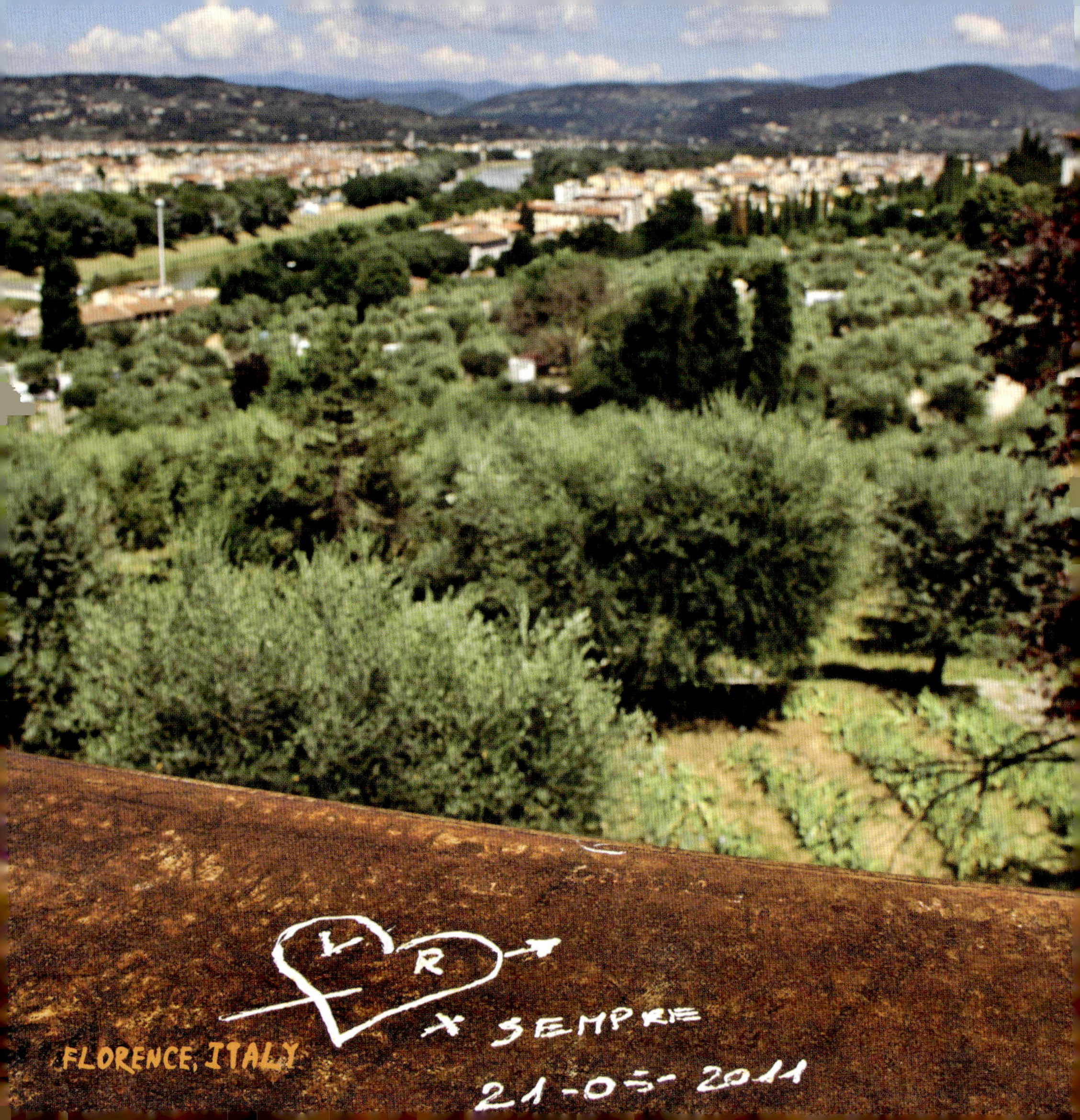

L R
X SEMPRE
FLORENCE, ITALY
21-05-2011

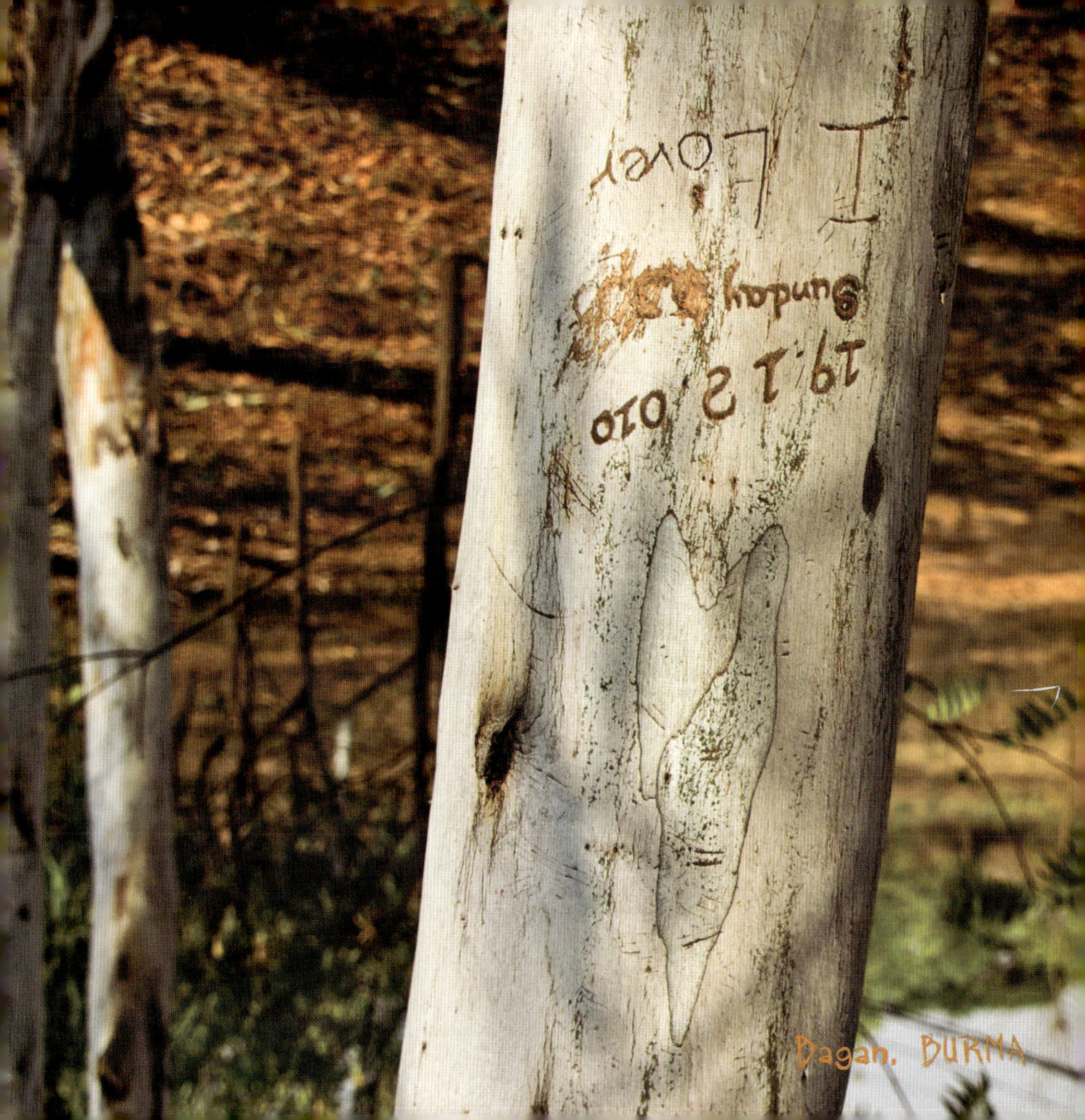
I Lover
Sunday
19.12.010
Bagan, BURMA

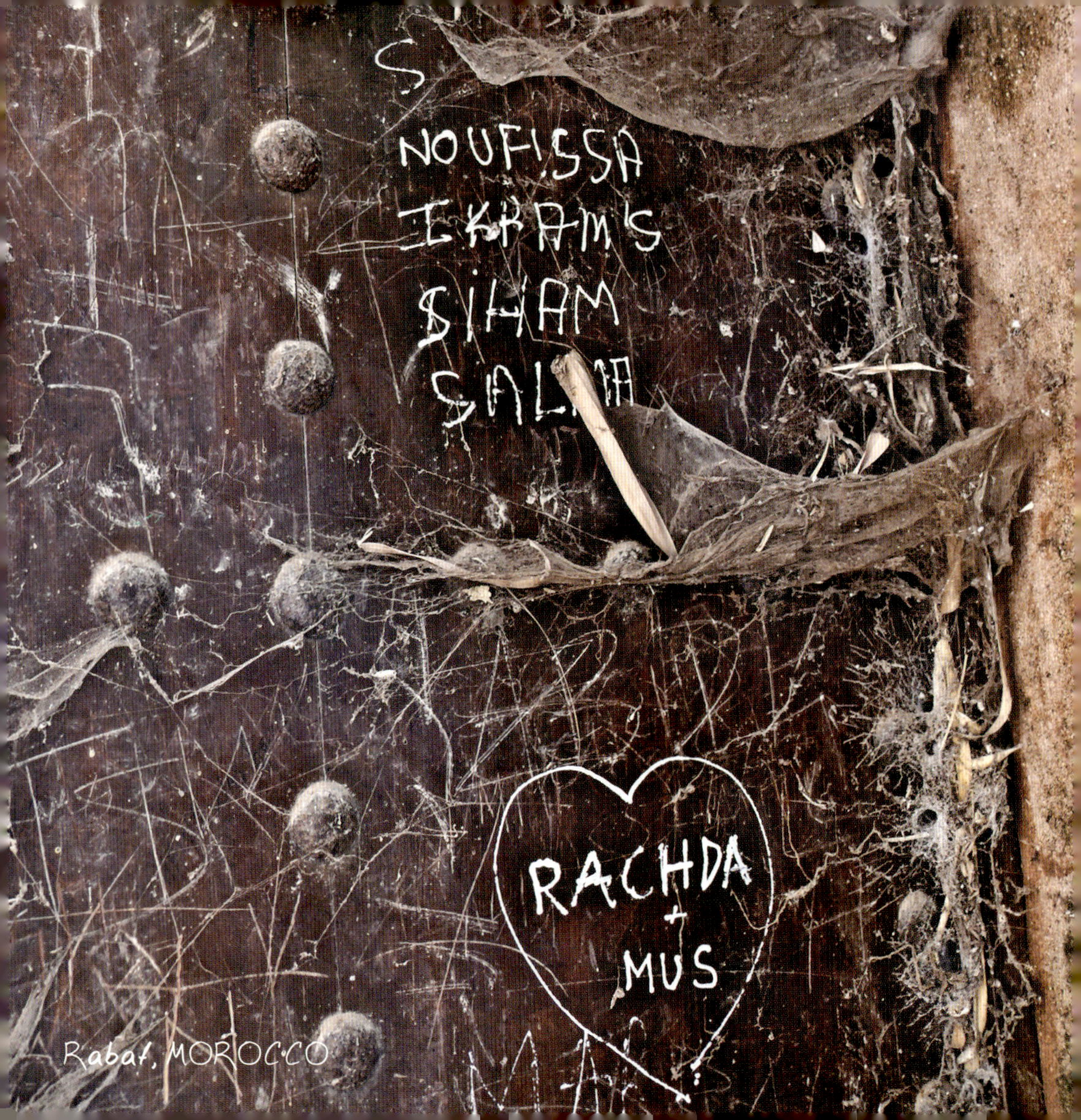

S
NOUFISSA
IKRAMS
SIHAM
SALMA
RACHDA
+
MUS
Rabat, MOROCCO

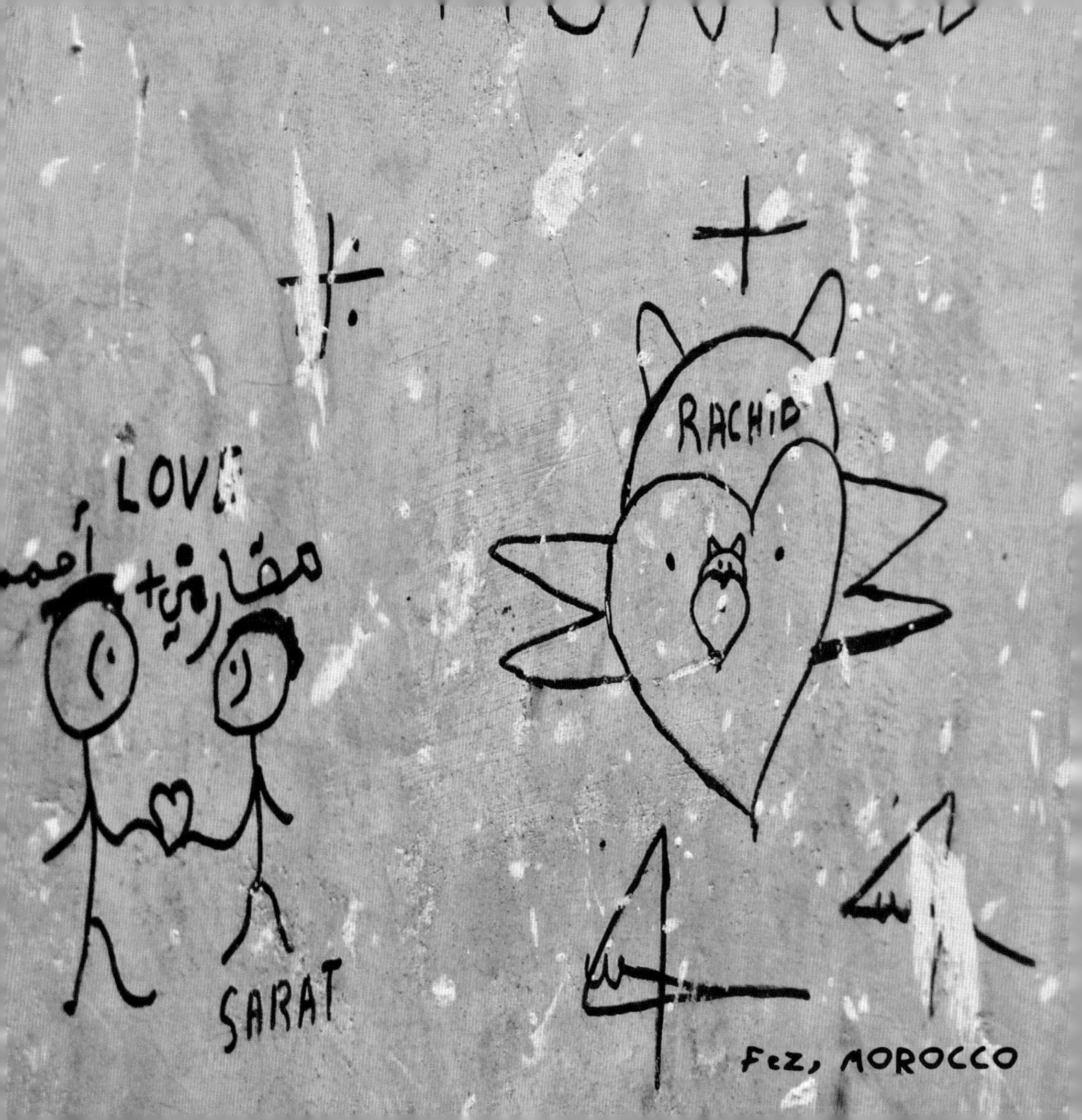

LOVE
مفارقني أحمد
SARAT
RACHID
Fez, MOROCCO

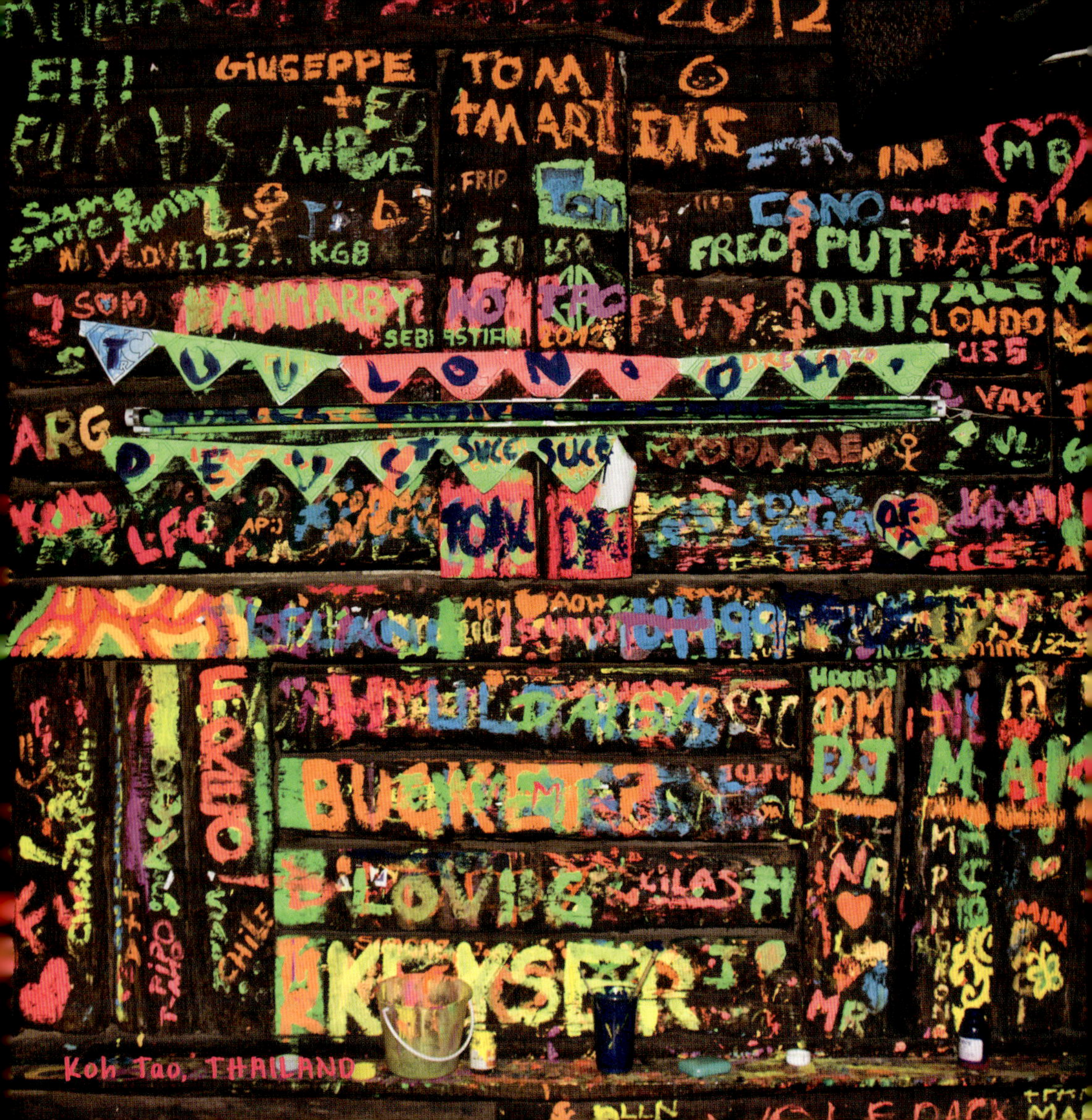
Koh Tao, THAILAND

COFFEE

TEA

others

ร้อน
- conpana 50 ฿
- Macchiato 50 ฿

40 ฿

40 ฿

...ha 50 ฿

e' 50 ฿

50 ฿

Macchiato 60 ฿

40 ฿/cup

...ea 55 ฿/pot

Earl Grey, Darjeeling
reakfast, Jasmine Green Tea
, Peppermint 50 ฿/cup
Strawberry, Lemon 50 ฿/cup
chai Tea 65฿ TAZO Organic chai Tea 80฿
Seasonings Sleepy Time, camomile
...us), Raspberry Zinger 60฿/pot
colate 50 ฿
...esh Milk 55 ฿
...azelnut or Caramel)

ICED Connect Cafe' coffee 60 ฿.

- Americano 55 ฿
- Caffe' Mocha 60 ฿
- Caffe' Latte' 60 ฿
- Caramel Macchiato 70 ฿   Iced Cappucino 60 ฿

- Iced Tea : Lemon 45 ฿
- THAI Iced Tea 55 ฿

- Iced Chocolate 60 ฿
- Iced Fresh Milk 65 ฿

(Vanilla / Caramel / Hazelnut Syrup)

FRAPPE' ปั่น

- Caffe' Latte' Frappe' 65 ฿
- Caffe' Mocha Frappe' 65 ฿
- Caramel Macchiato Frappe' 79 ฿
- Caffe' Brownie Frappe' 85 ฿
- Thai Tea Frappe' 65 ฿
- Chocolate Frappe' 65 ฿
  Chocolate + Brownie Frappe' 85 ฿

★ Singha Beer 60 ฿
★ Heineken Beer ฿
★ Bottle Water 20 ฿

Limenade Soda 65 ฿

Fresh
APPLE

POPULAR

- Blueber...
- Man...
- Apricot

Hungry

① with
② with
③ with

★ Cereal wi...
♥ Toast &
♥ Toast &

Chiang Rai THAILAND

Add 10 ฿ Marshmallows

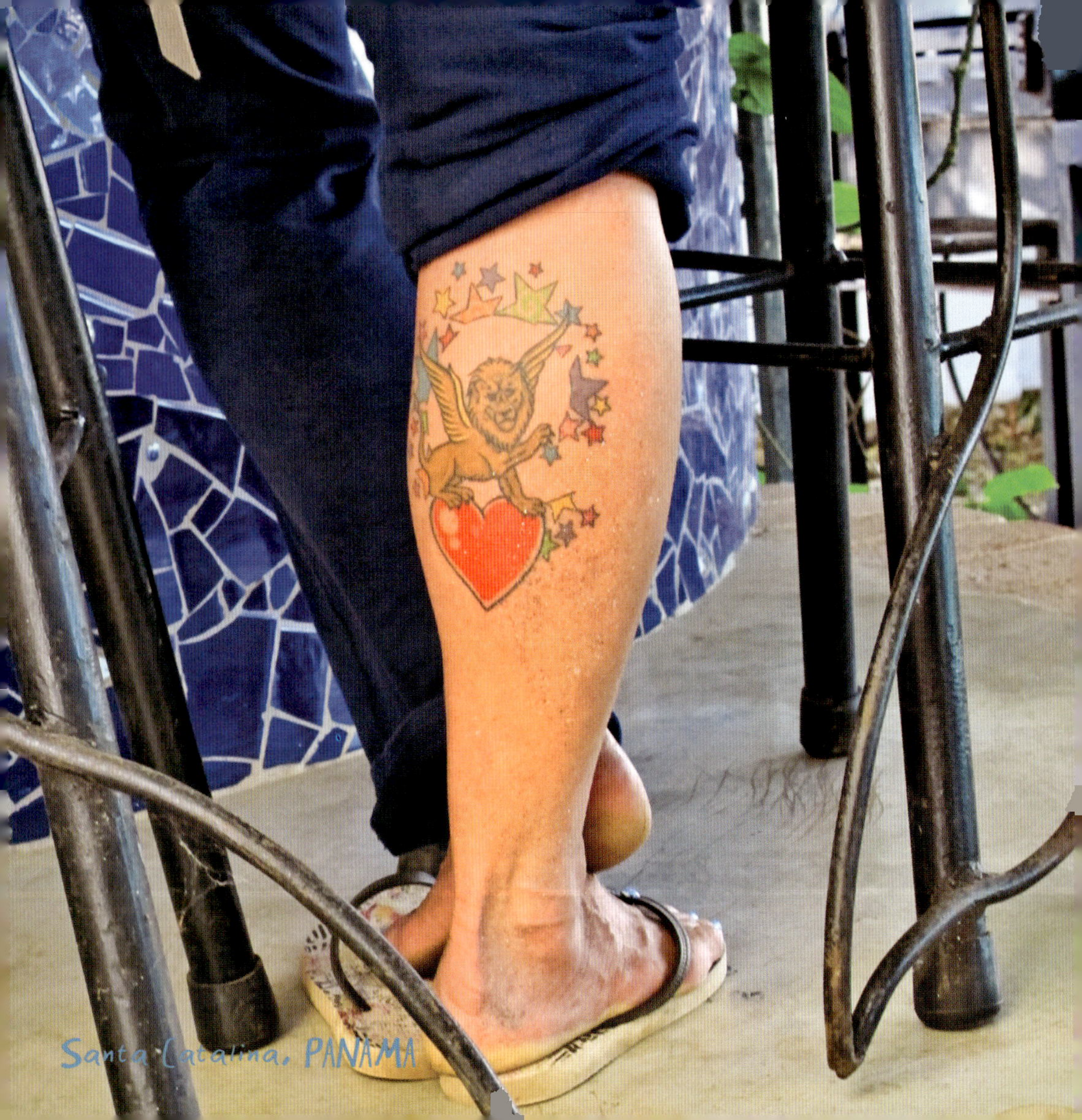
Santa Catalina, PANAMA

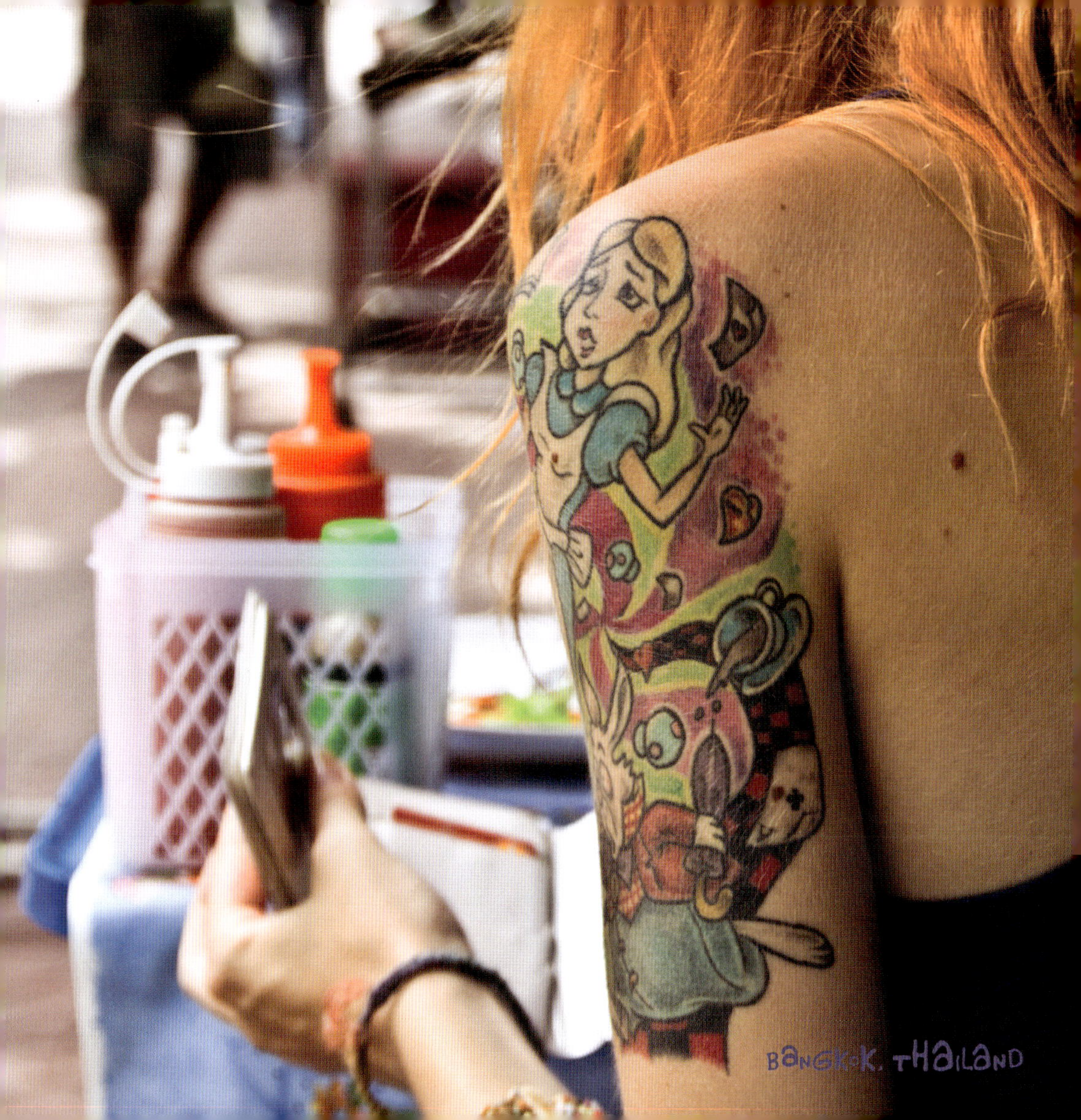
BANGKOK. THAILAND

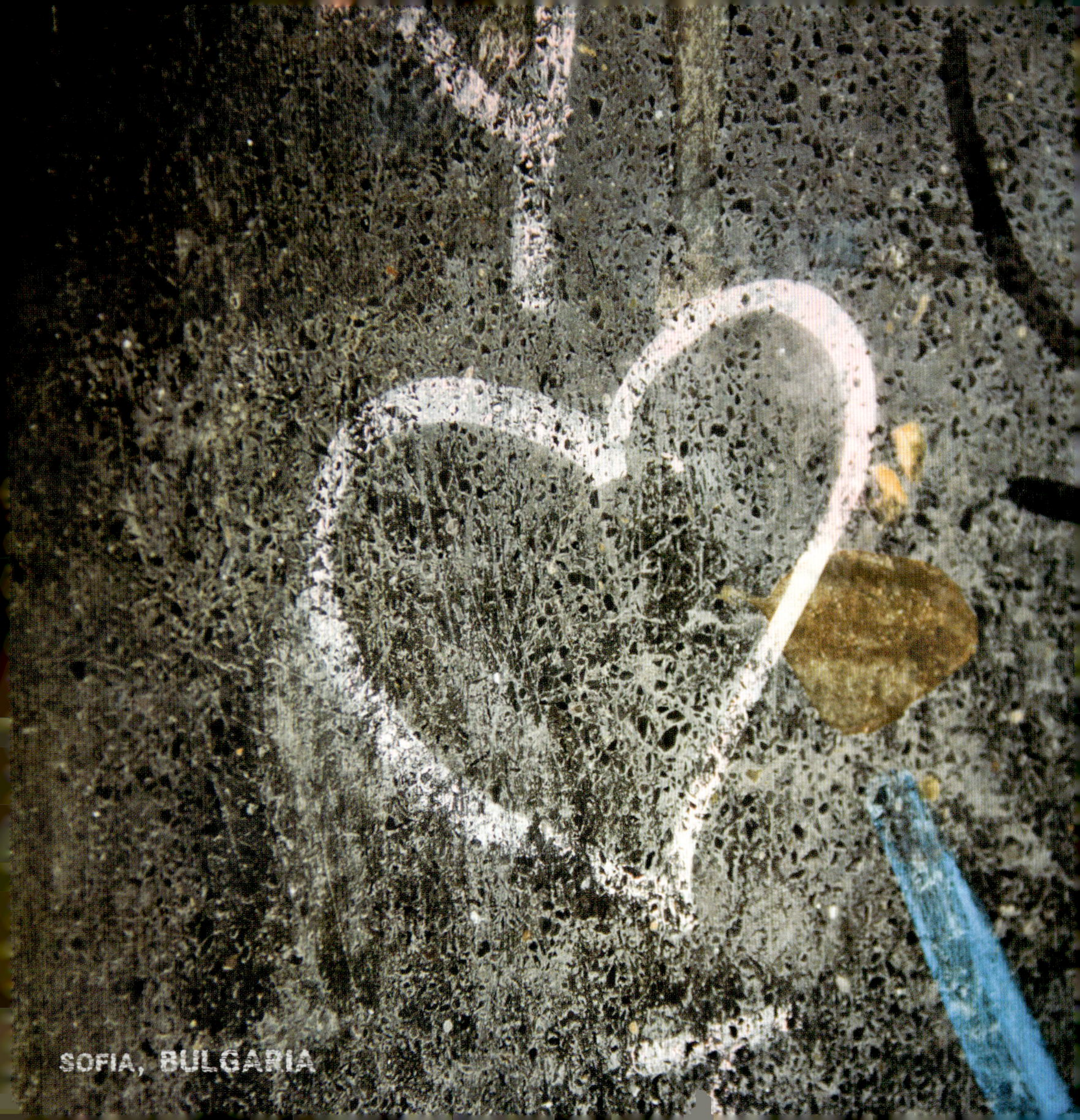
SOFIA, BULGARIA

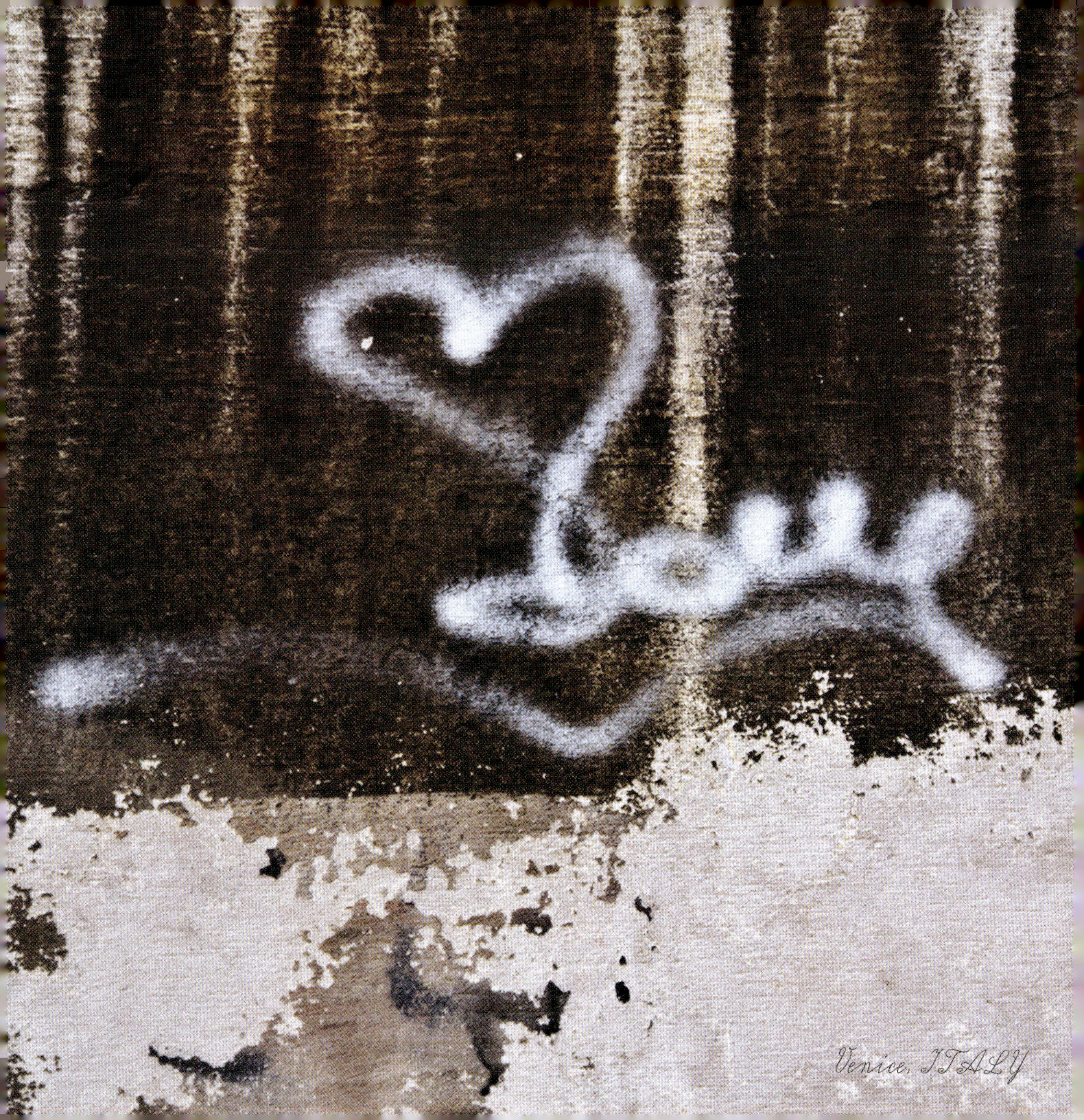
Venice, ITALY

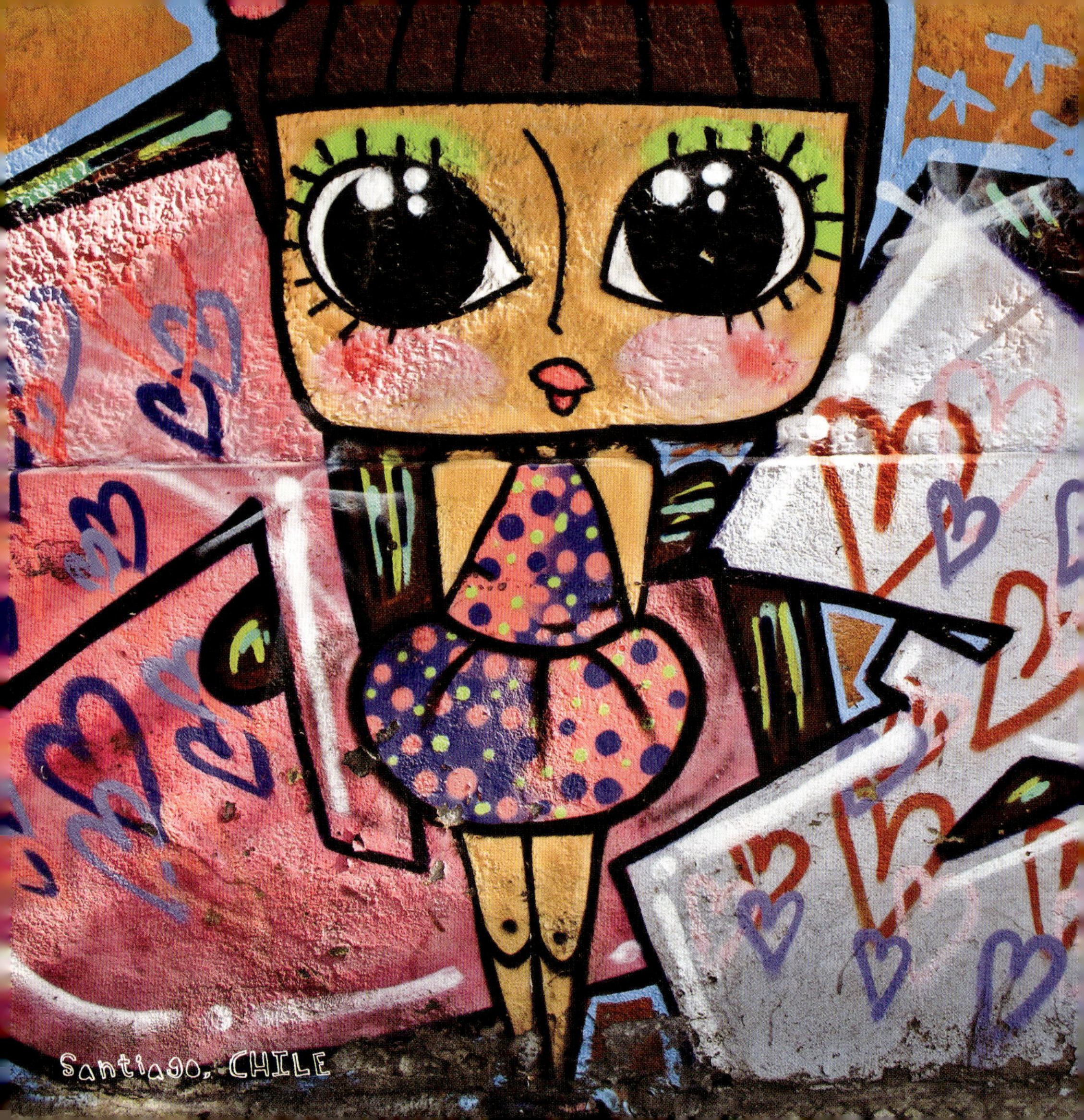

Santiago, CHILE

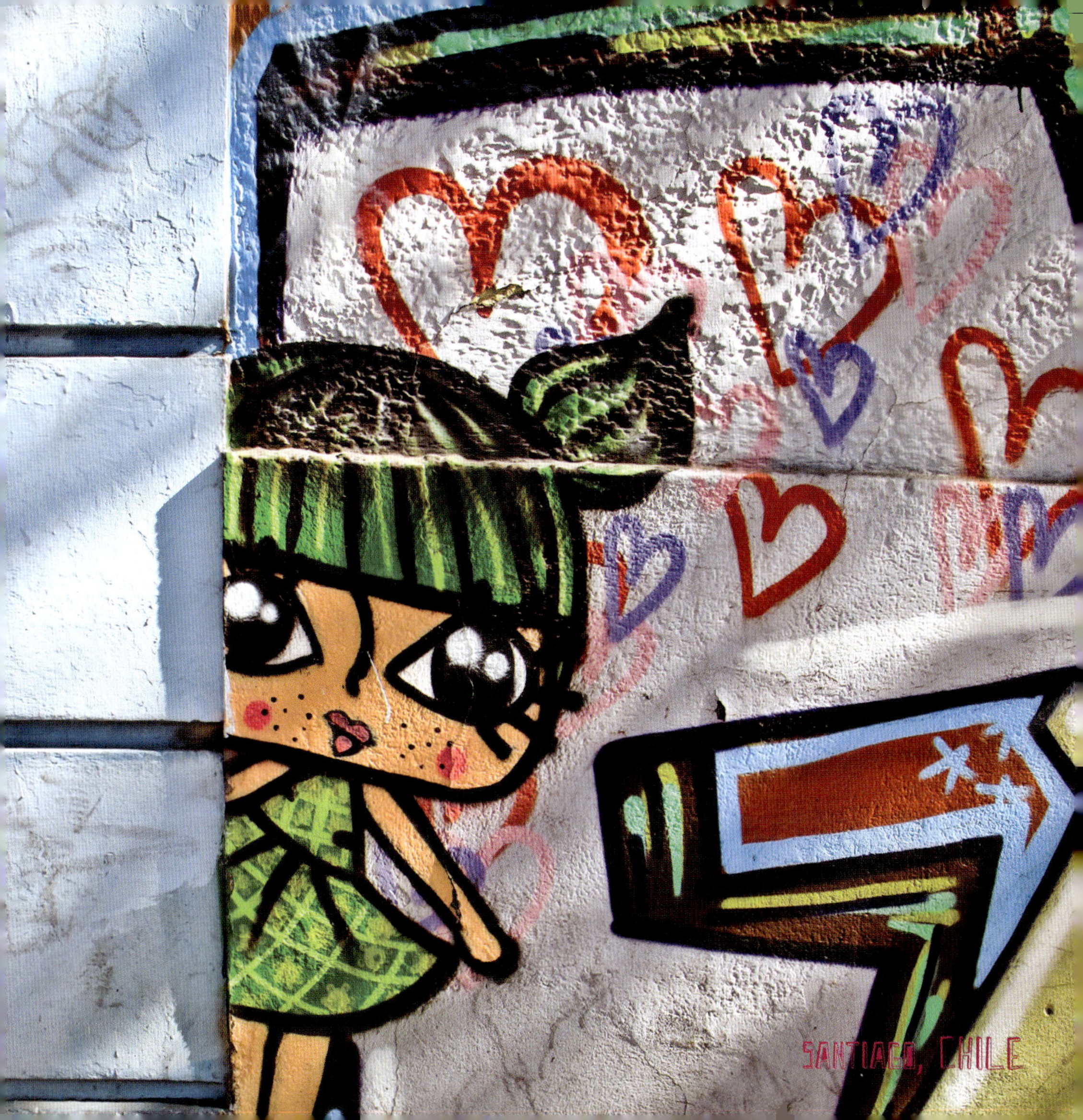

SANTIAGO, CHILE

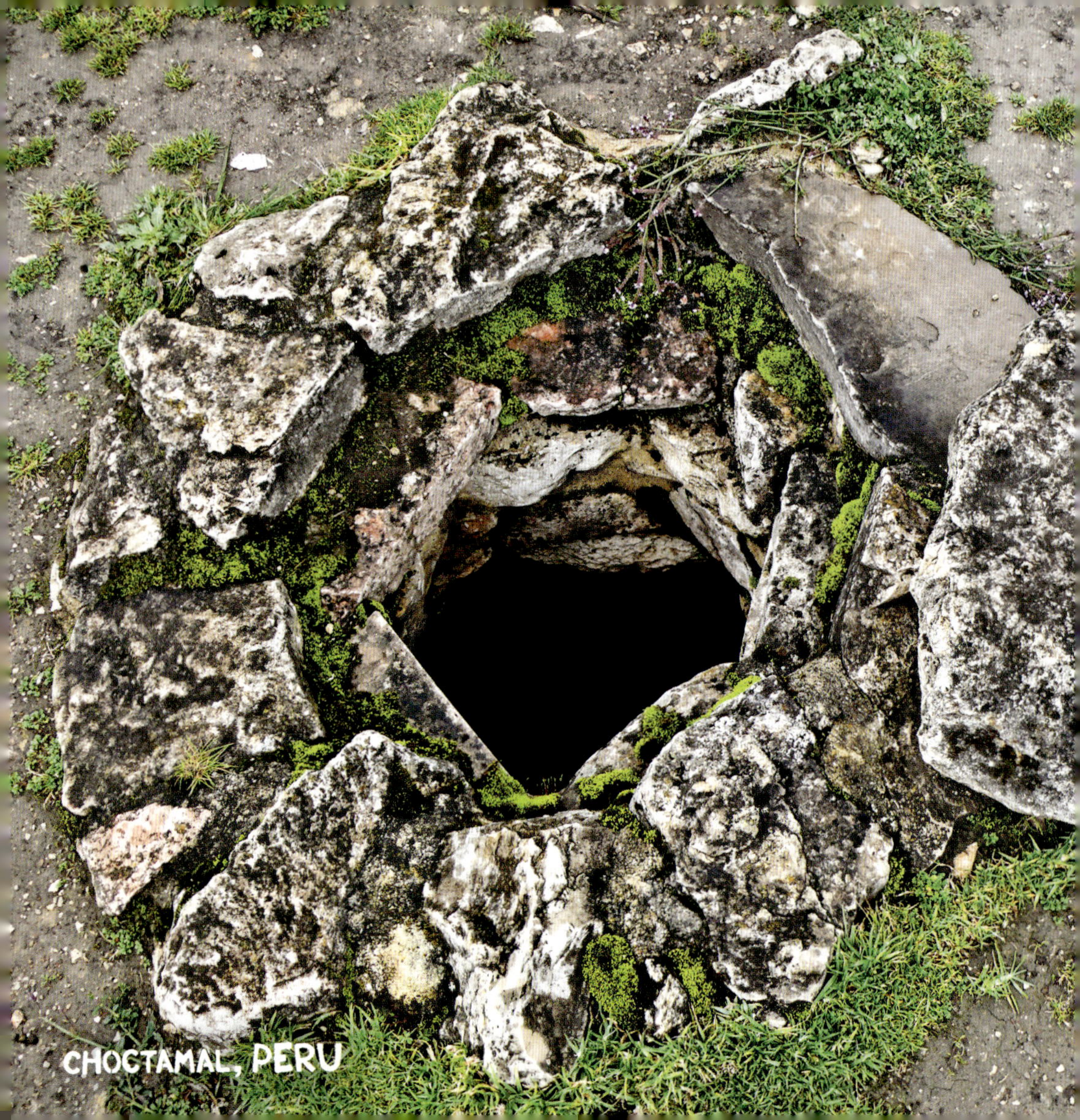

CHOCTAMAL, PERU

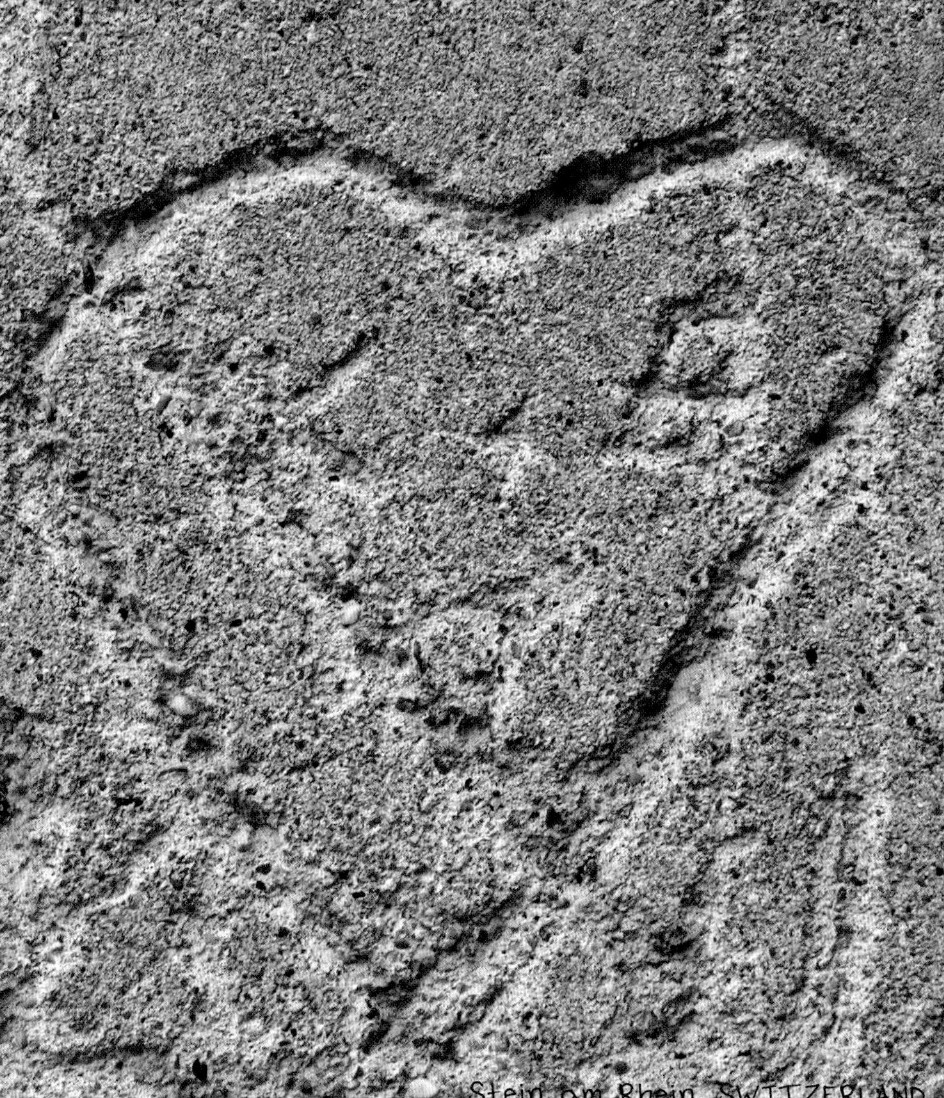
Stein am Rhein, SWITZERLAND

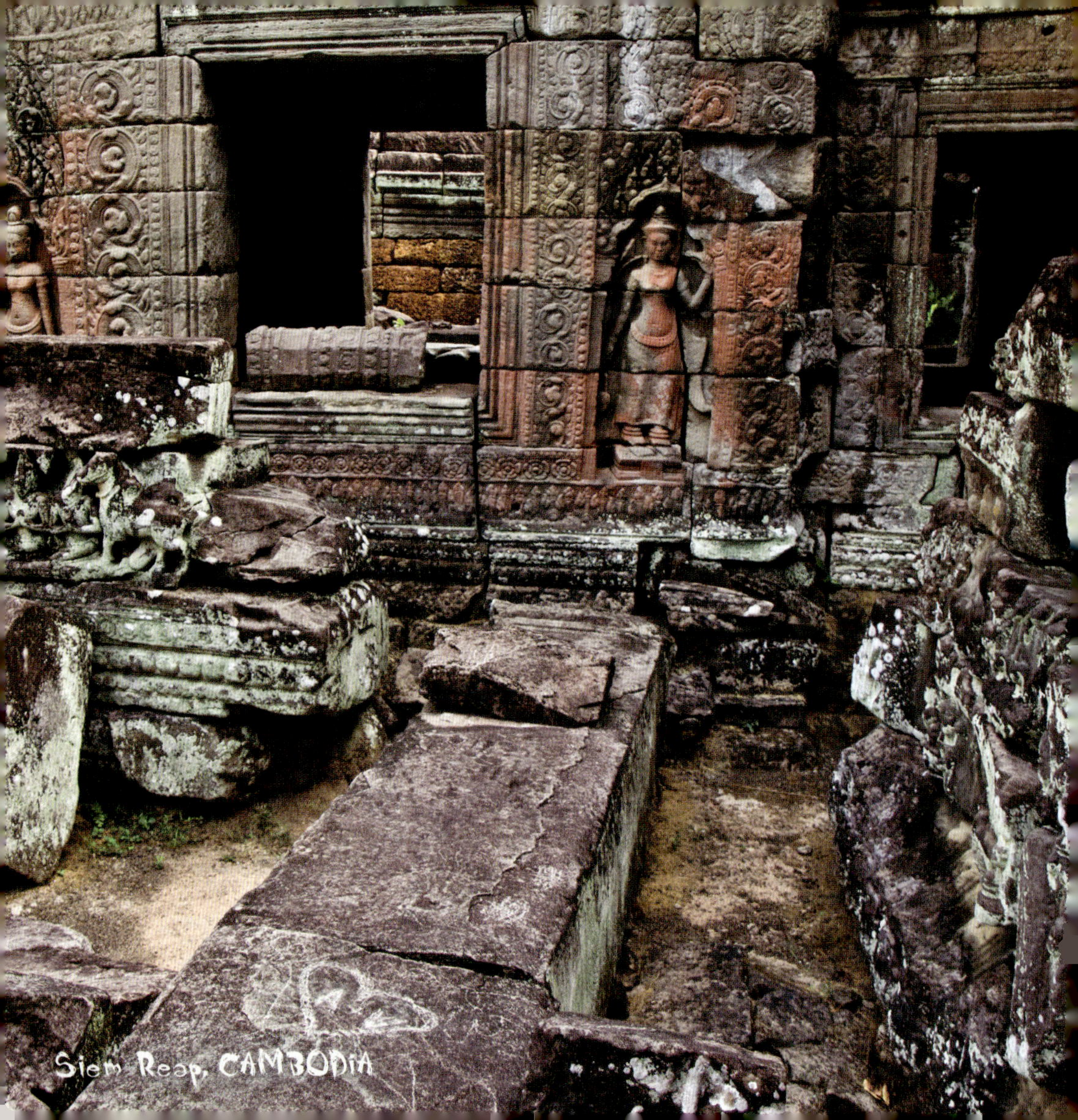
Siem Reap, CAMBODIA

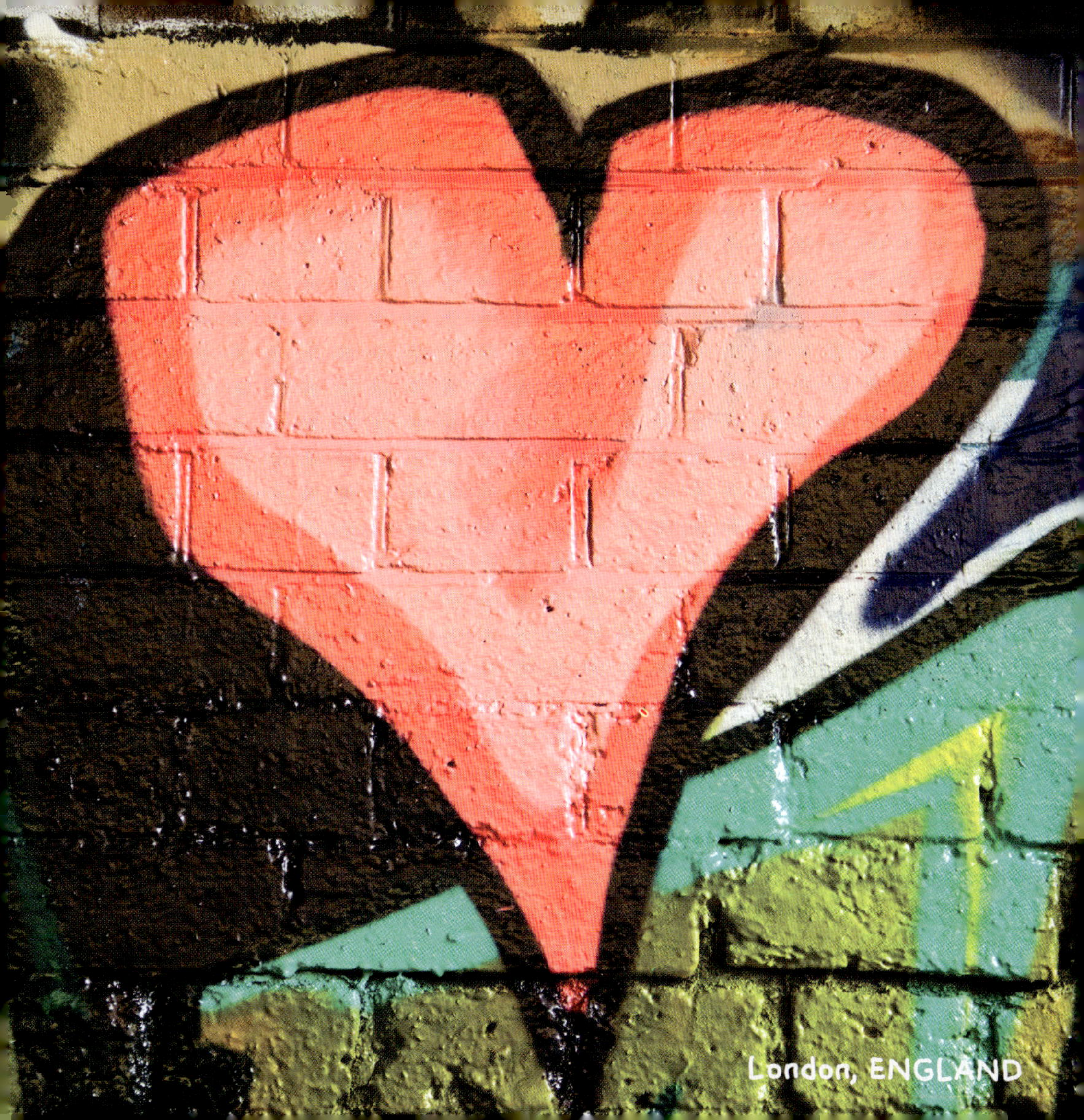
London, ENGLAND

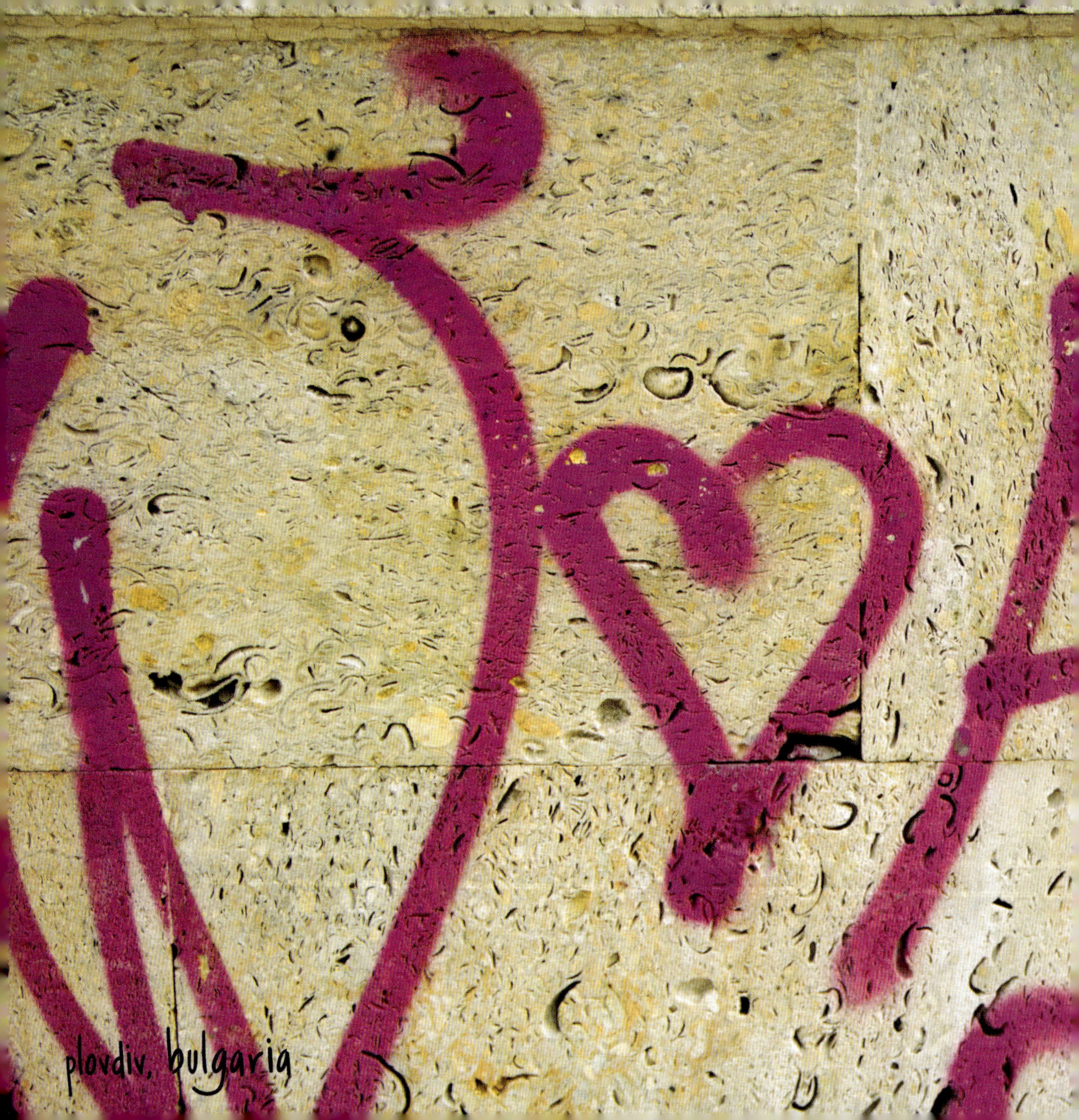
plovdiv, bulgaria

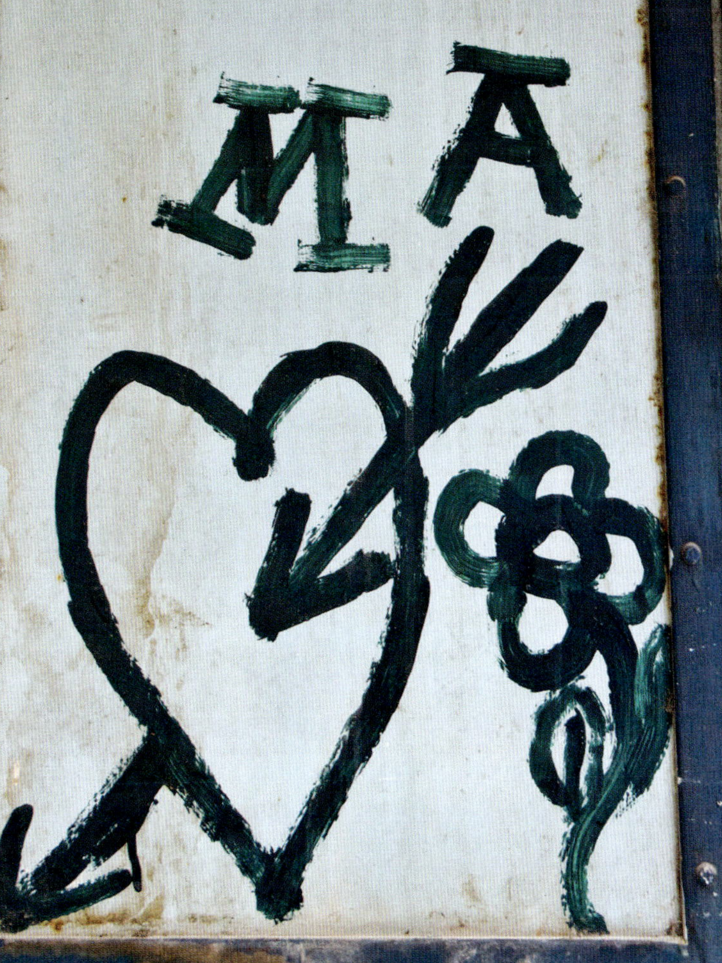
MA
JERUSALEM ISRAEL

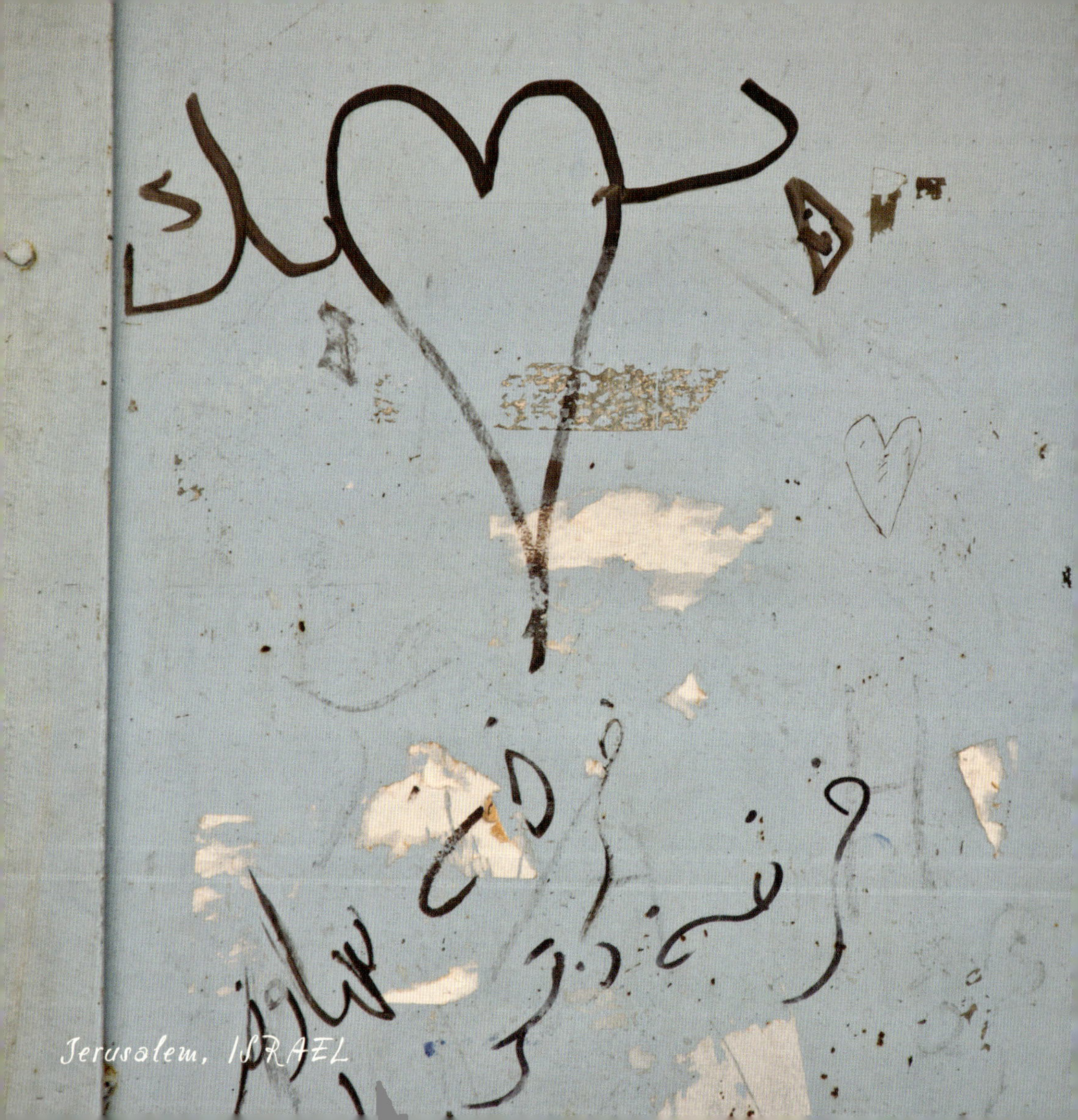

Jerusalem, ISRAEL

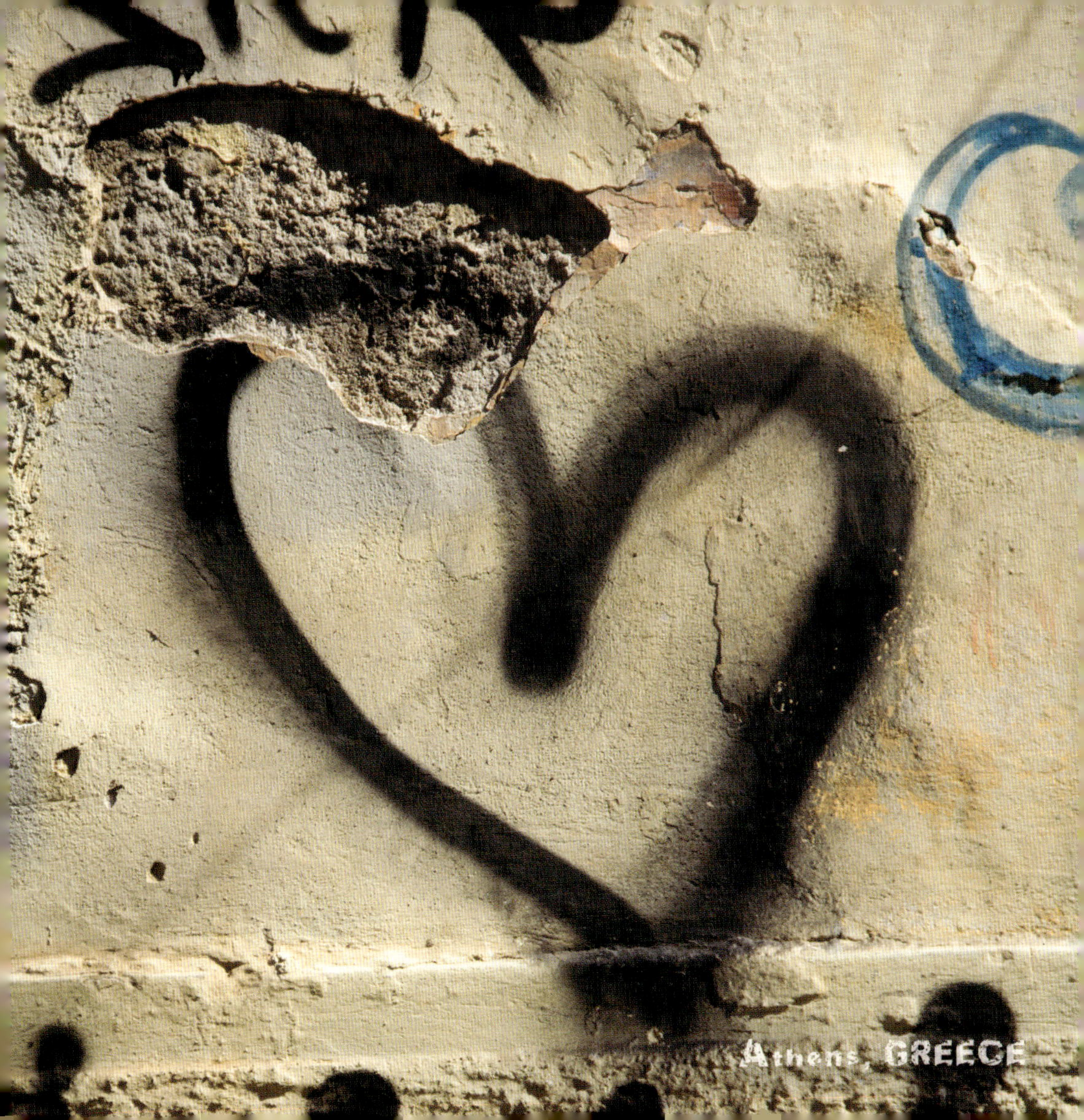

Athens, GREECE

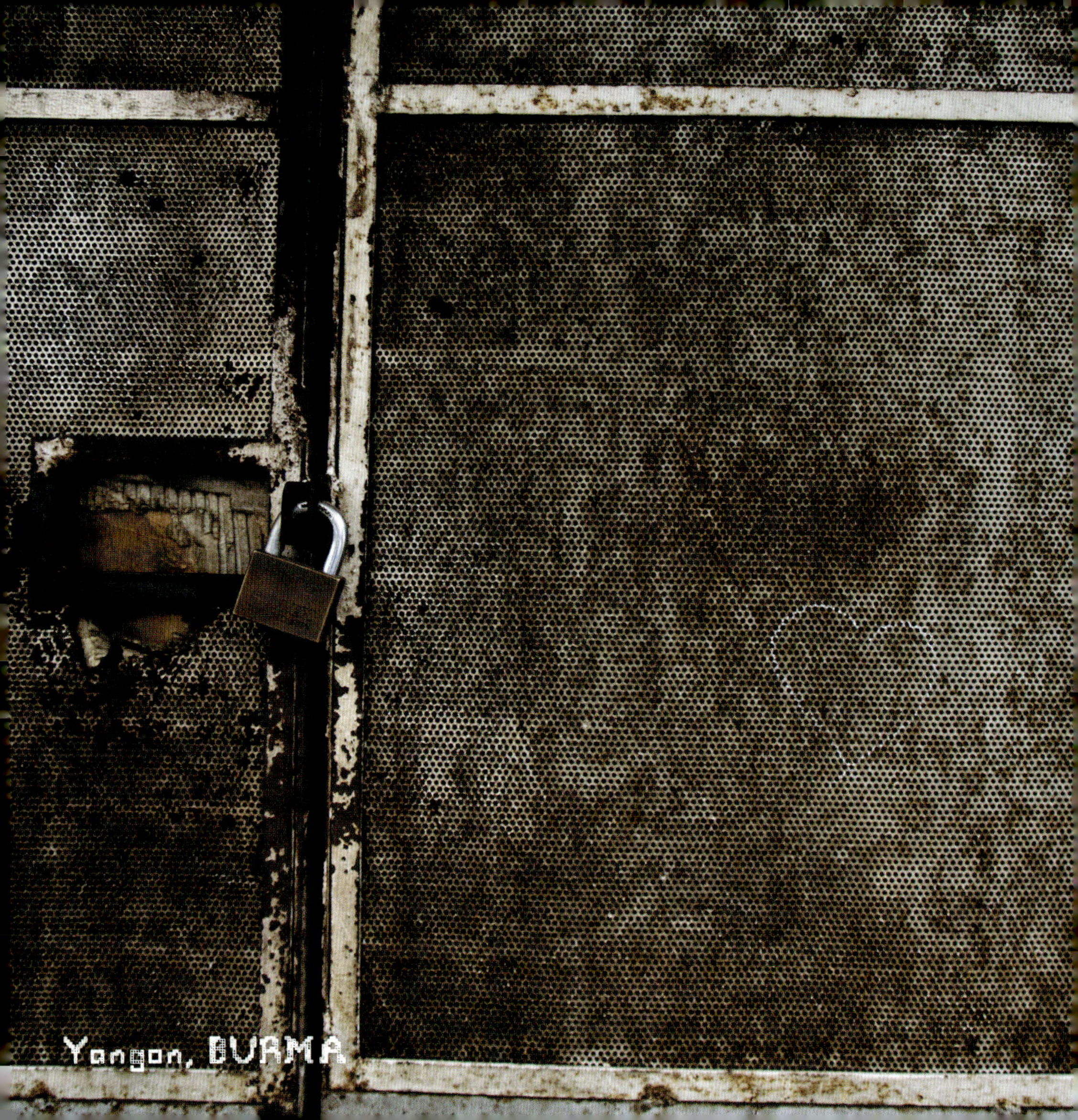

Yangon, BURMA

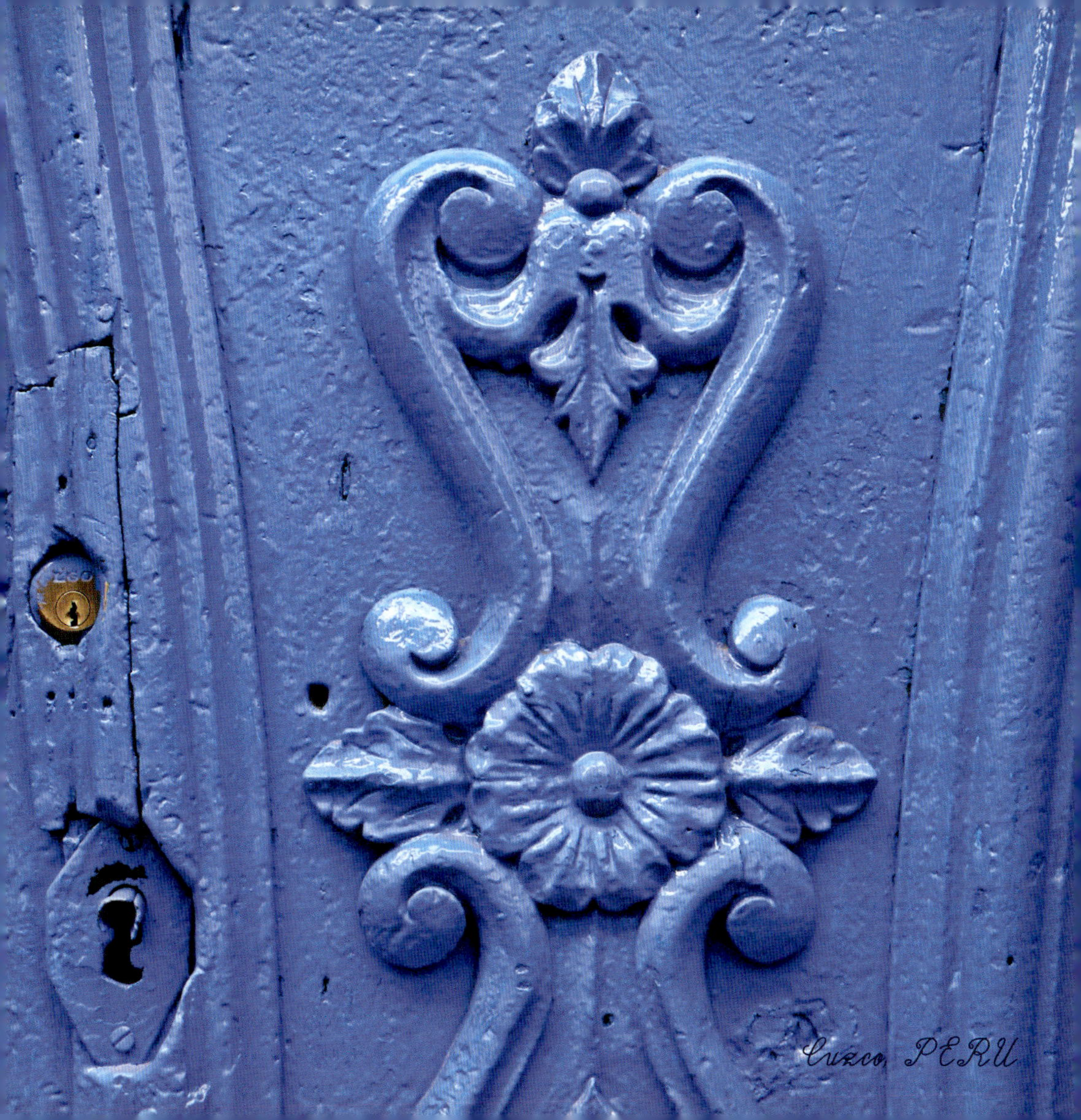

Cuzco, PERU

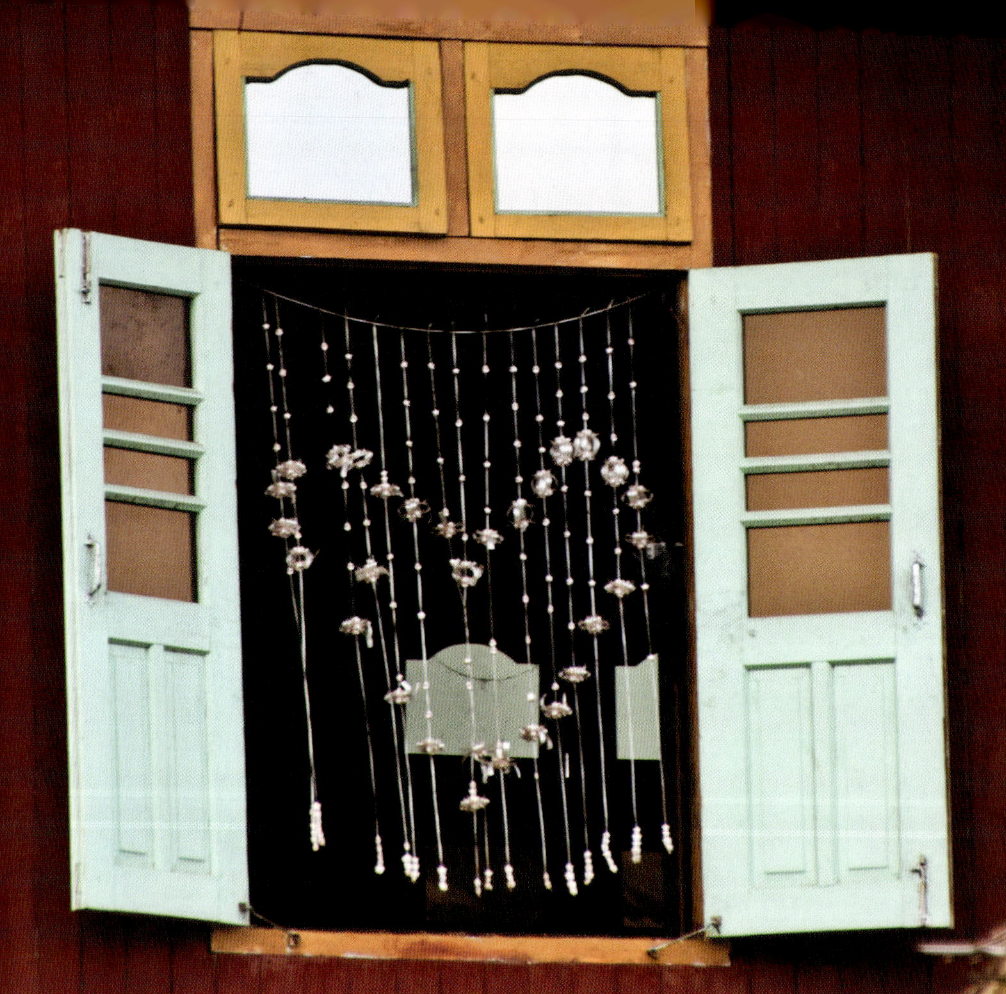
INLE LAKE. BURMA

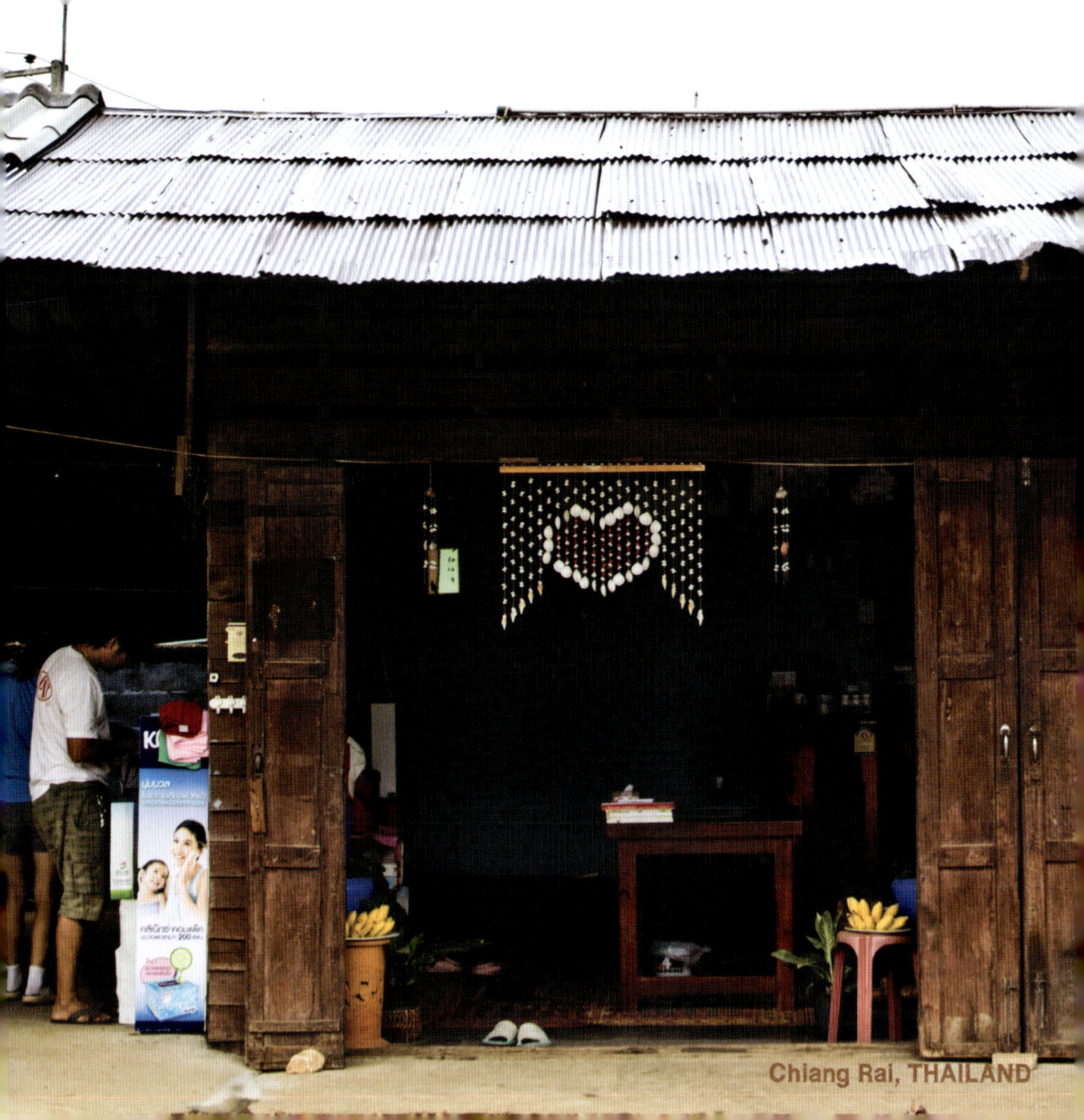

Chiang Rai, THAILAND

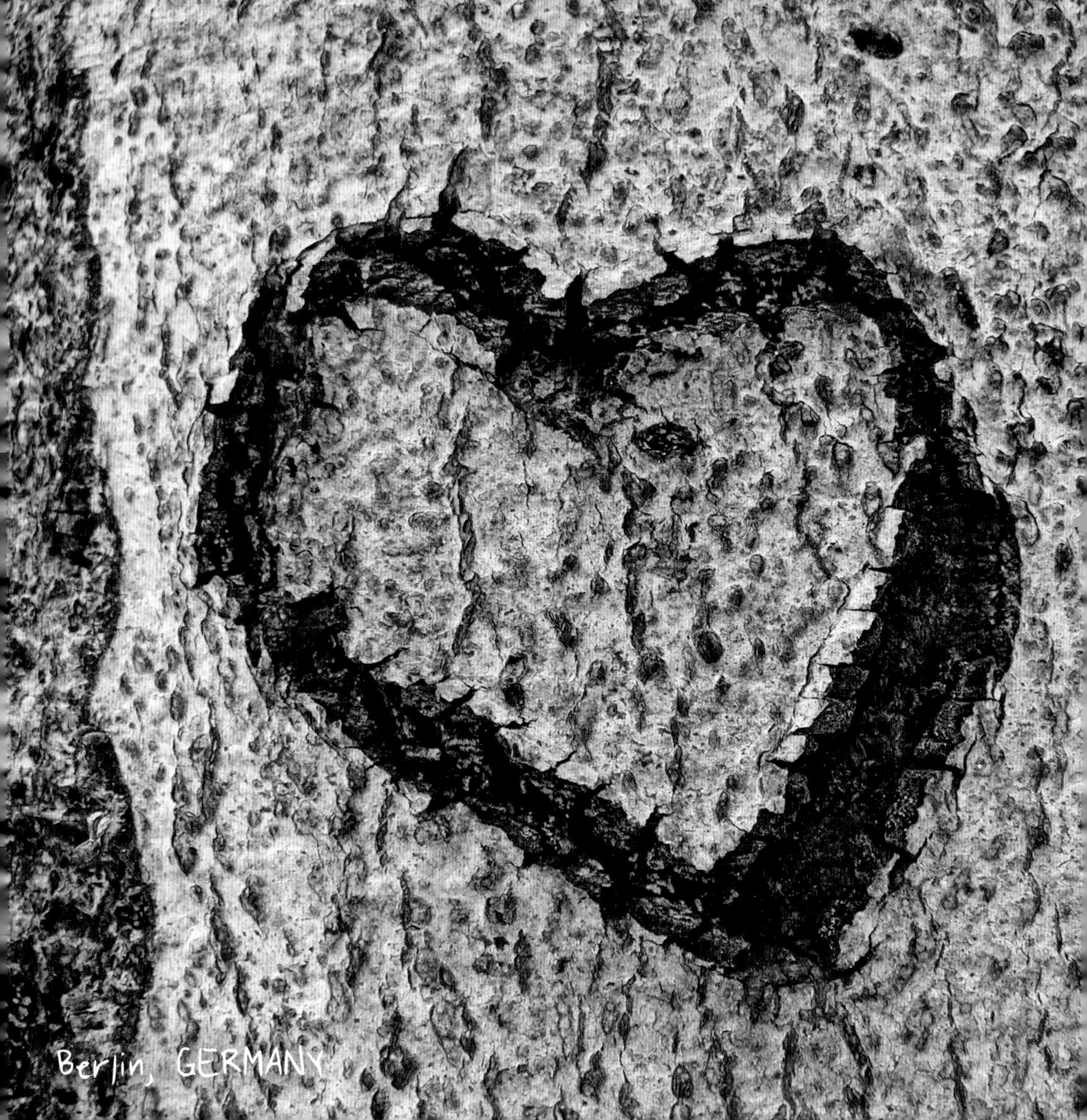
Berlin, GERMANY

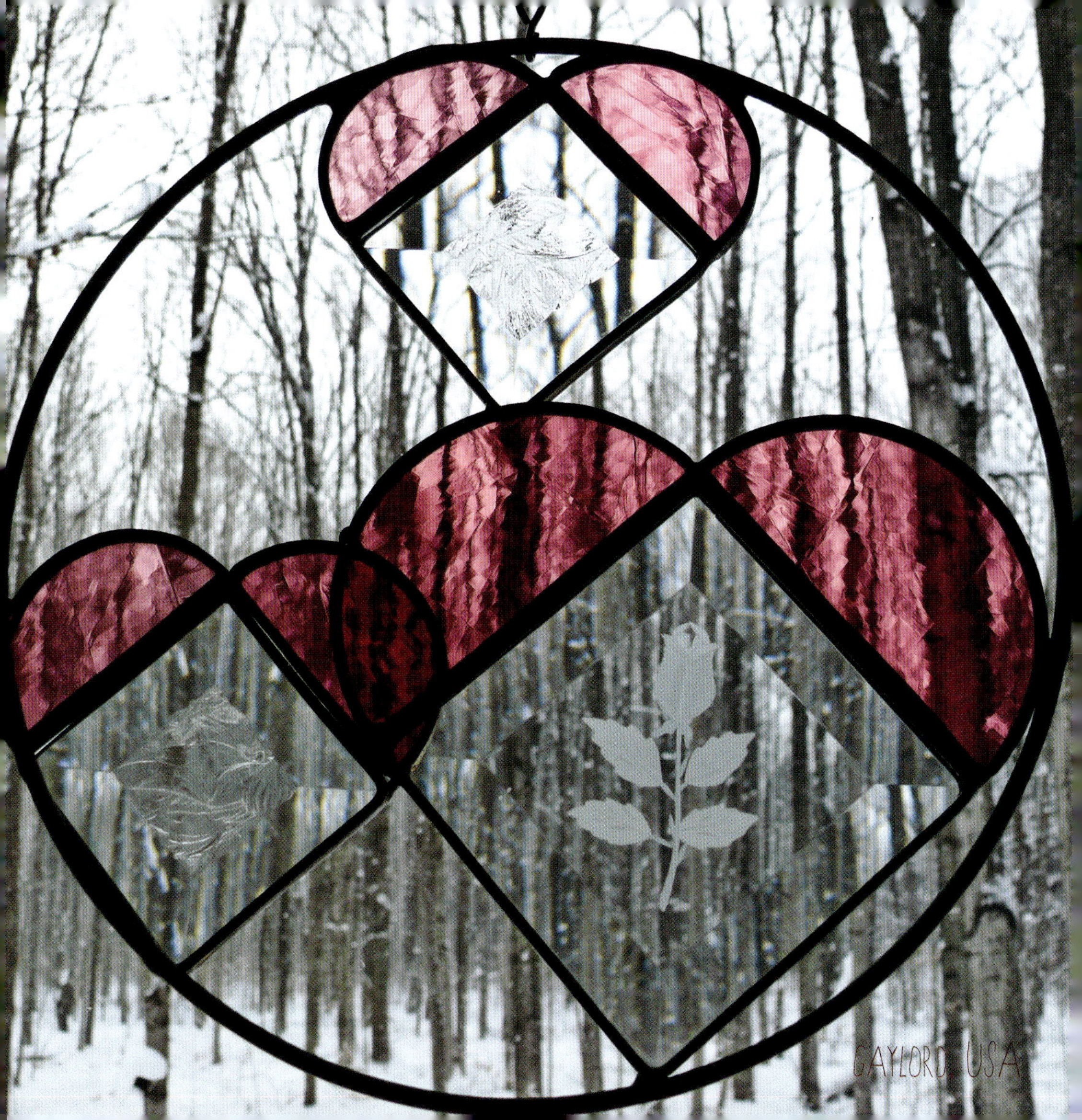
GAYLORD USA

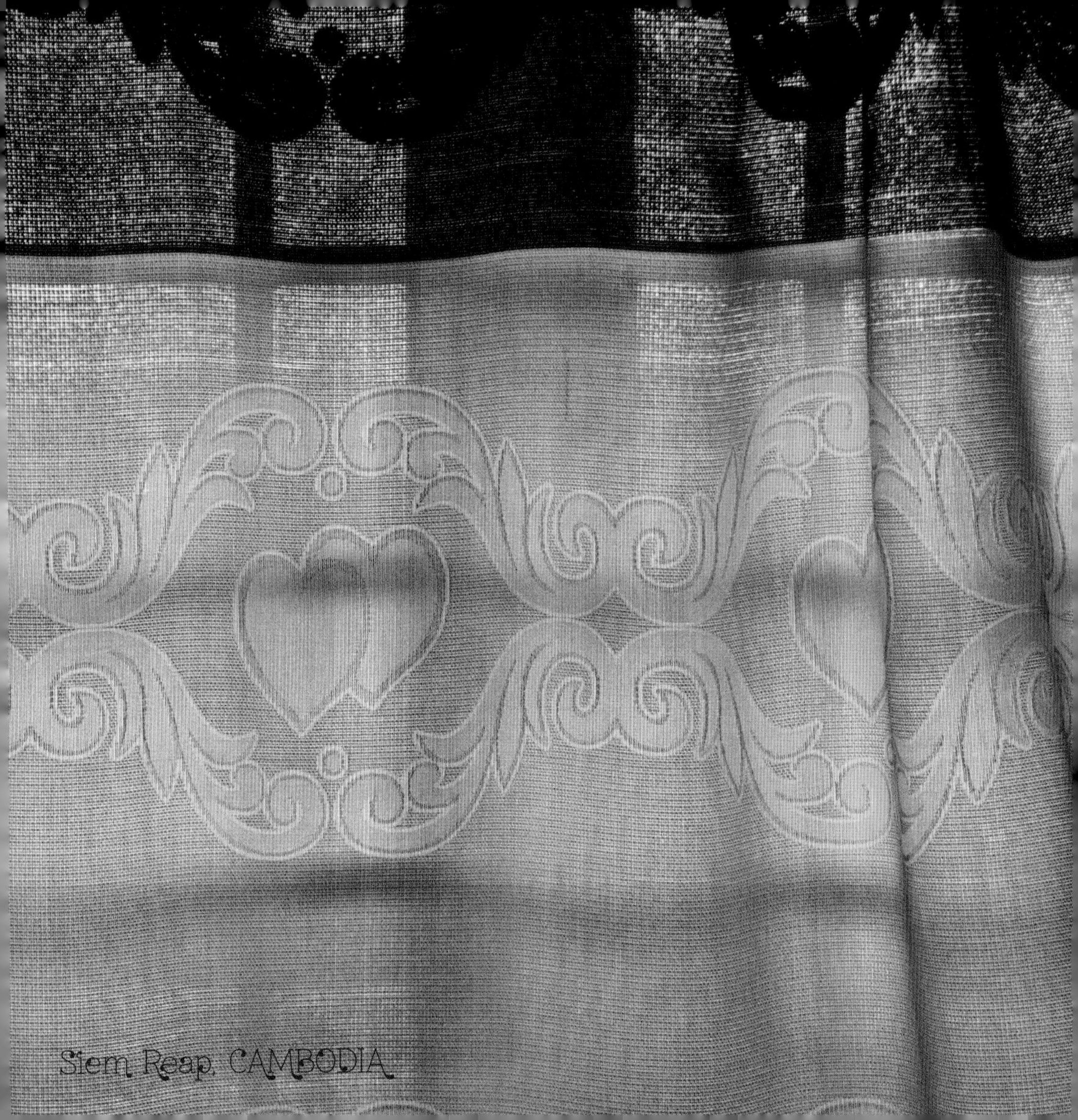
Siem Reap, CAMBODIA

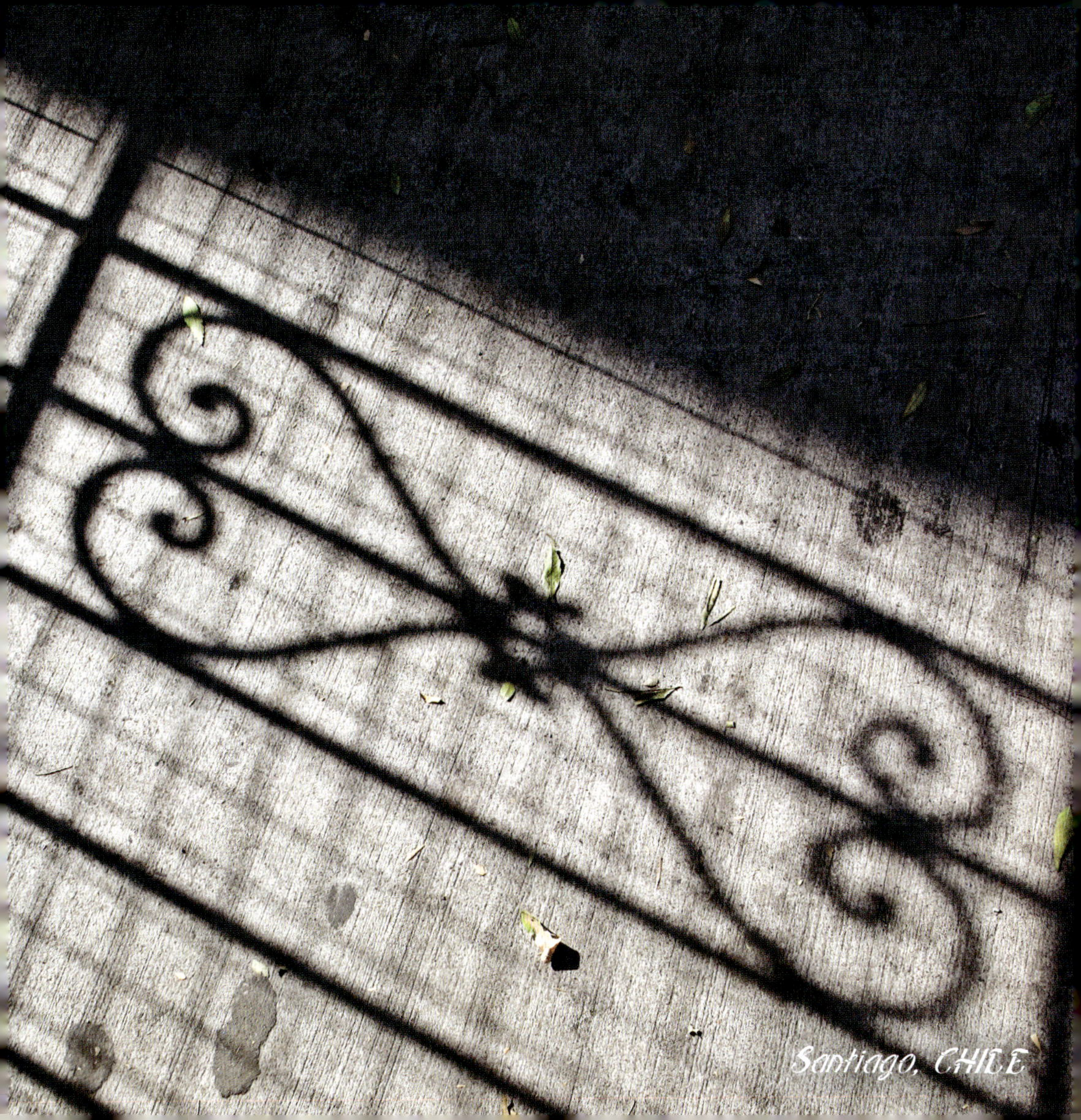
Santiago, CHILE

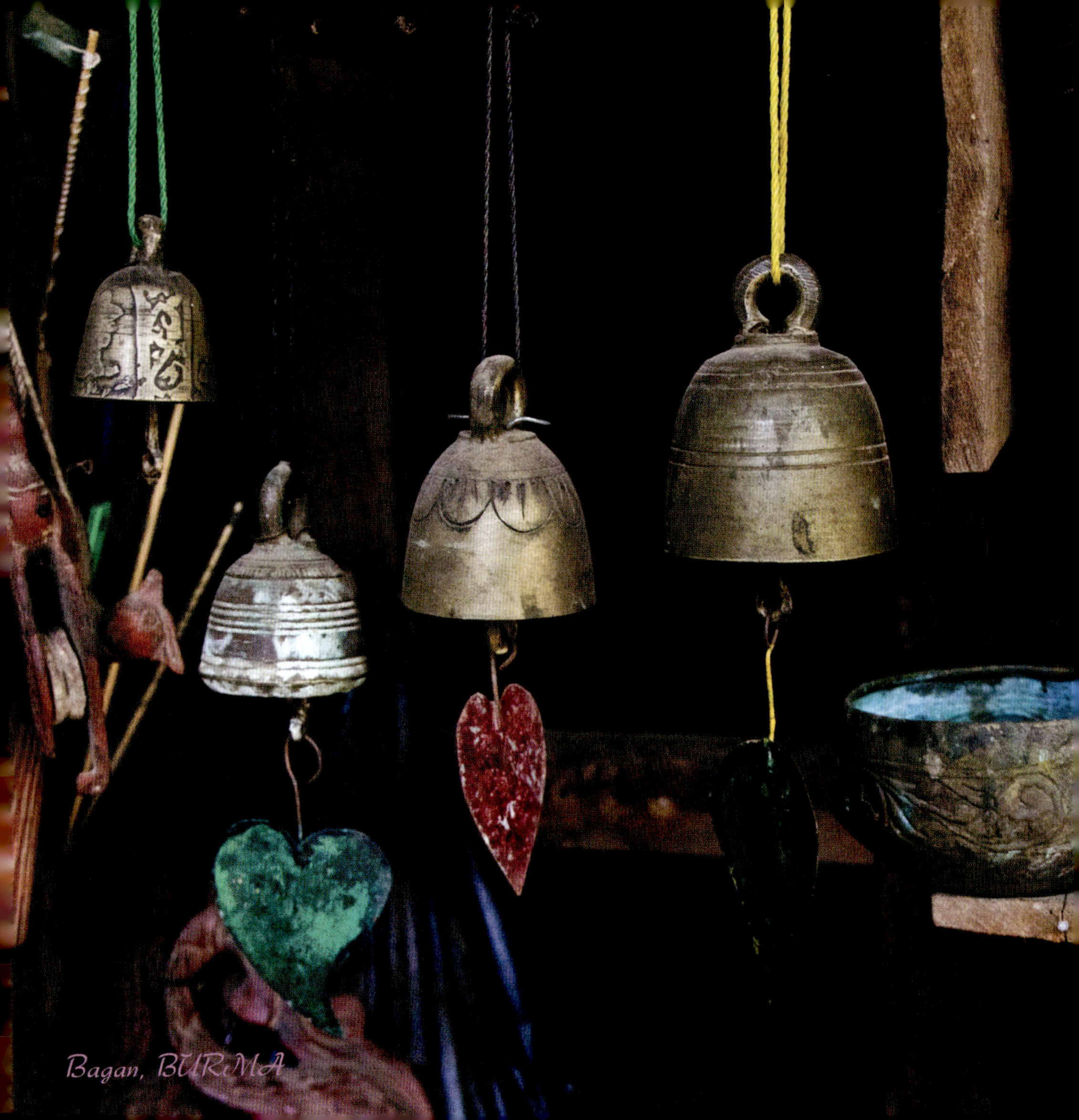
Bagan, BURMA

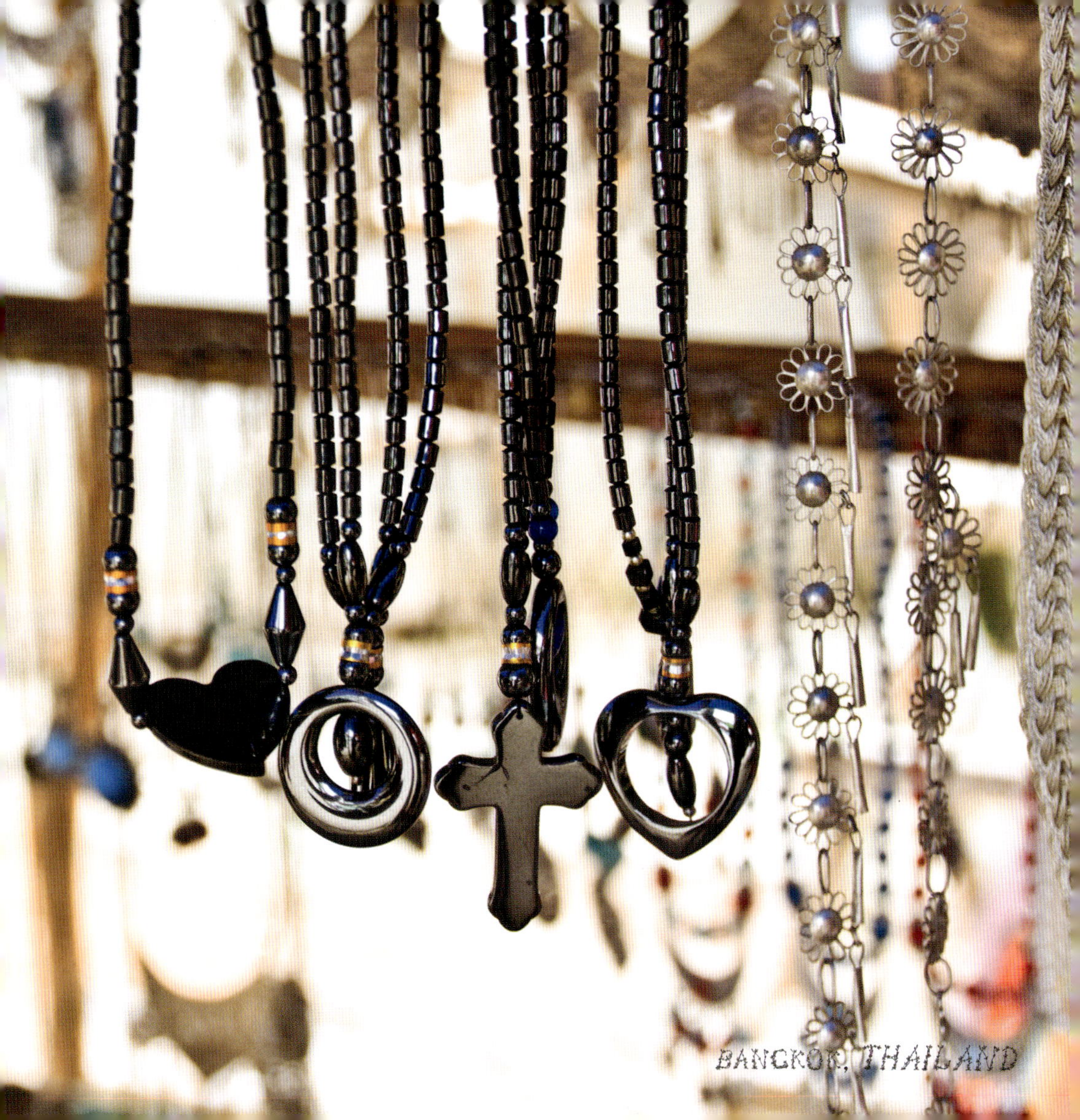

BANGKOK, THAILAND

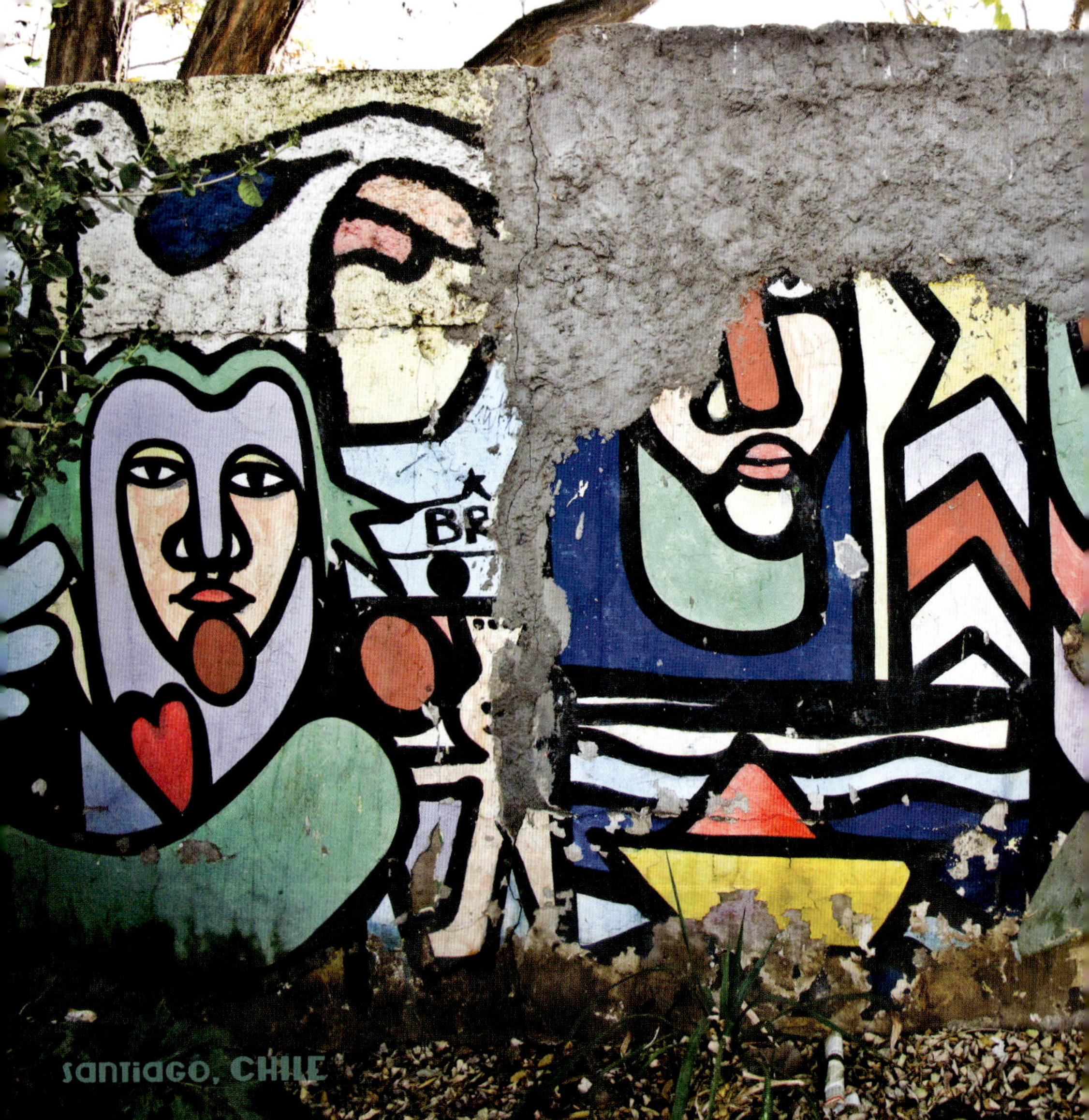
BR
santiago, CHILE

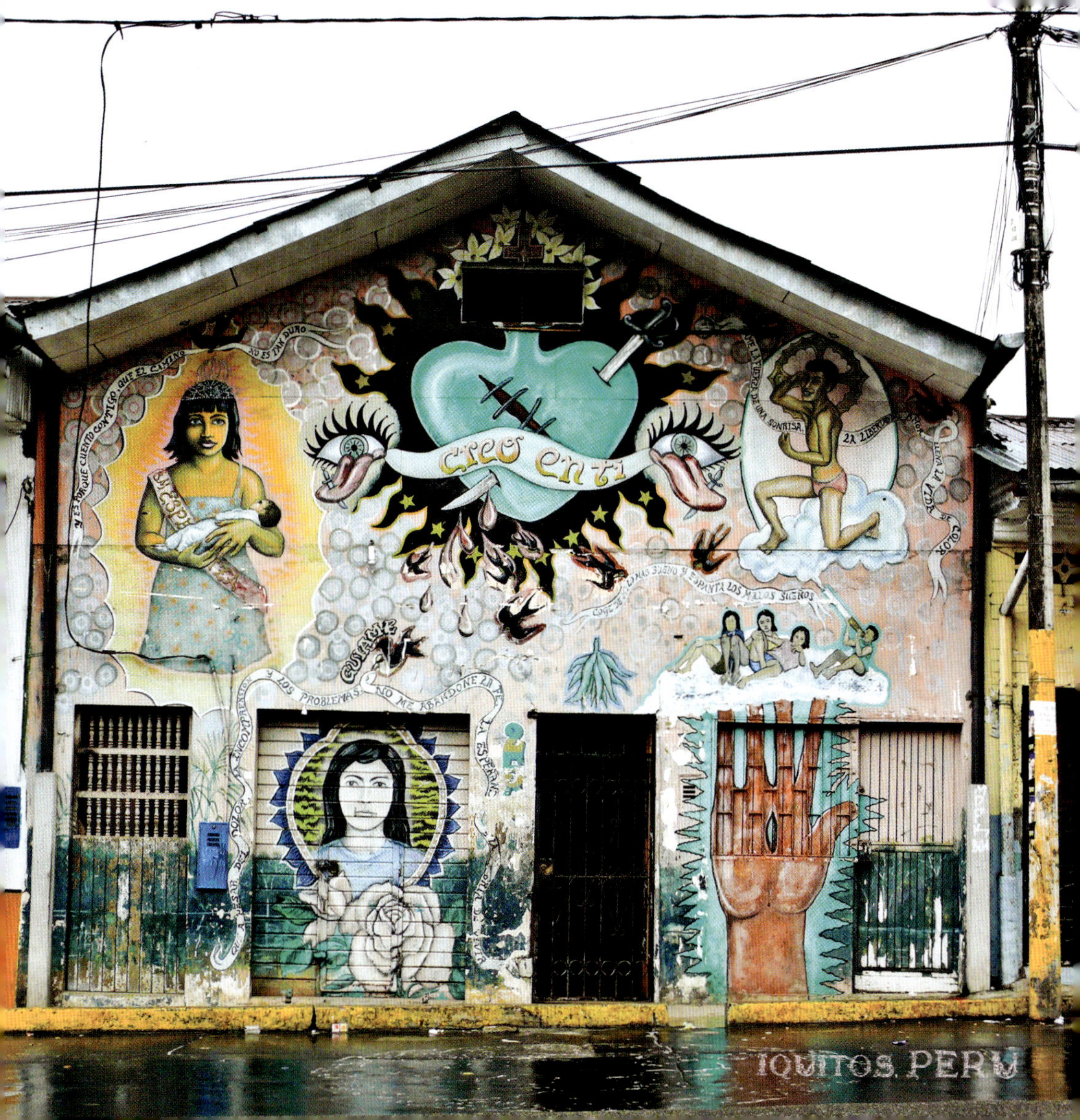
creo en ti
IQUITOS PERU

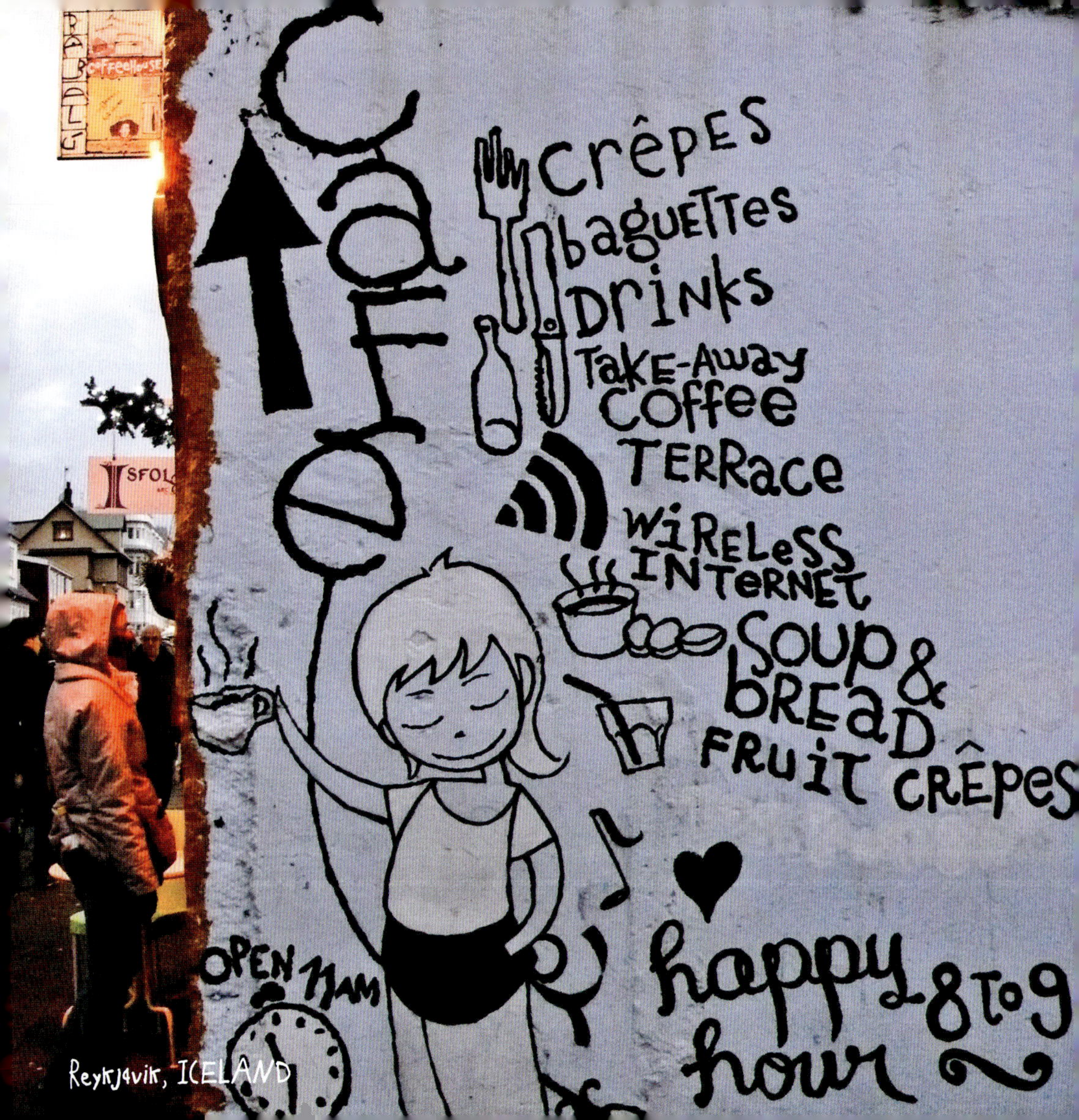

Café
crêpes
baguettes
drinks
Take-Away
Coffee
Terrace
Wireless
Internet
Soup &
Bread
Fruit crêpes
happy 8 to 9
hour
Open 11am
Reykjavik, ICELAND

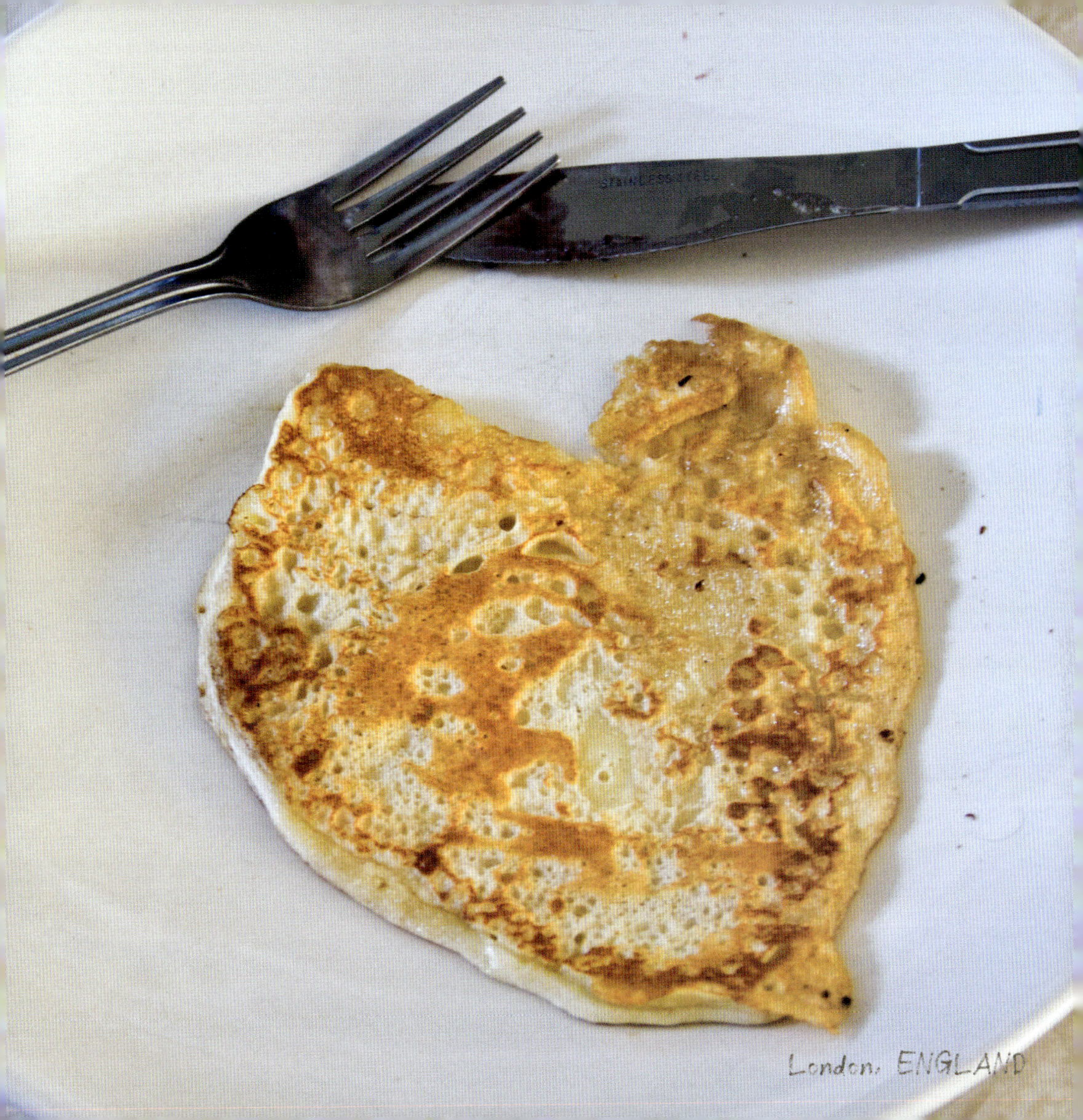
London, ENGLAND

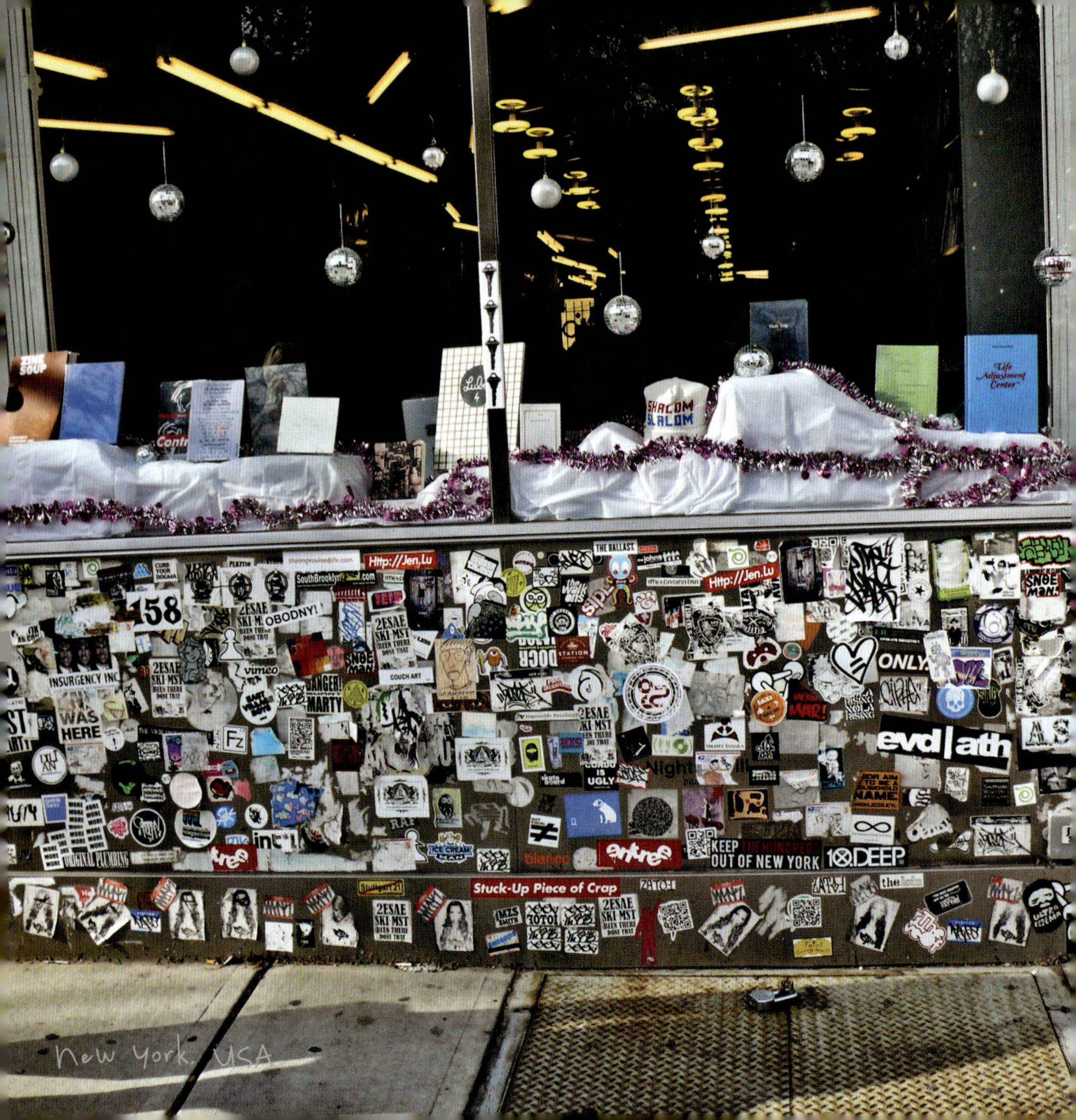

New York, USA

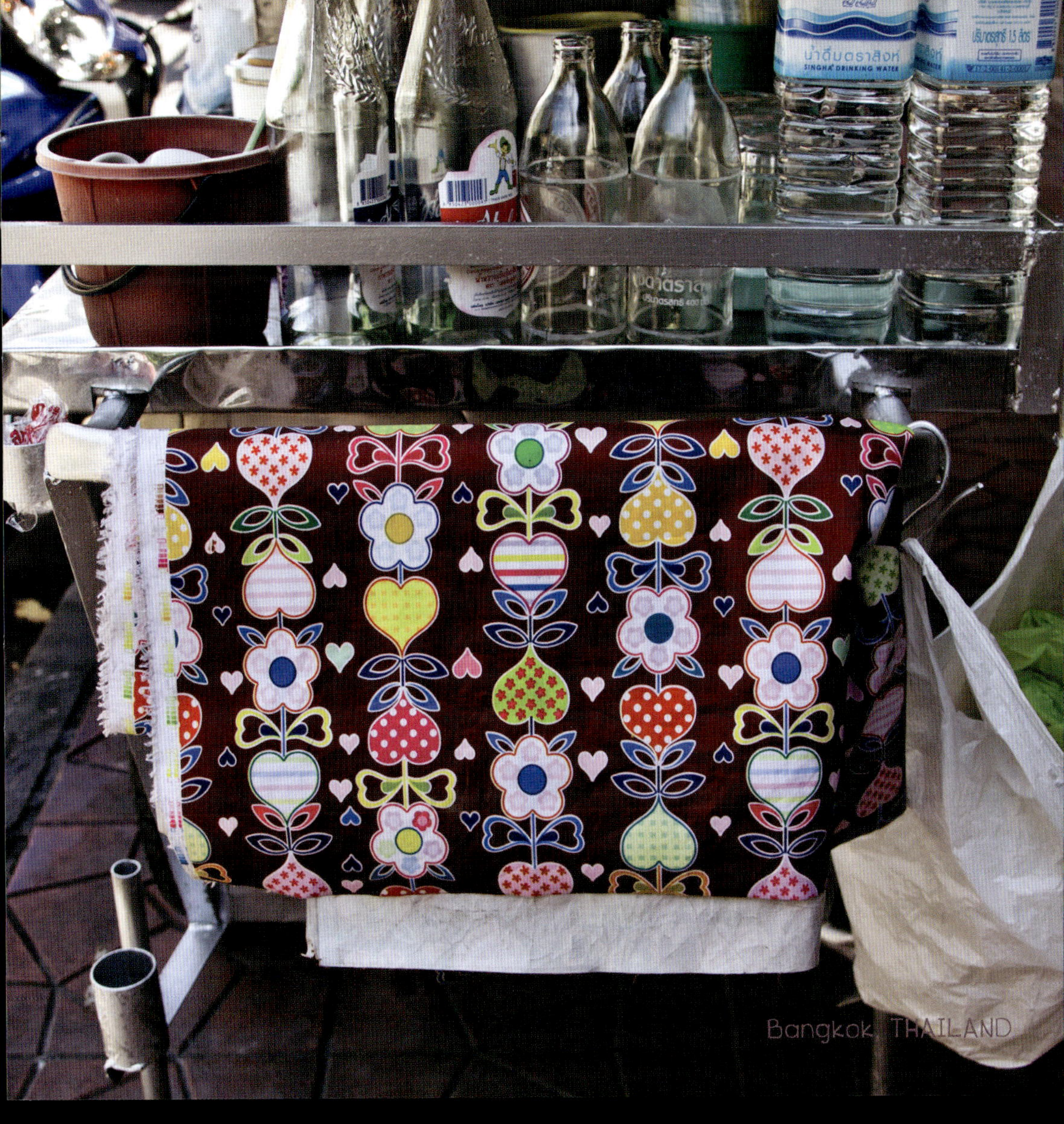
Bangkok THAILAND

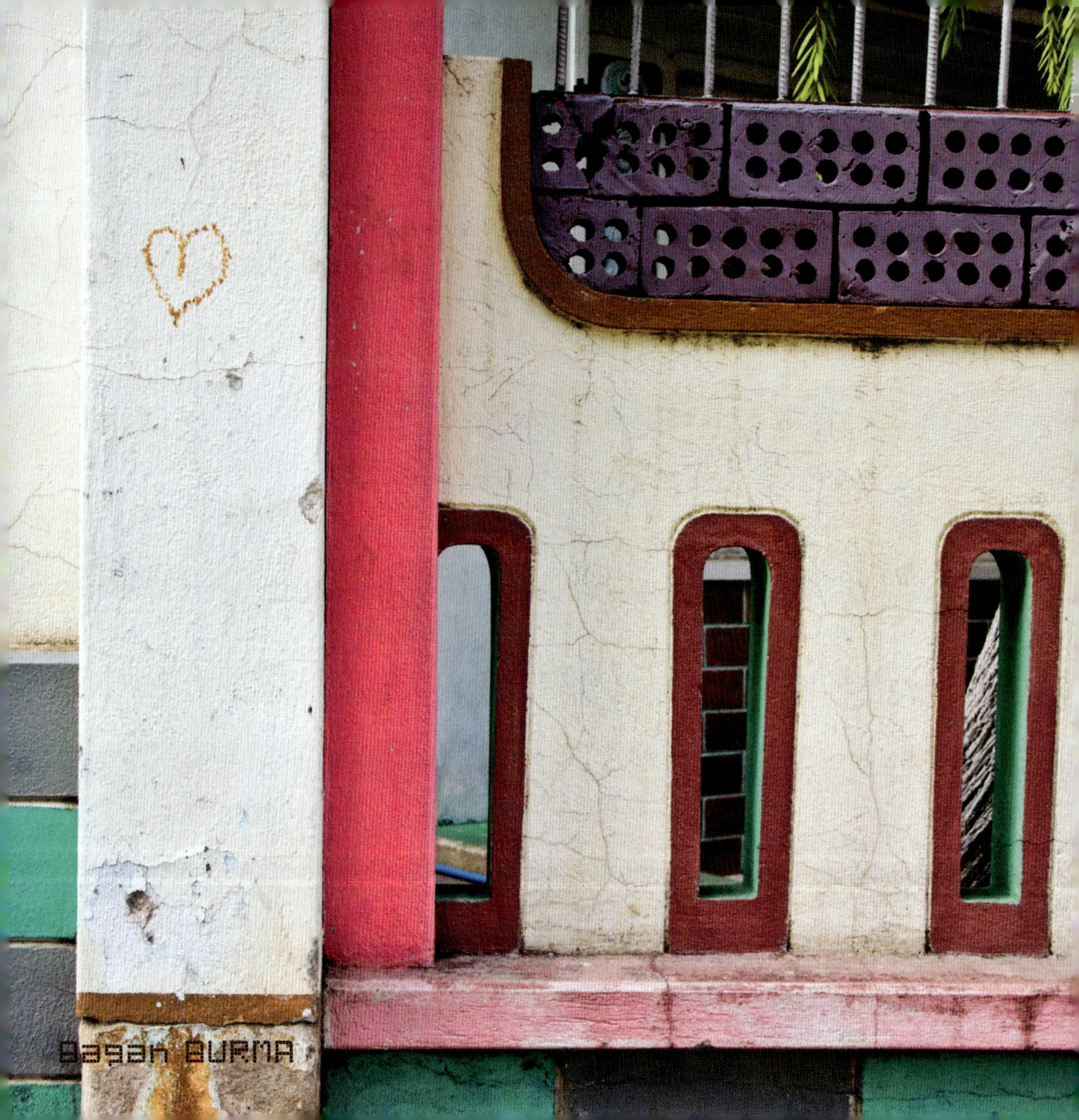

Bagan BURMA

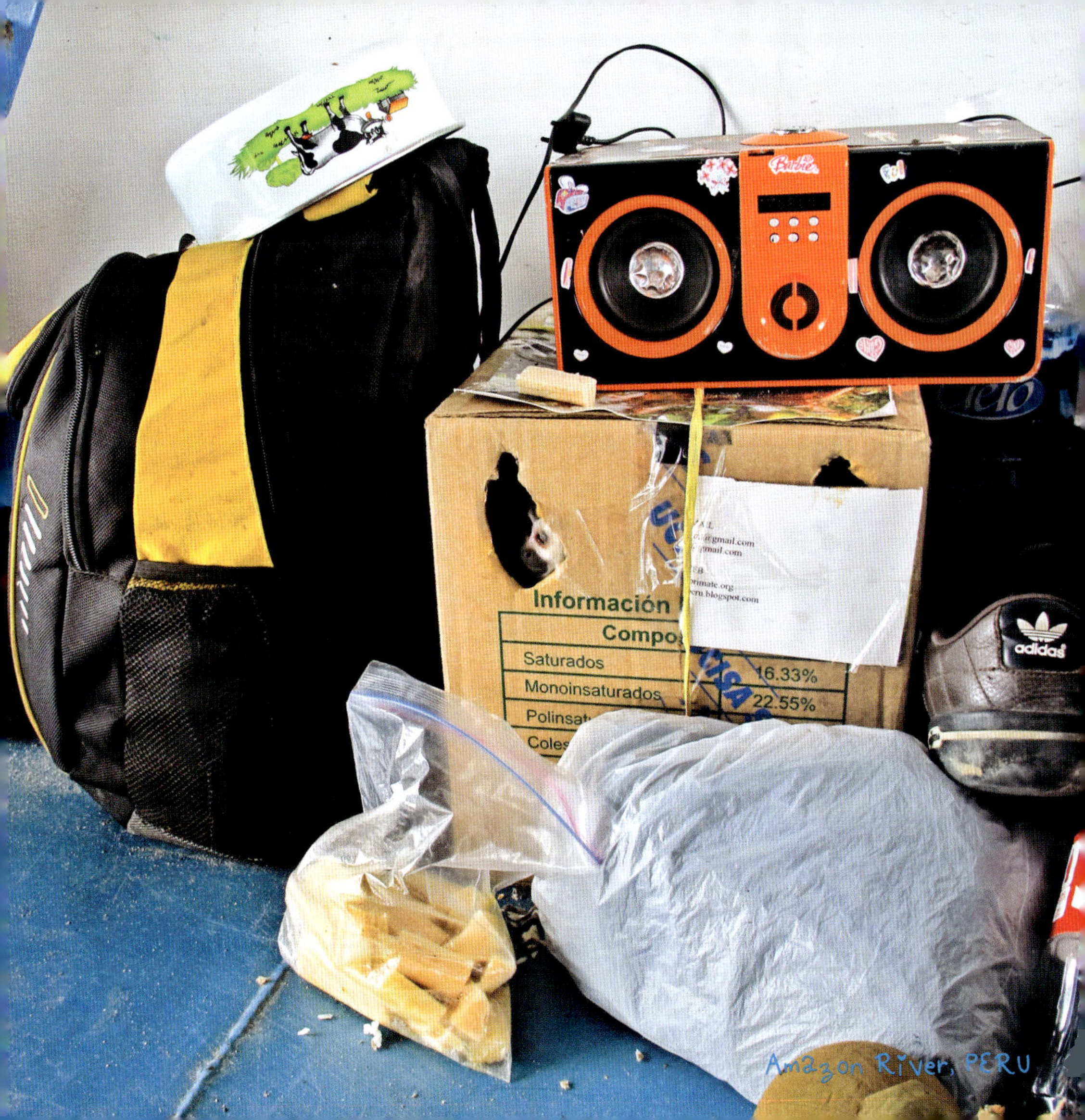

Barbie
Información
Compos
Saturados
16.33%
Monoinsaturados
22.55%
Polinsat
Coles
@gmail.com
@gmail.com
primate.org
peru.blogspot.com
adidas
ielo
Amazon River, PERU

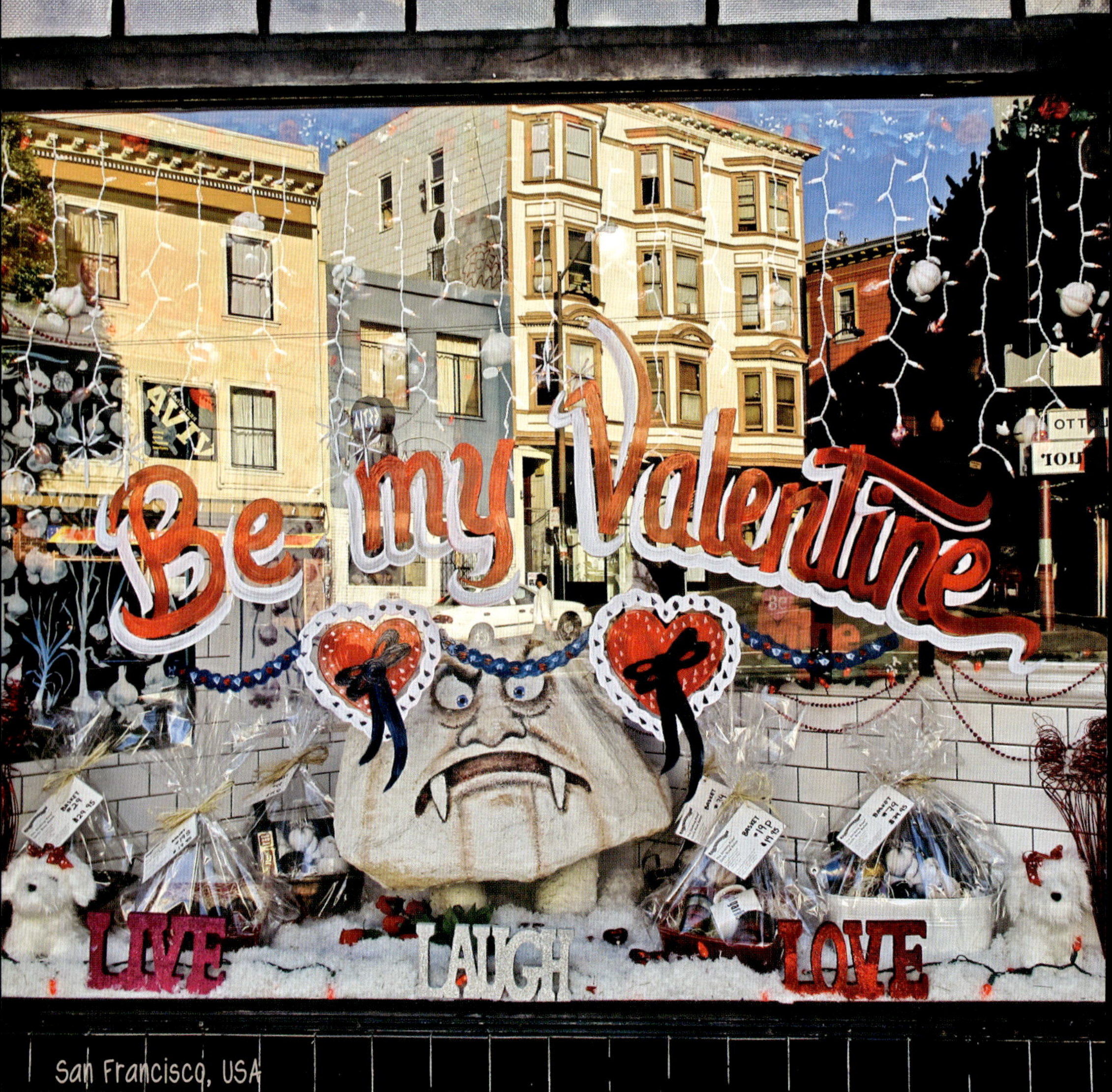
Be my Valentine
LIVE
LAUGH
LOVE
San Francisco, USA

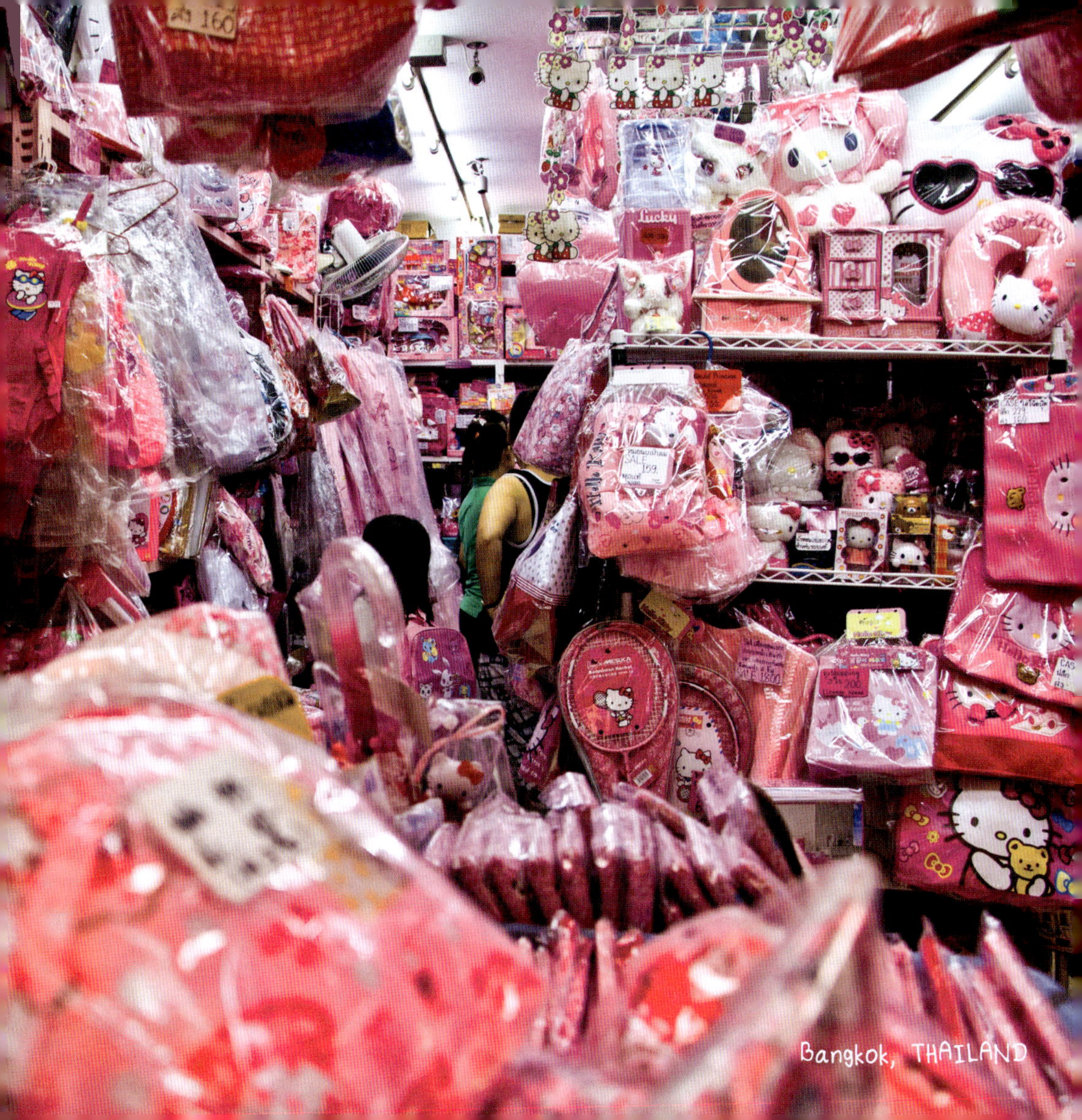
160
lucky
Hello Kitty
SALE 169
Bangkok, THAILAND

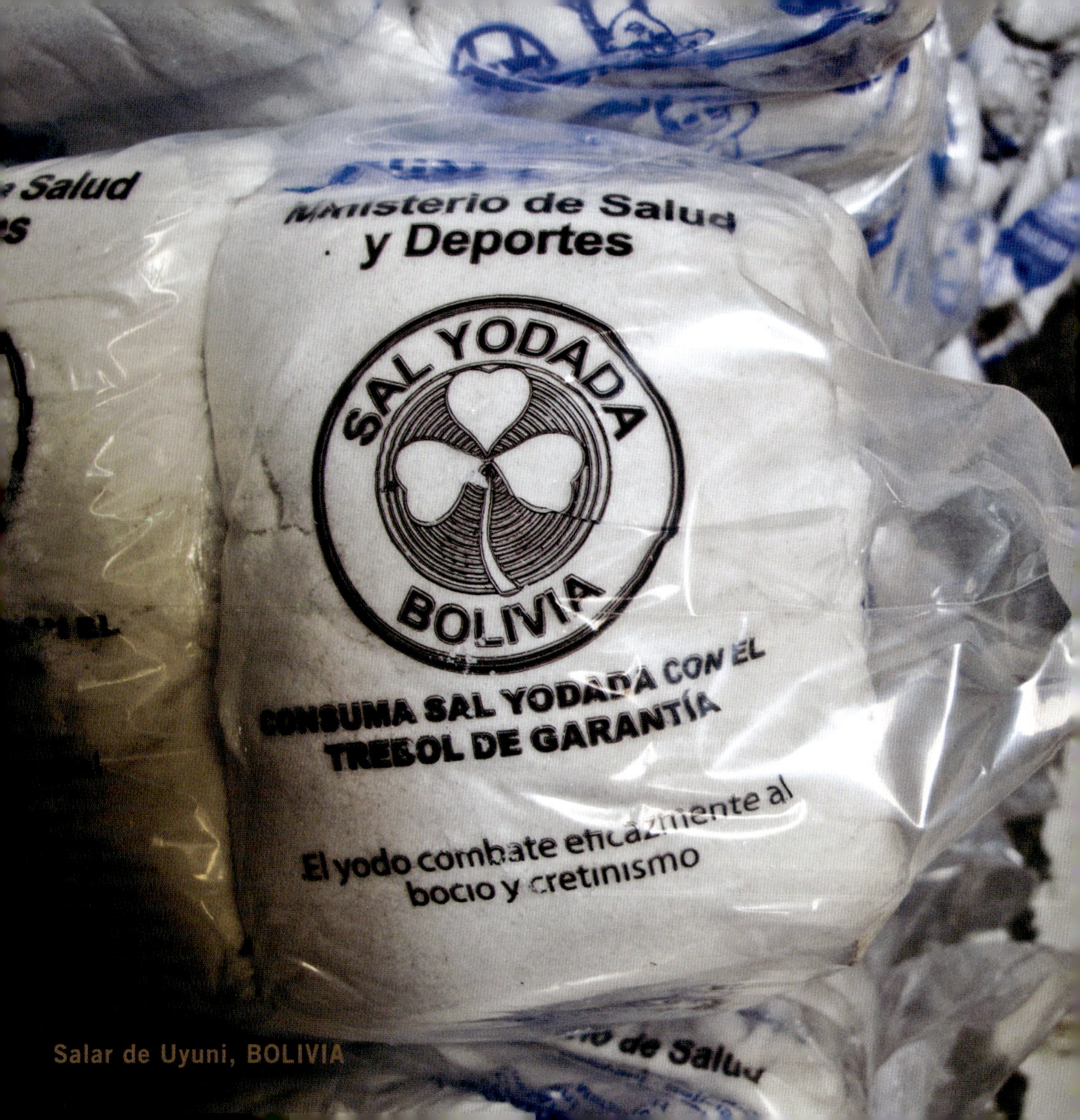

Salar de Uyuni, BOLIVIA

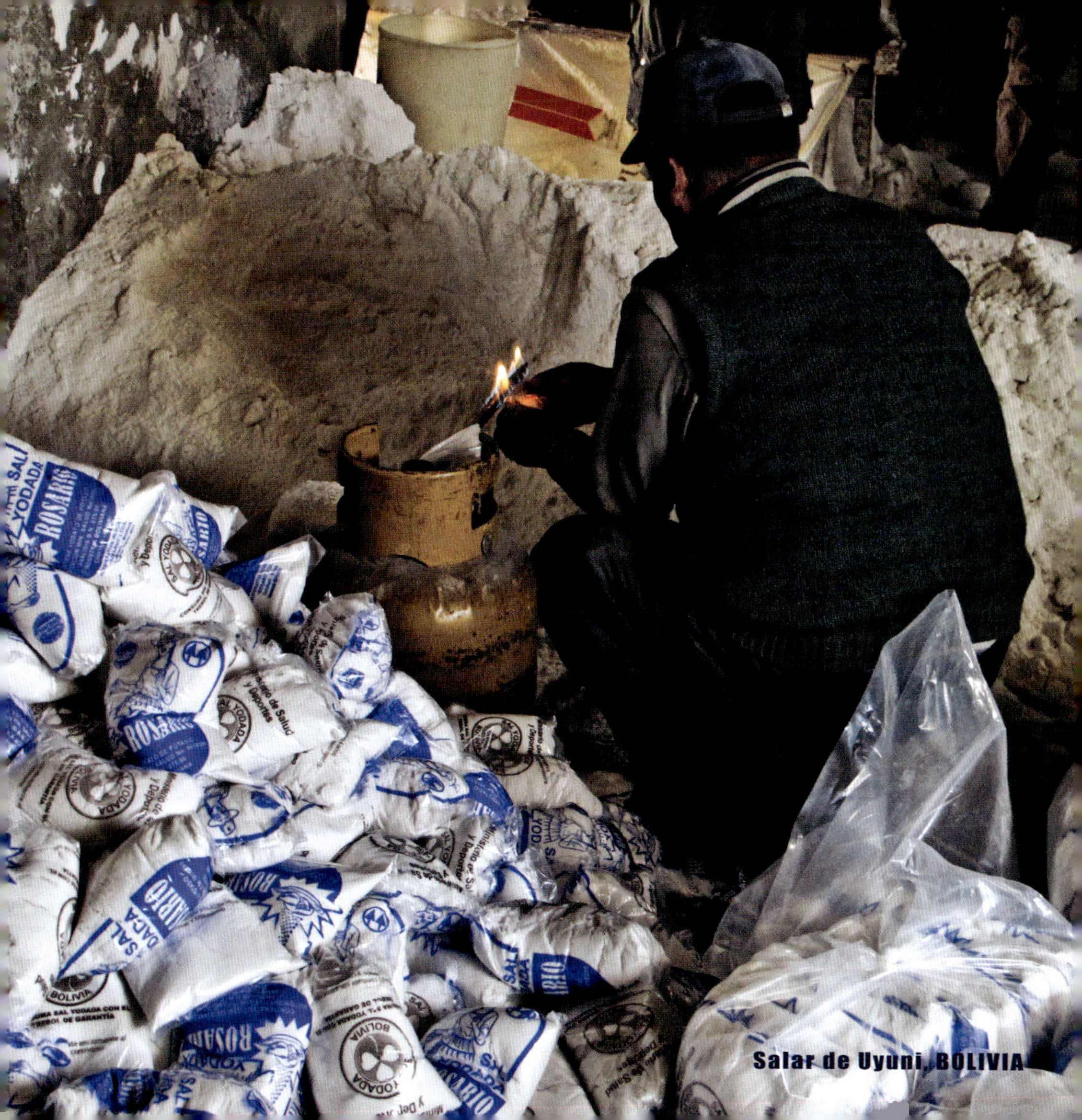
Salar de Uyuni, BOLIVIA

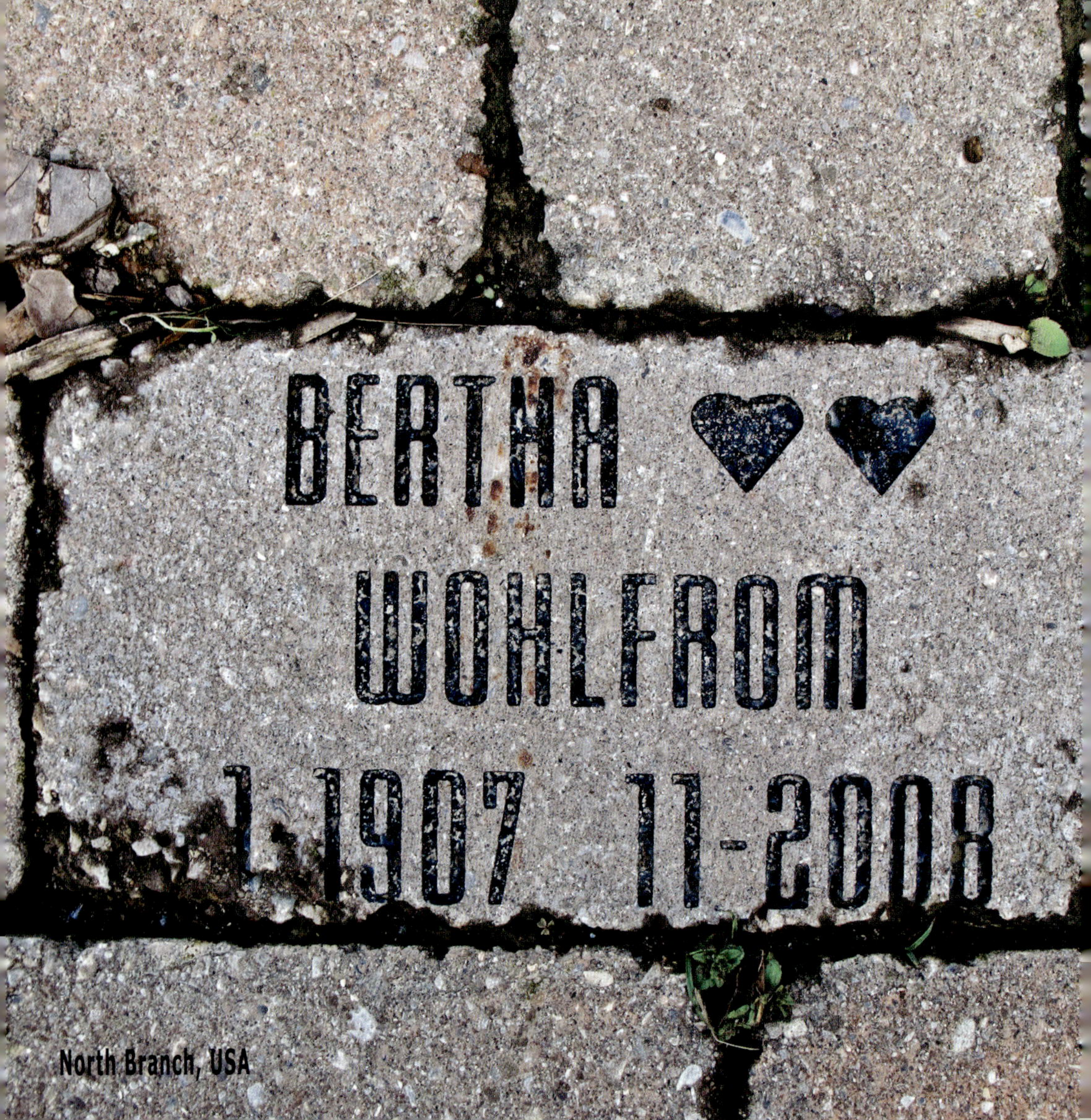

North Branch, USA

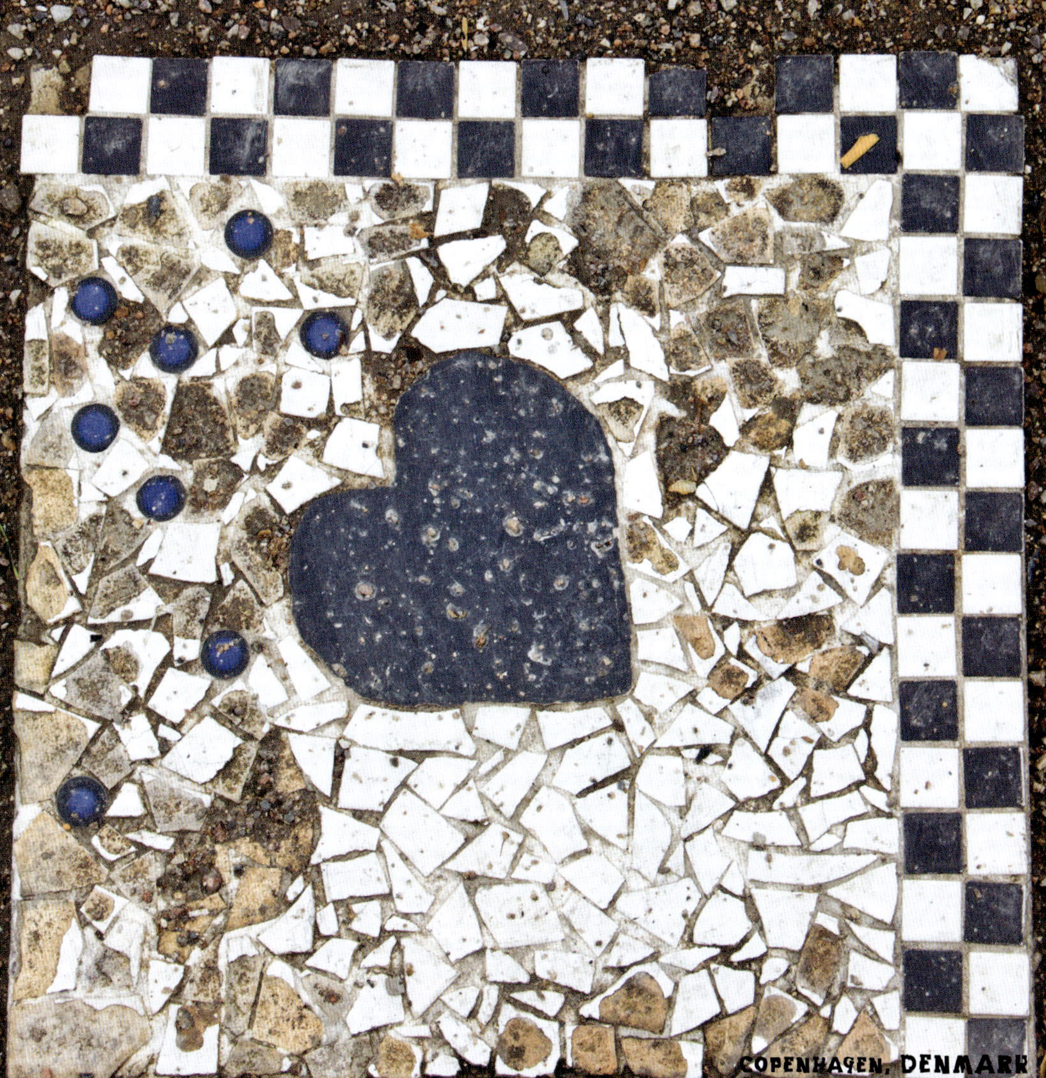

COPENHAGEN, DENMARK

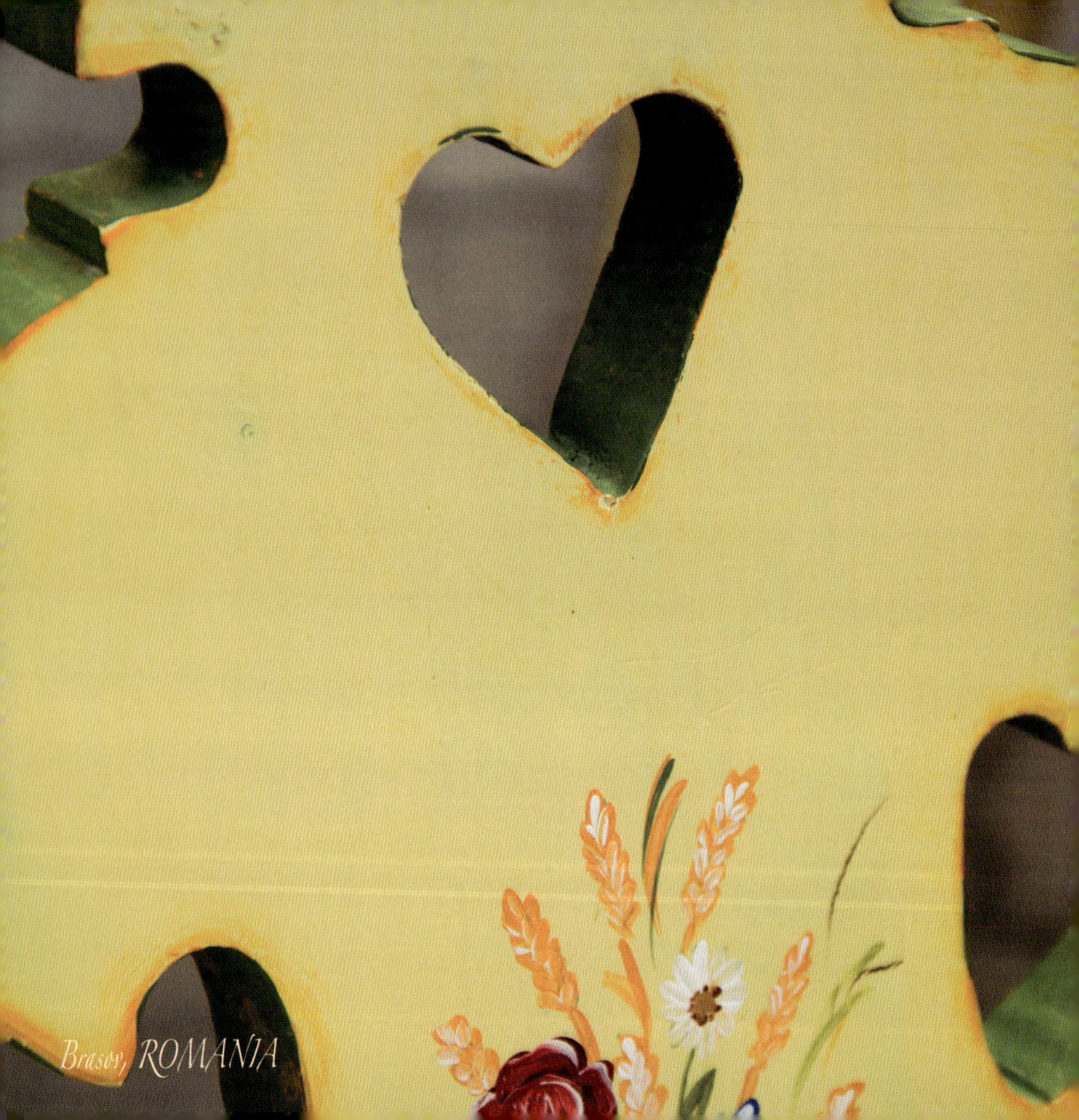
Brasov, ROMANIA

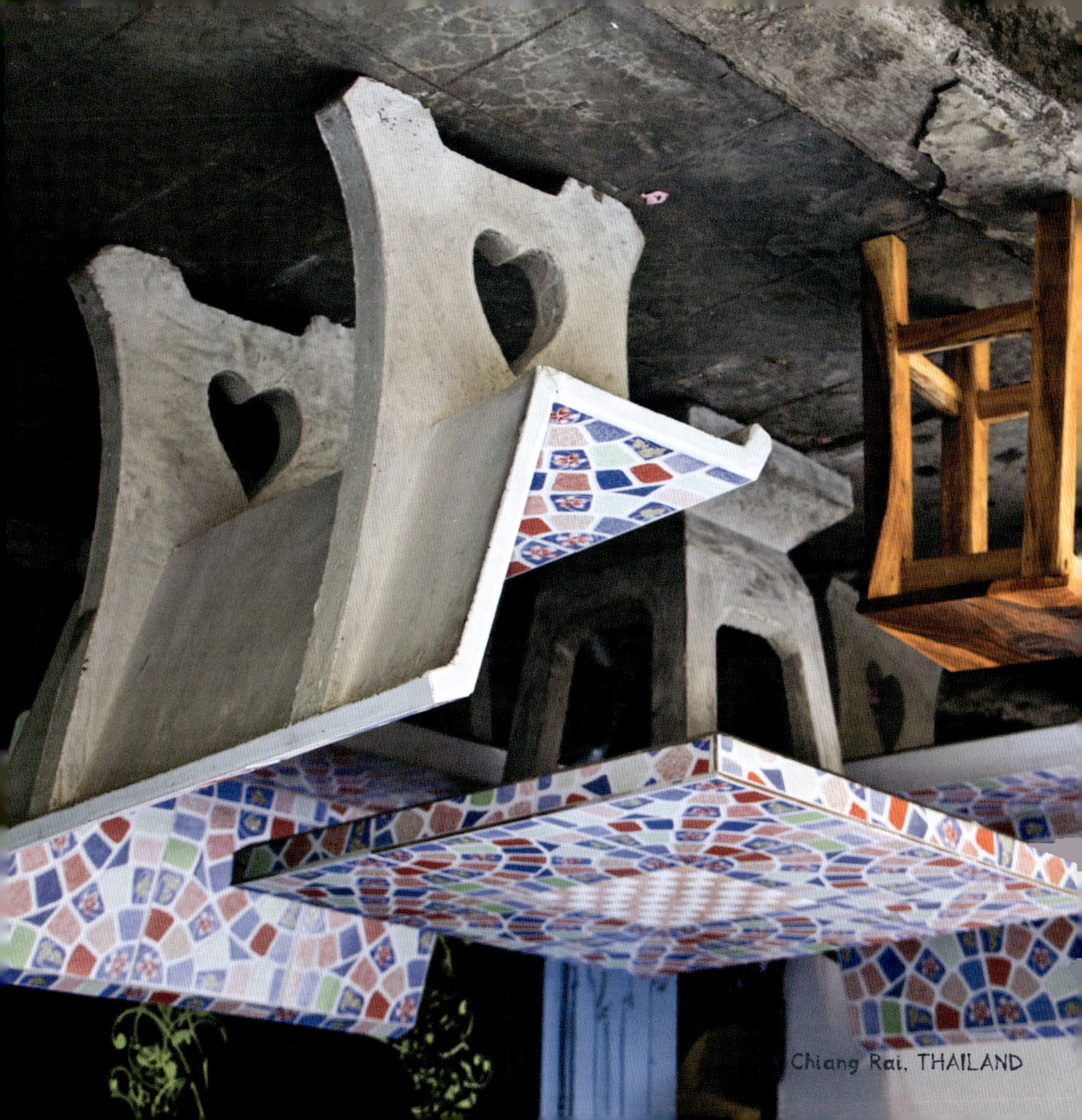
Chiang Rai, THAILAND

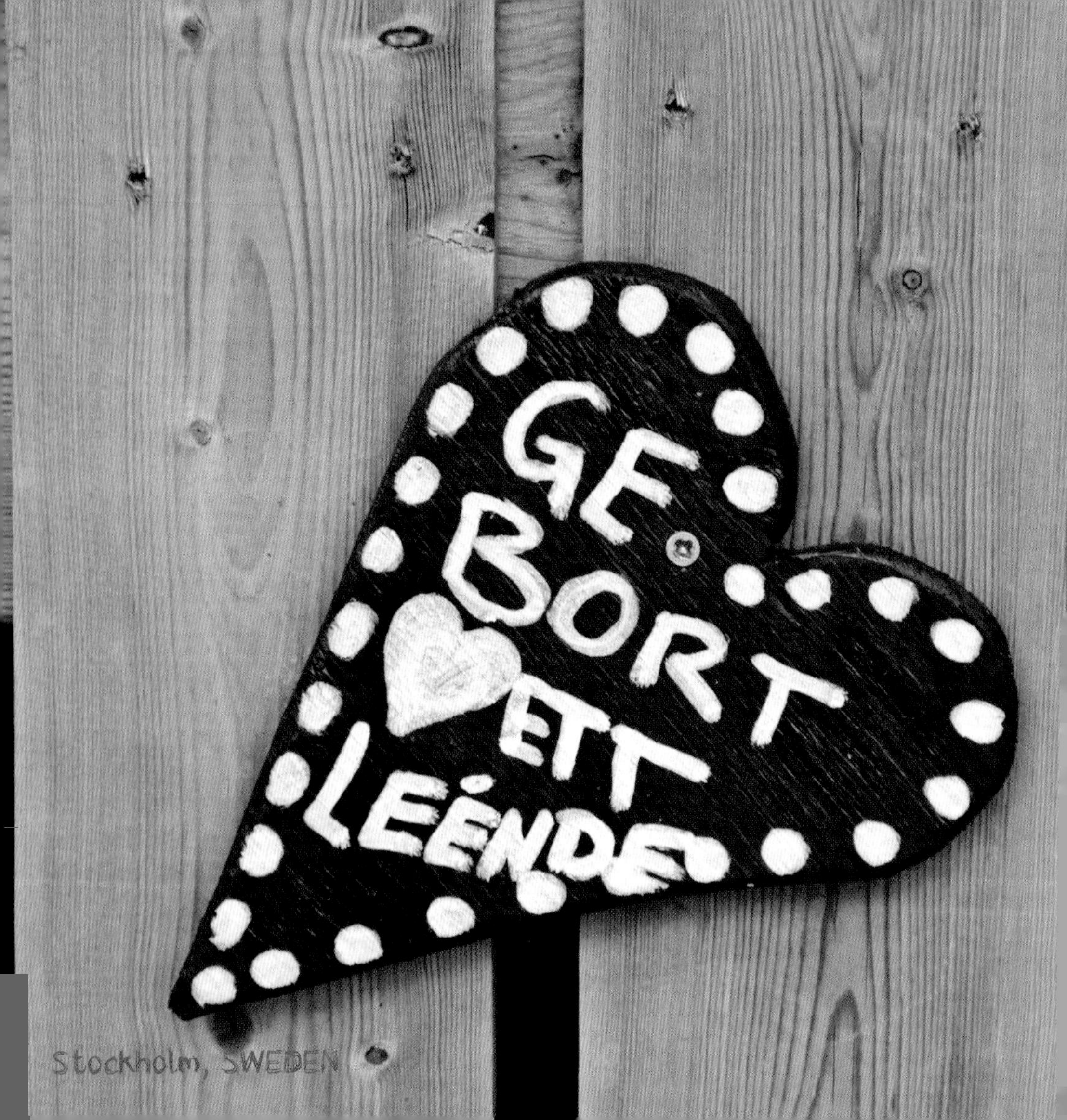

Stockholm, SWEDEN

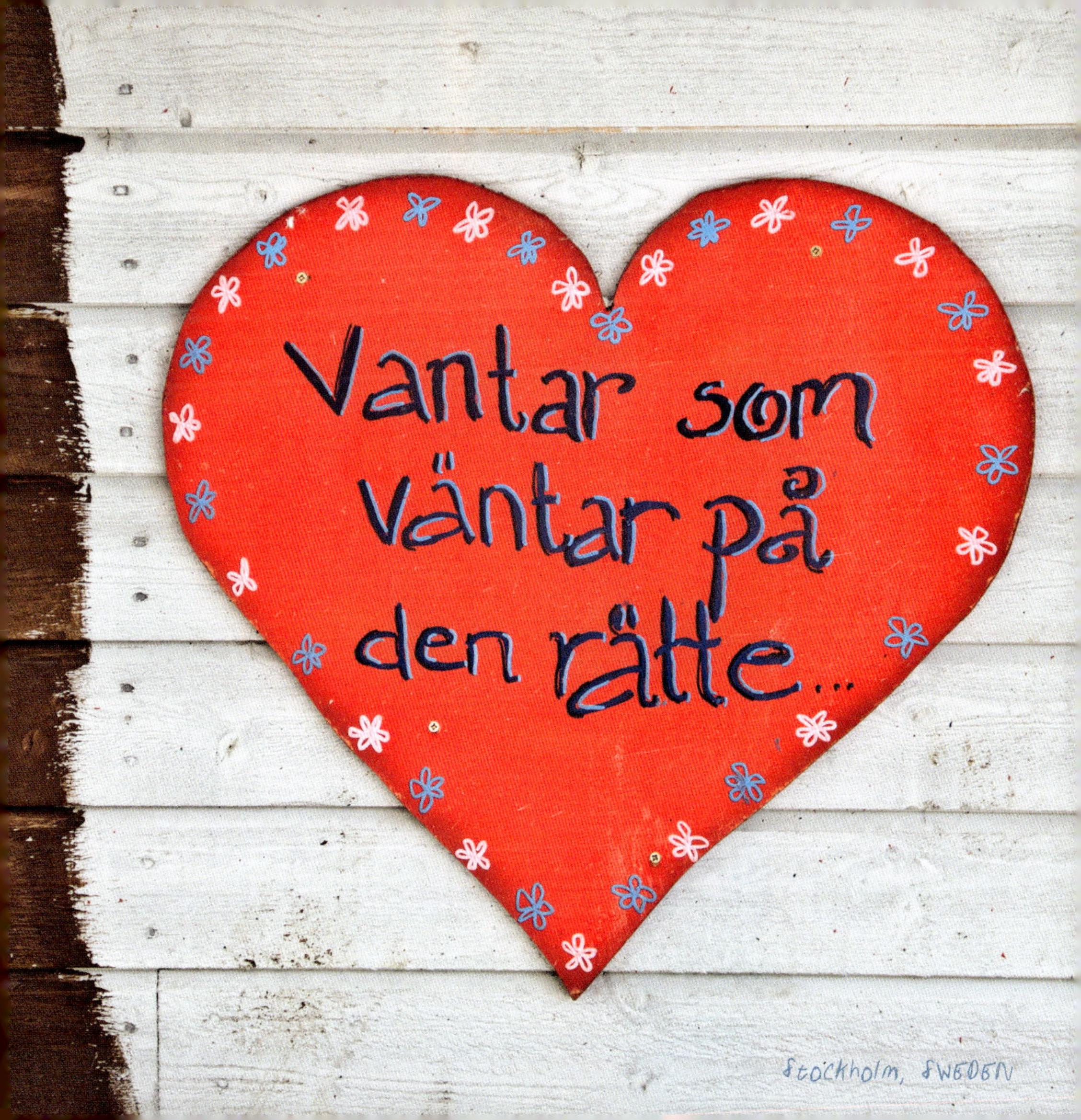

Vantar som
väntar på
den rätte...
Stockholm, SWEDEN

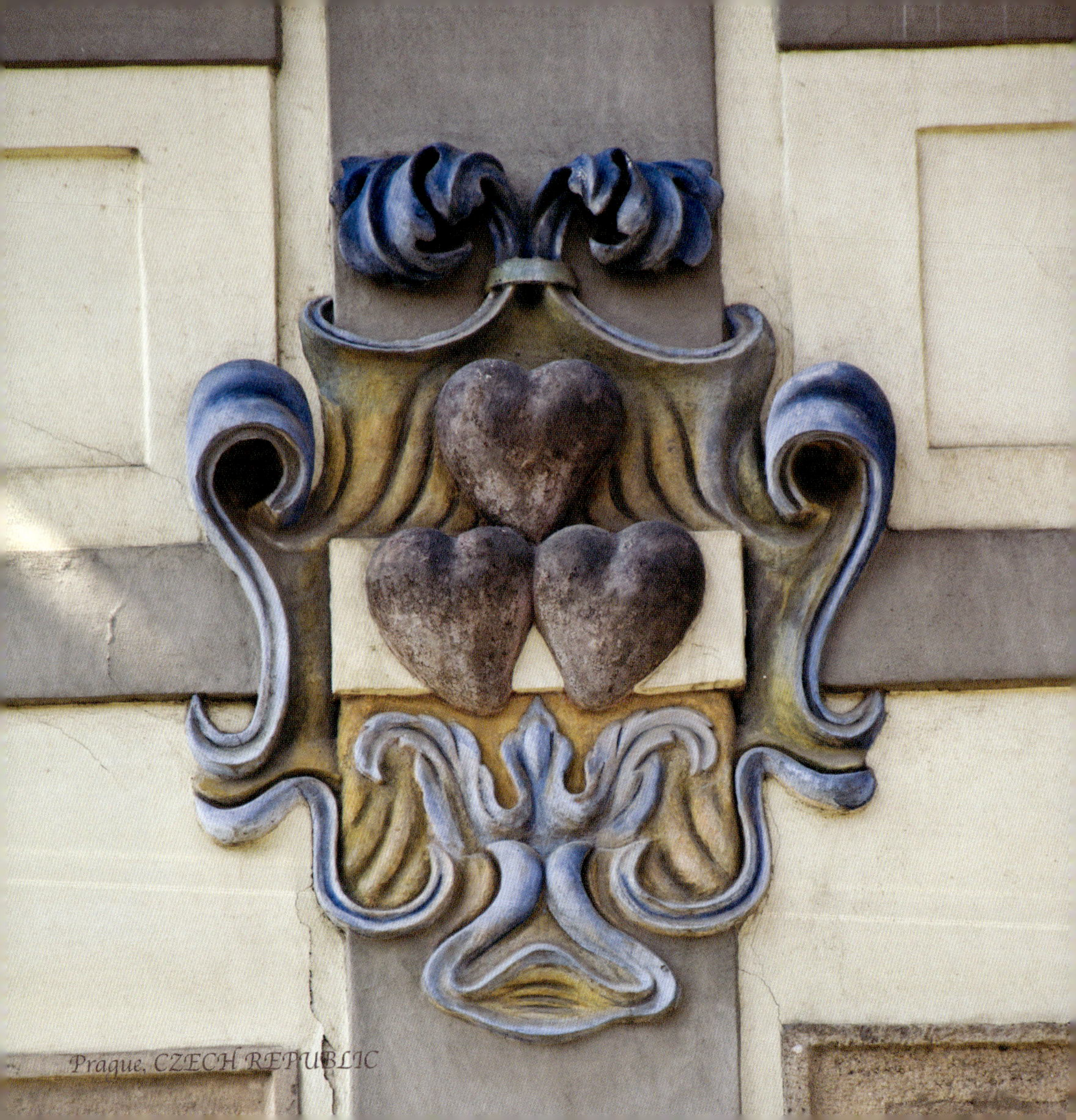
Prague. CZECH REPUBLIC

BRIGHTON, ENGLAND

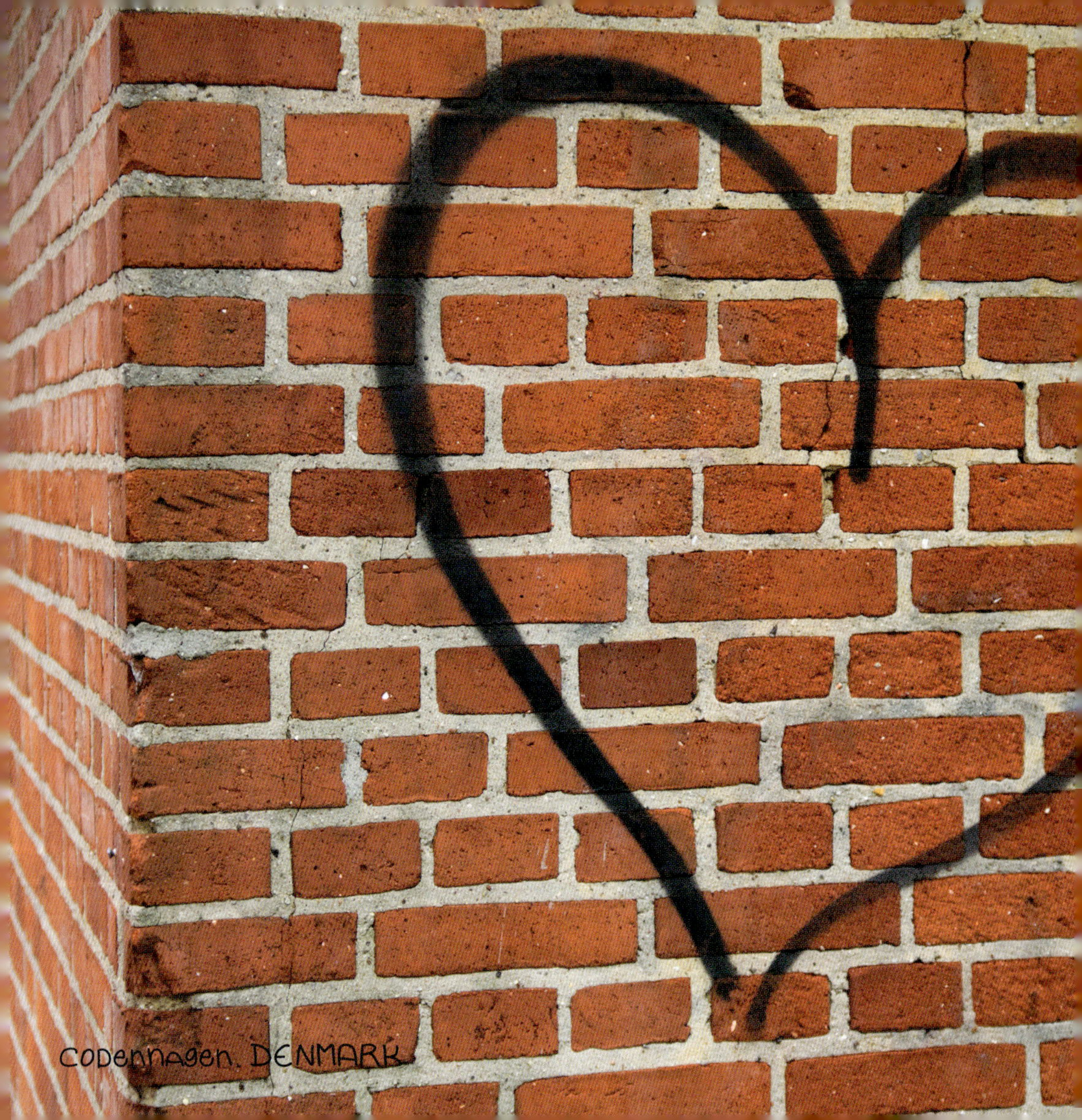

Copenhagen. DENMARK

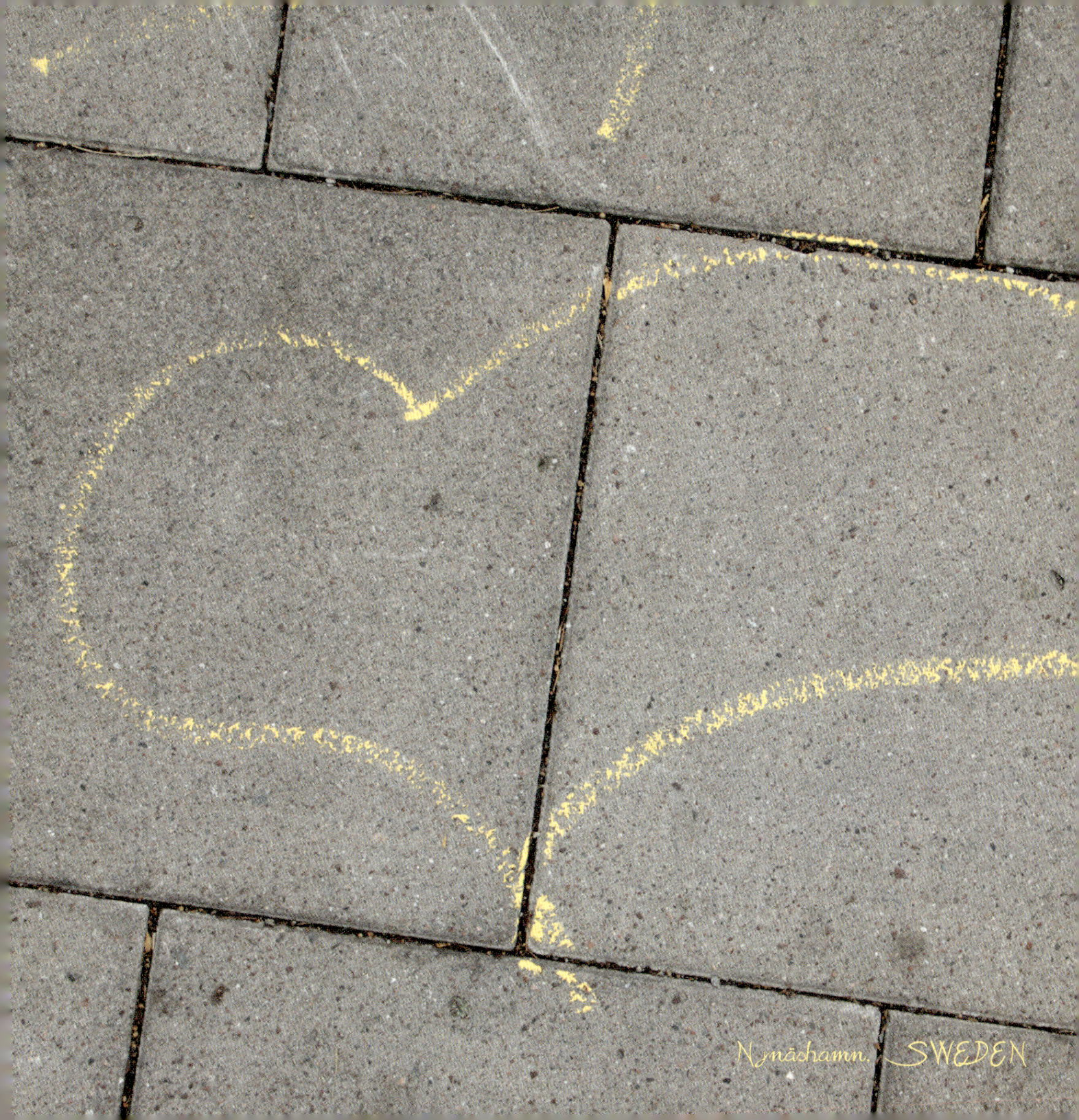
Nynäshamn. SWEDEN

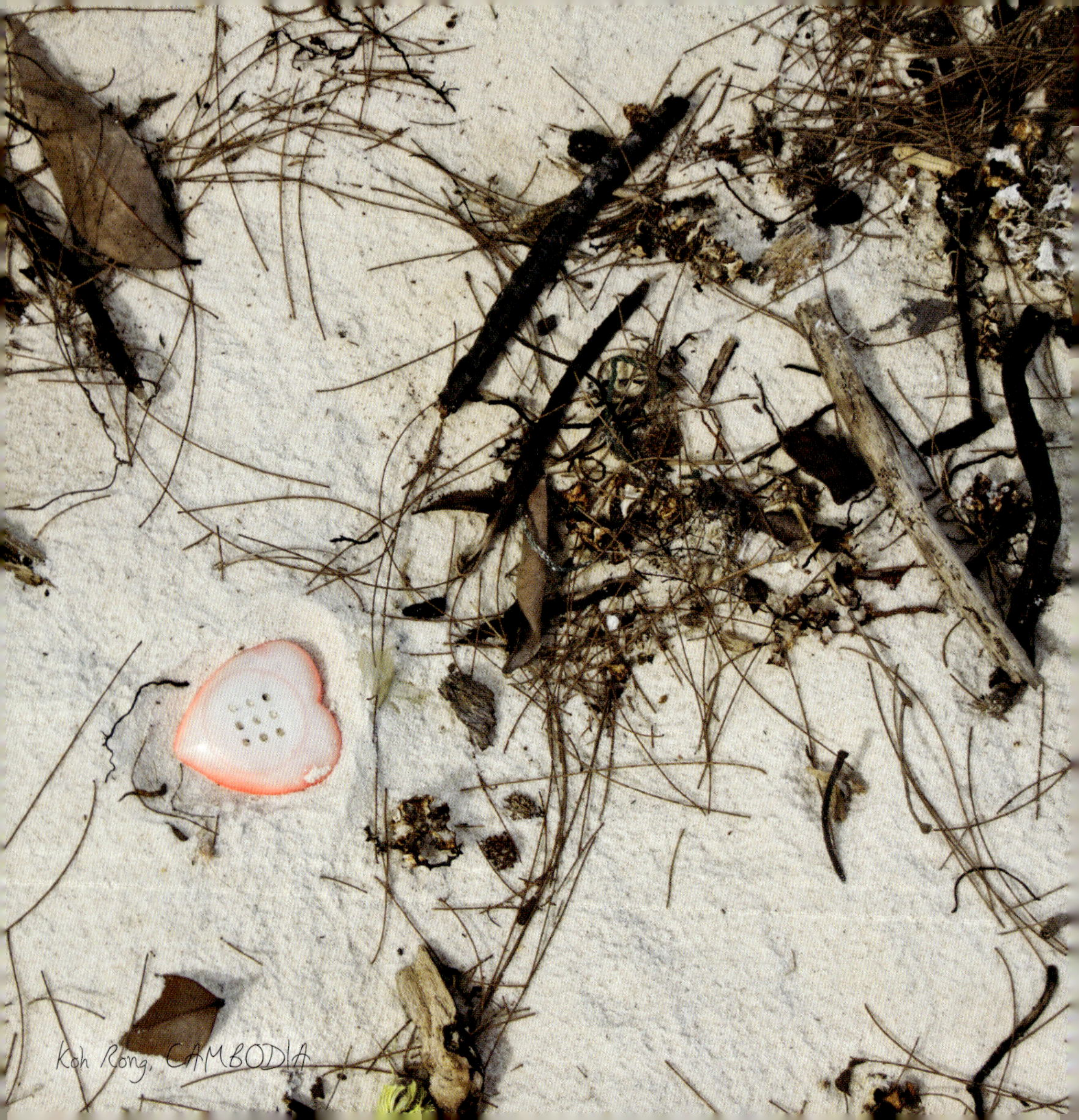
Koh Rong, CAMBODIA

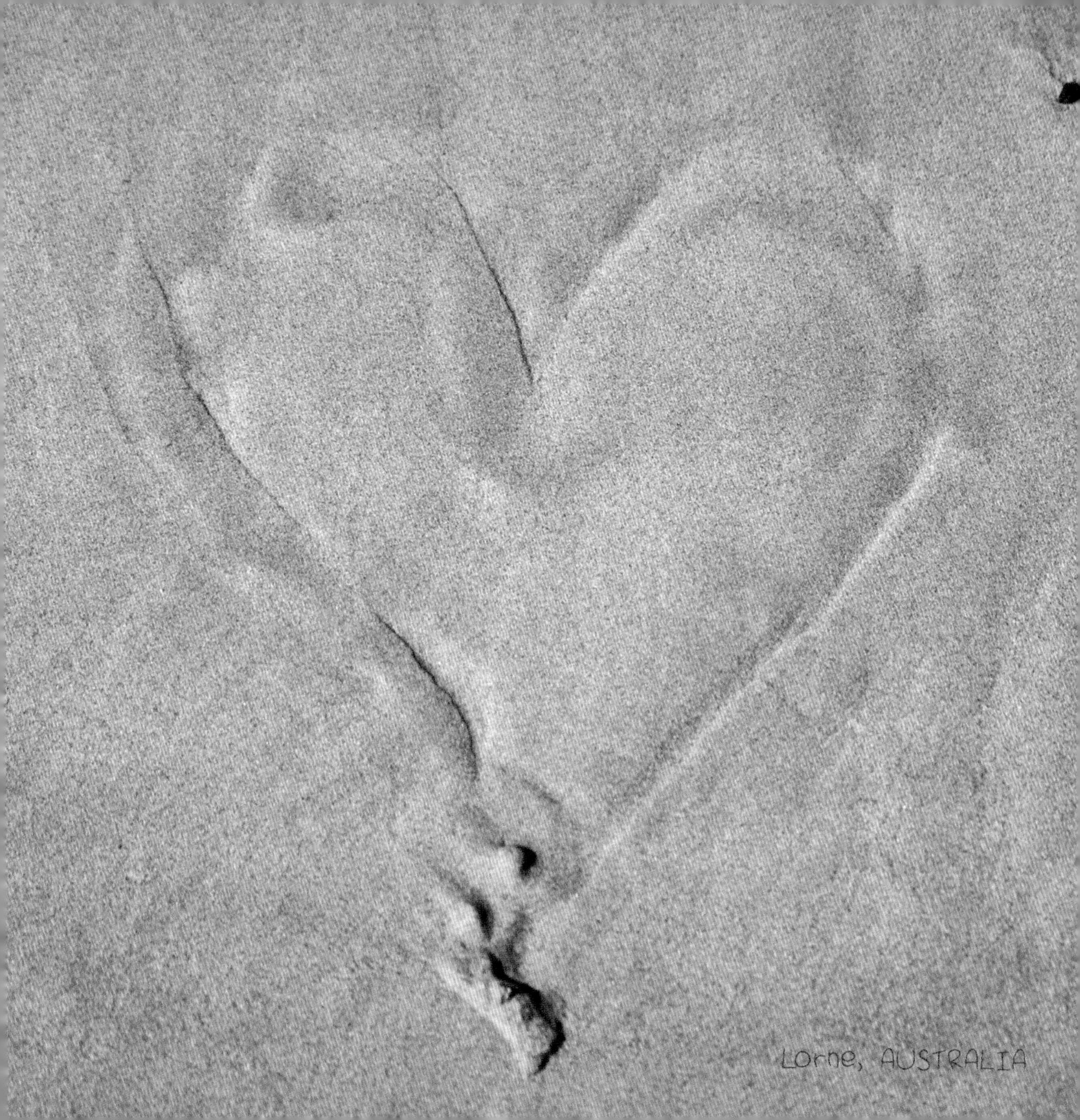

Lorne, AUSTRALIA

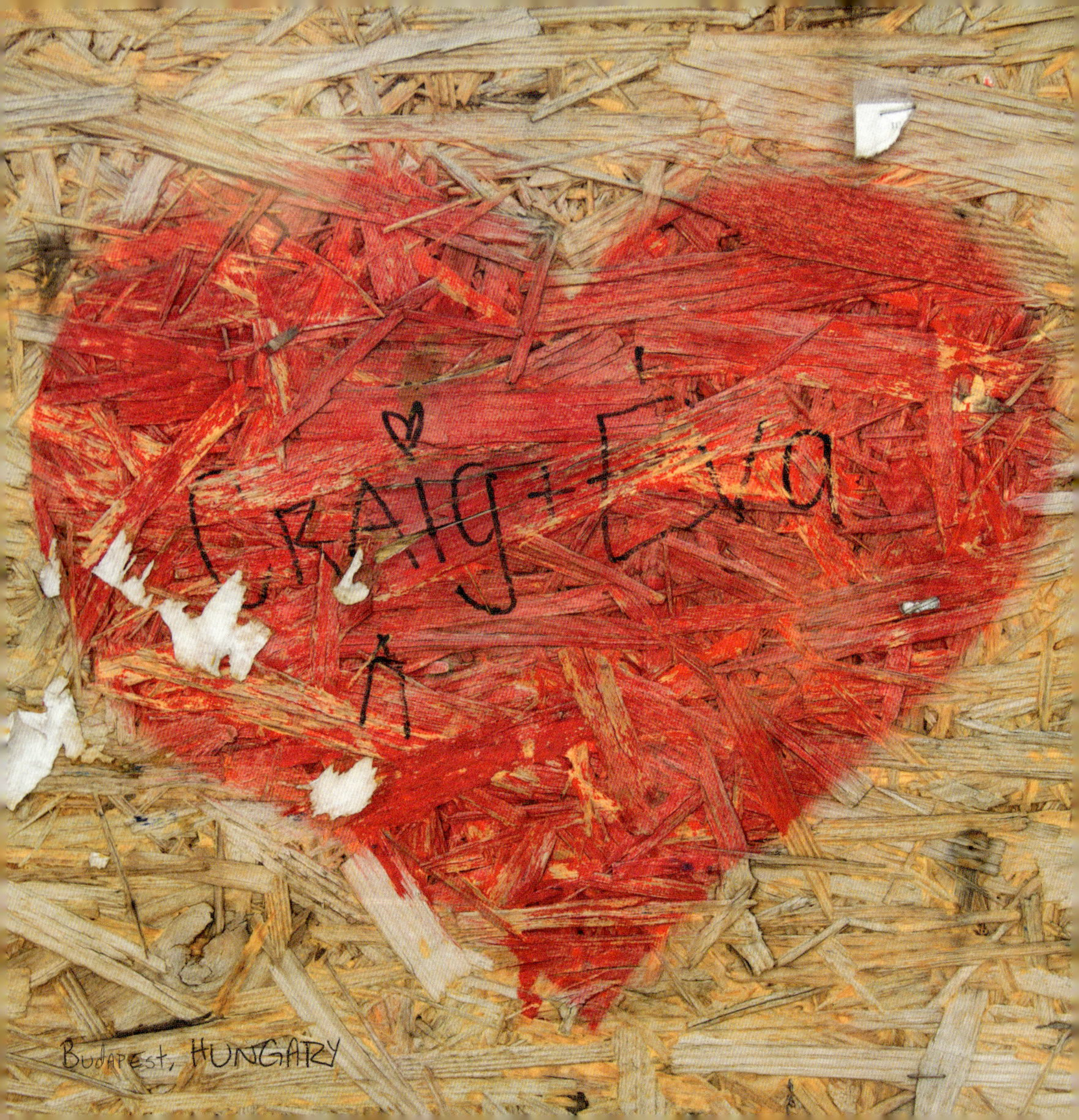
CRAIG + Eva
Budapest, HUNGARY

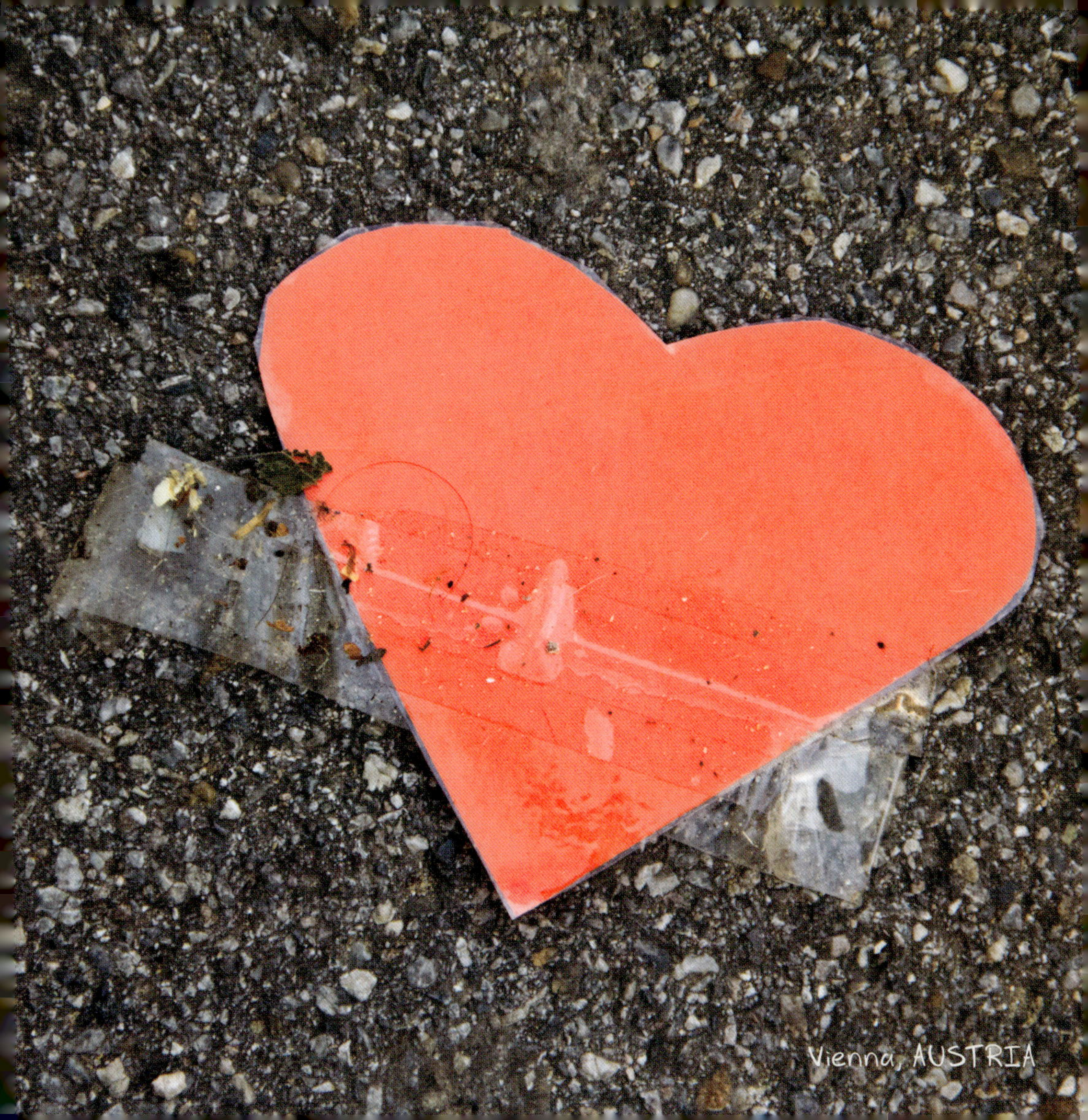
Vienna, AUSTRIA

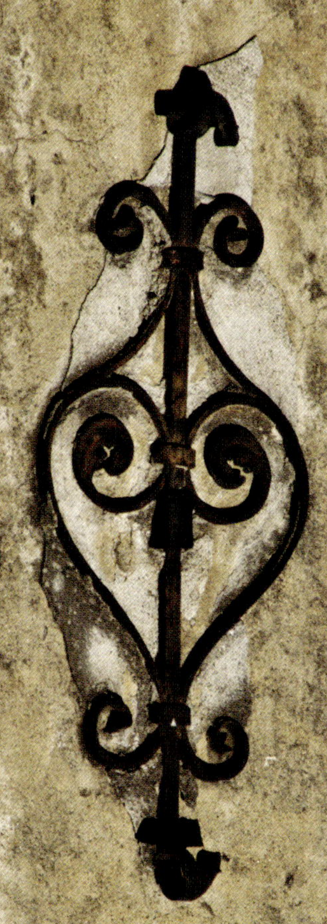

Brasov, ROMANIA

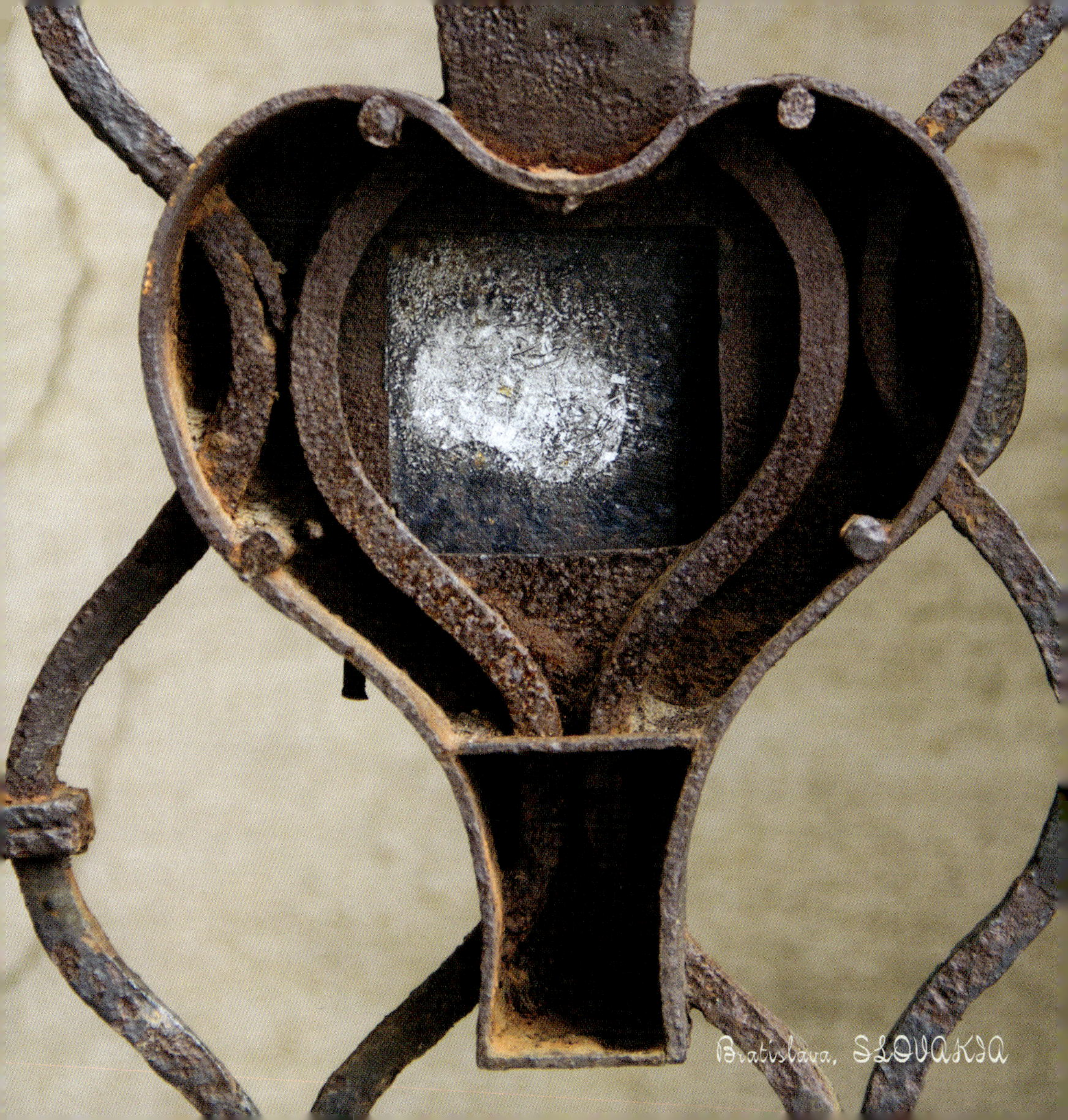
Bratislava, SLOVAKIA

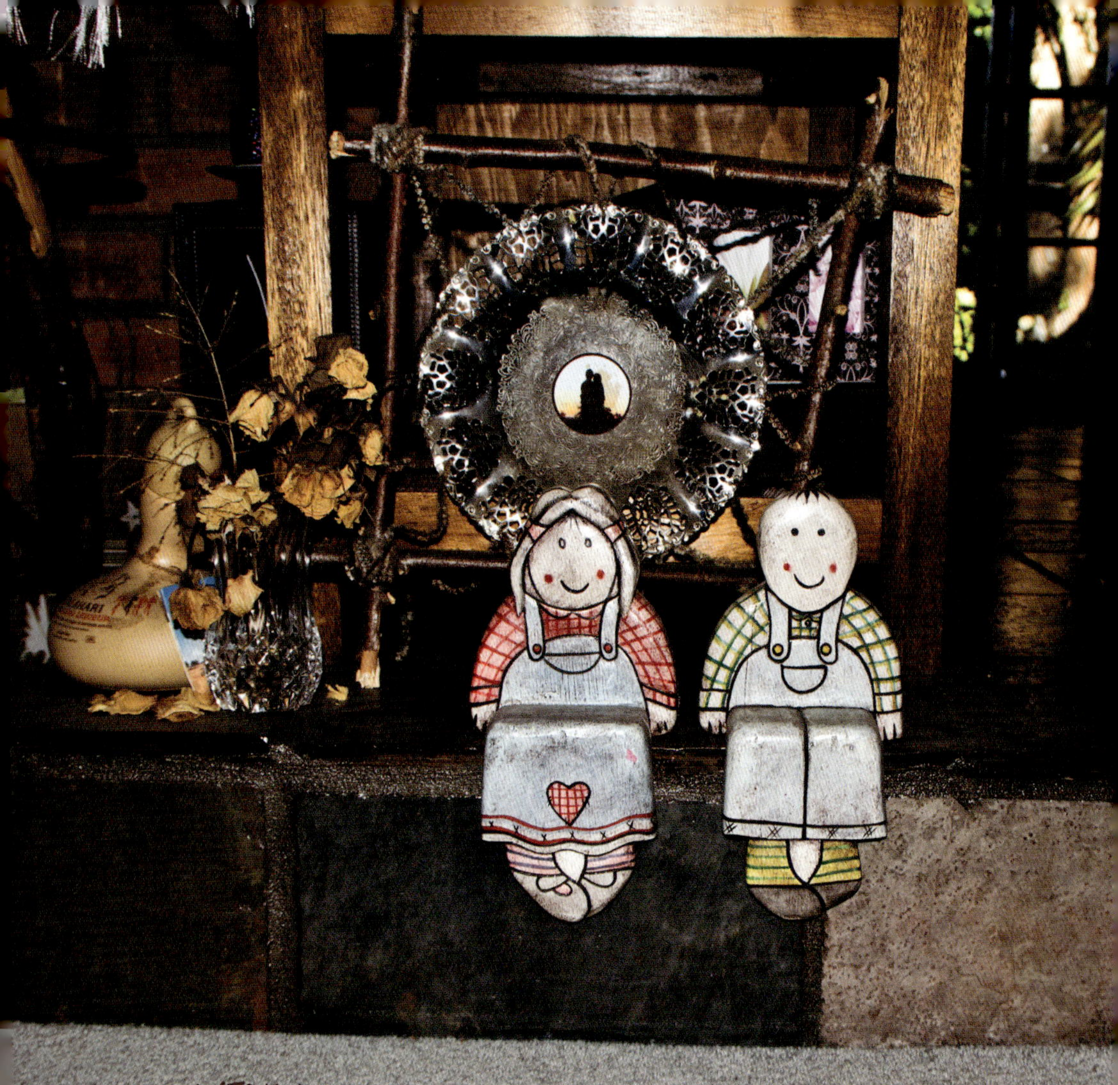

BUNINYONG, AUSTRALIA

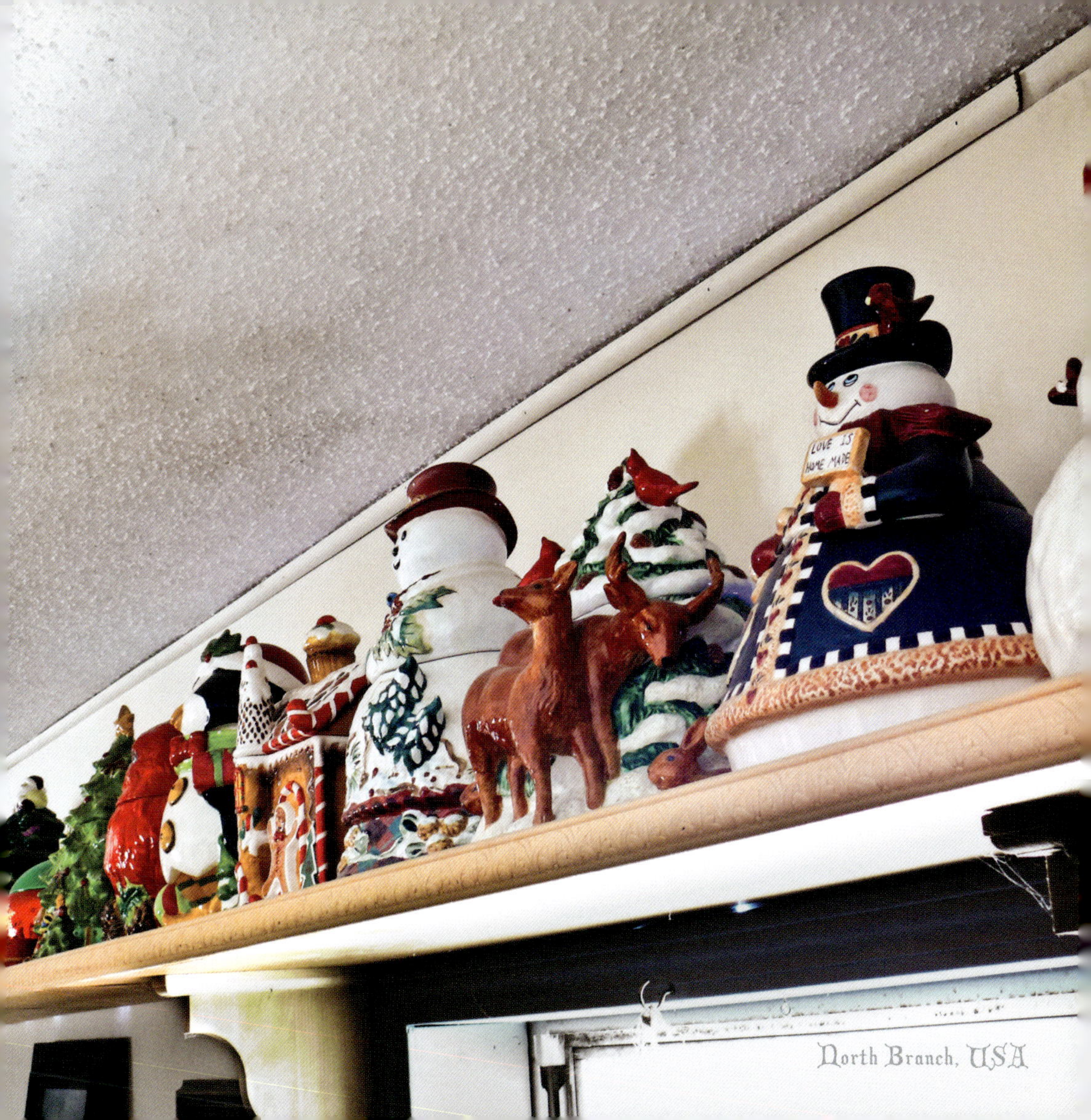

LOVE IS HOME MADE
North Branch, USA

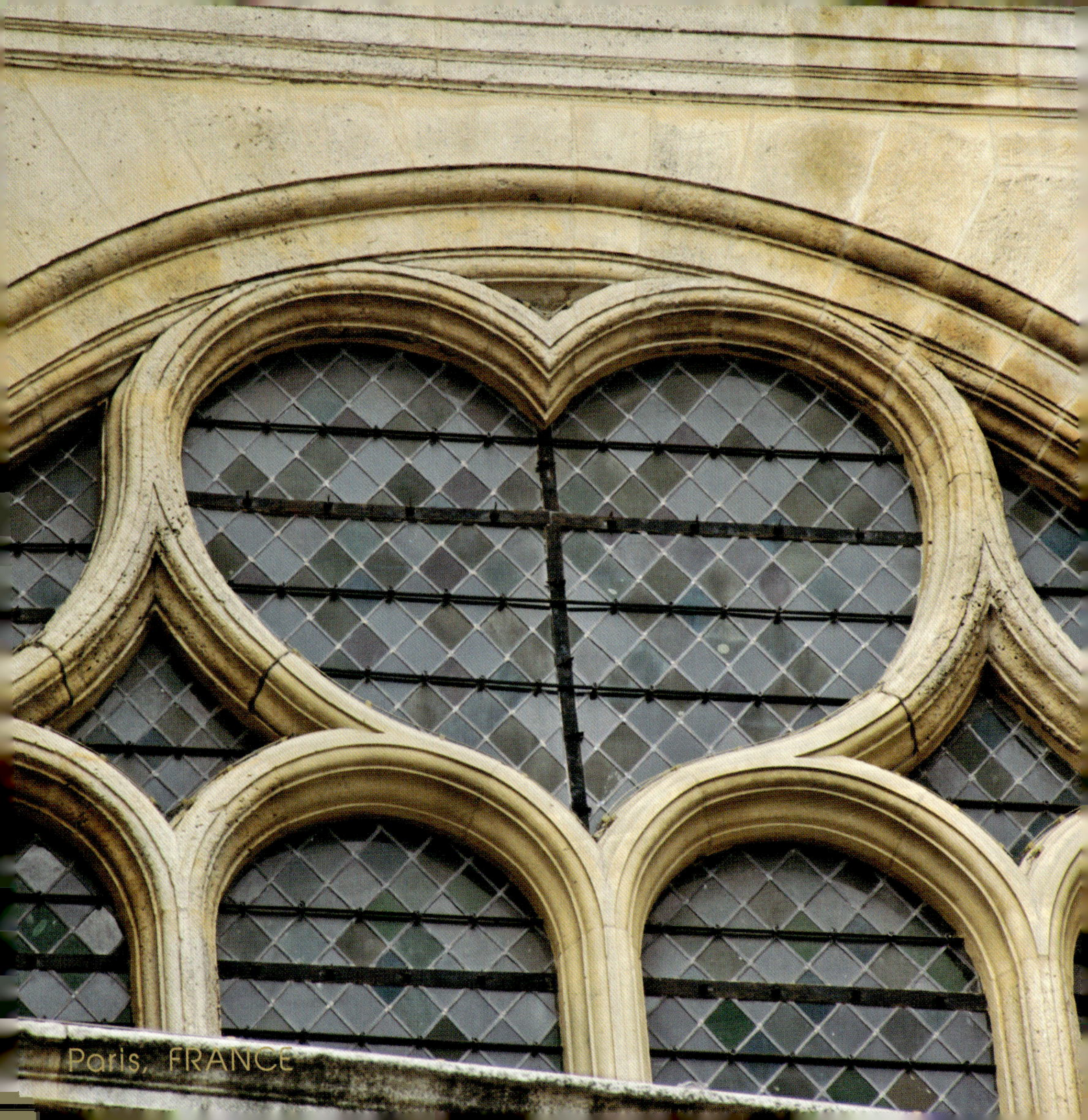
Paris, FRANCE

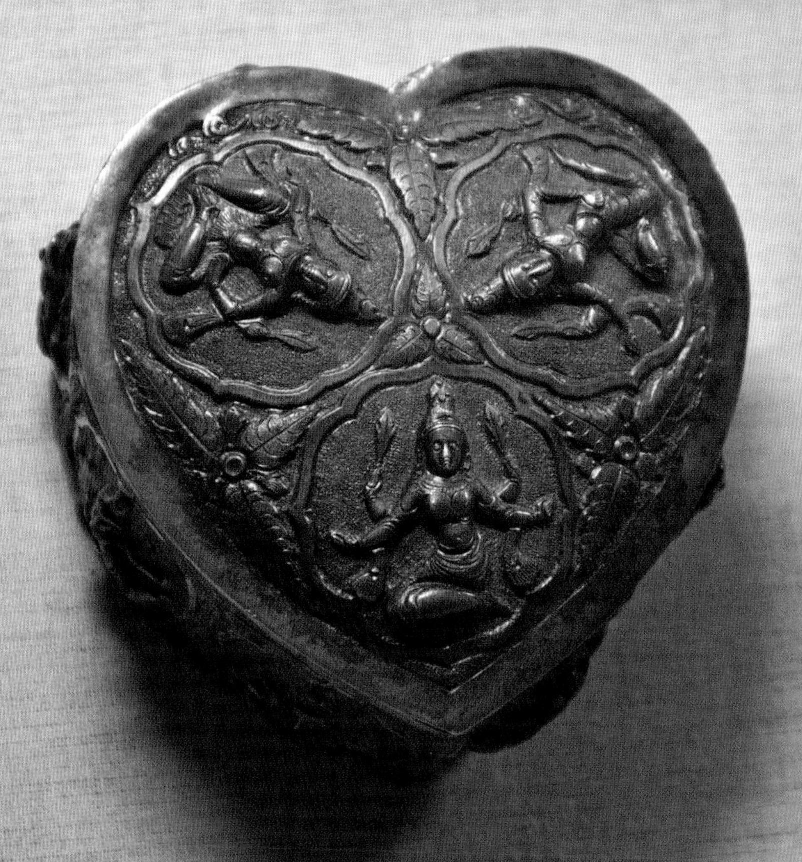
Jodhpur, INDIA

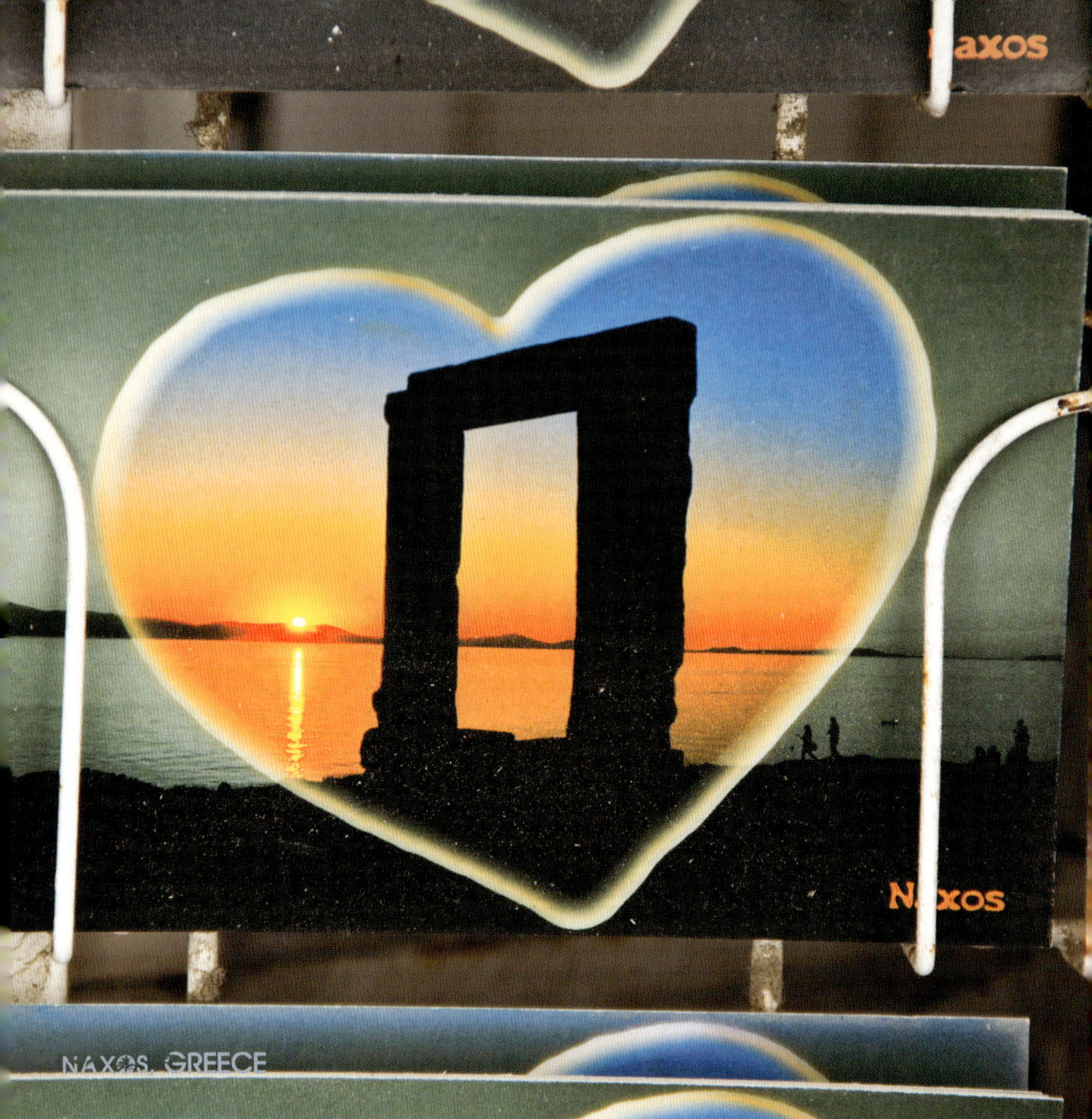
Naxos
Naxos
NAXOS, GREECE

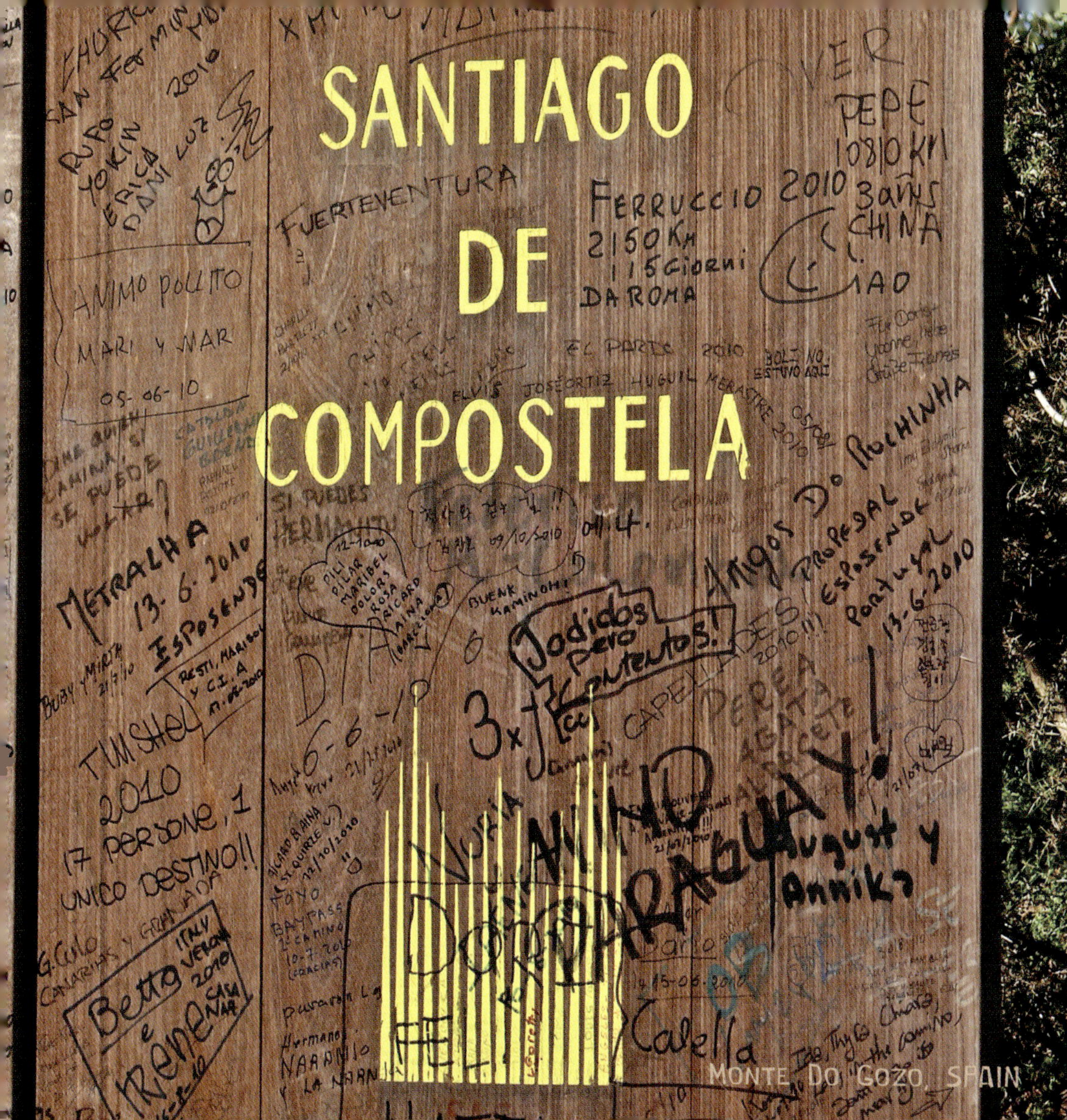
SANTIAGO
DE
COMPOSTELA
Ferruccio 2010
2150 Km
115 Giorni
DA ROMA
VER PEPE
10810 KM
3 ANOS
CHINA
CIAO
FUERTEVENTURA
ANIMO POLLITO
MARI Y MAR
05-06-10
METRALHA 13.6.2010
TIMSHEL 2010
17 PERSONE, 1 UNICO DESTINO!!
Betto ITALY VERONA 2010
IRENE
Jodidos pero contentos!
3 x
PARAGUAY!
Amigos Do Rochinha
ESPOSENDE PORTUGAL 13-6-2010
MONTE DO GOZO, SPAIN

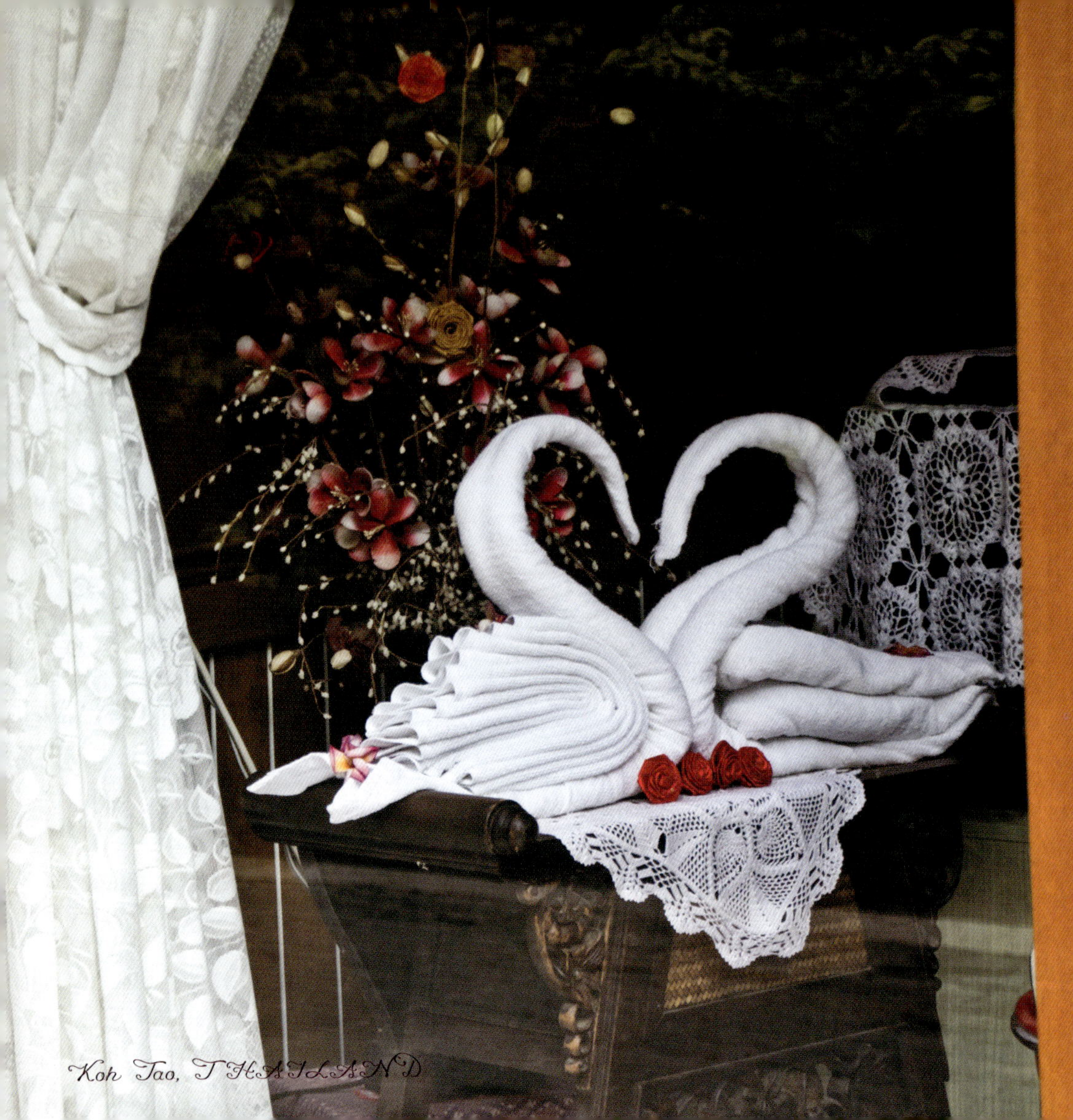

Koh Tao, THAILAND

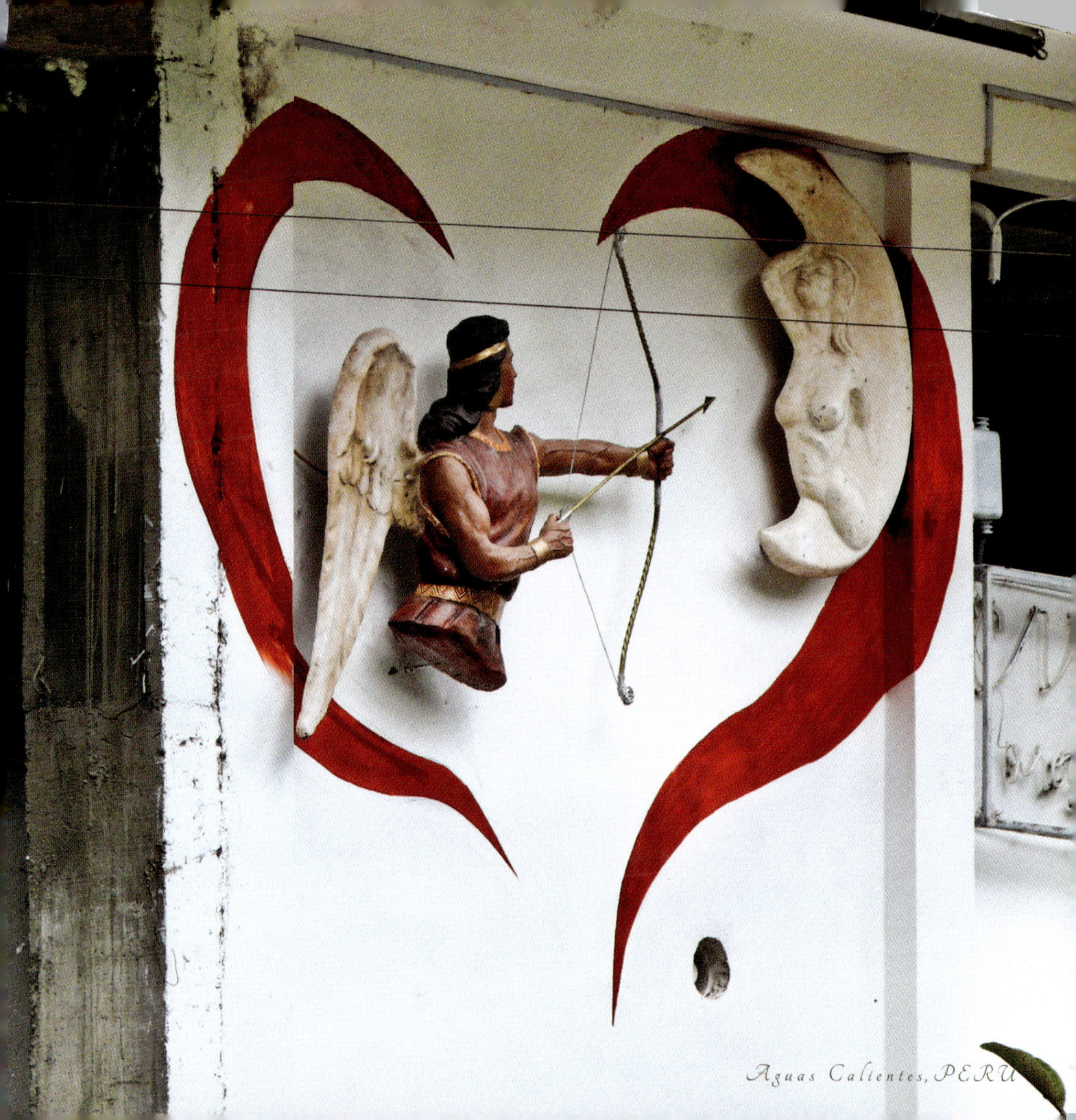

Aguas Calientes, PERU

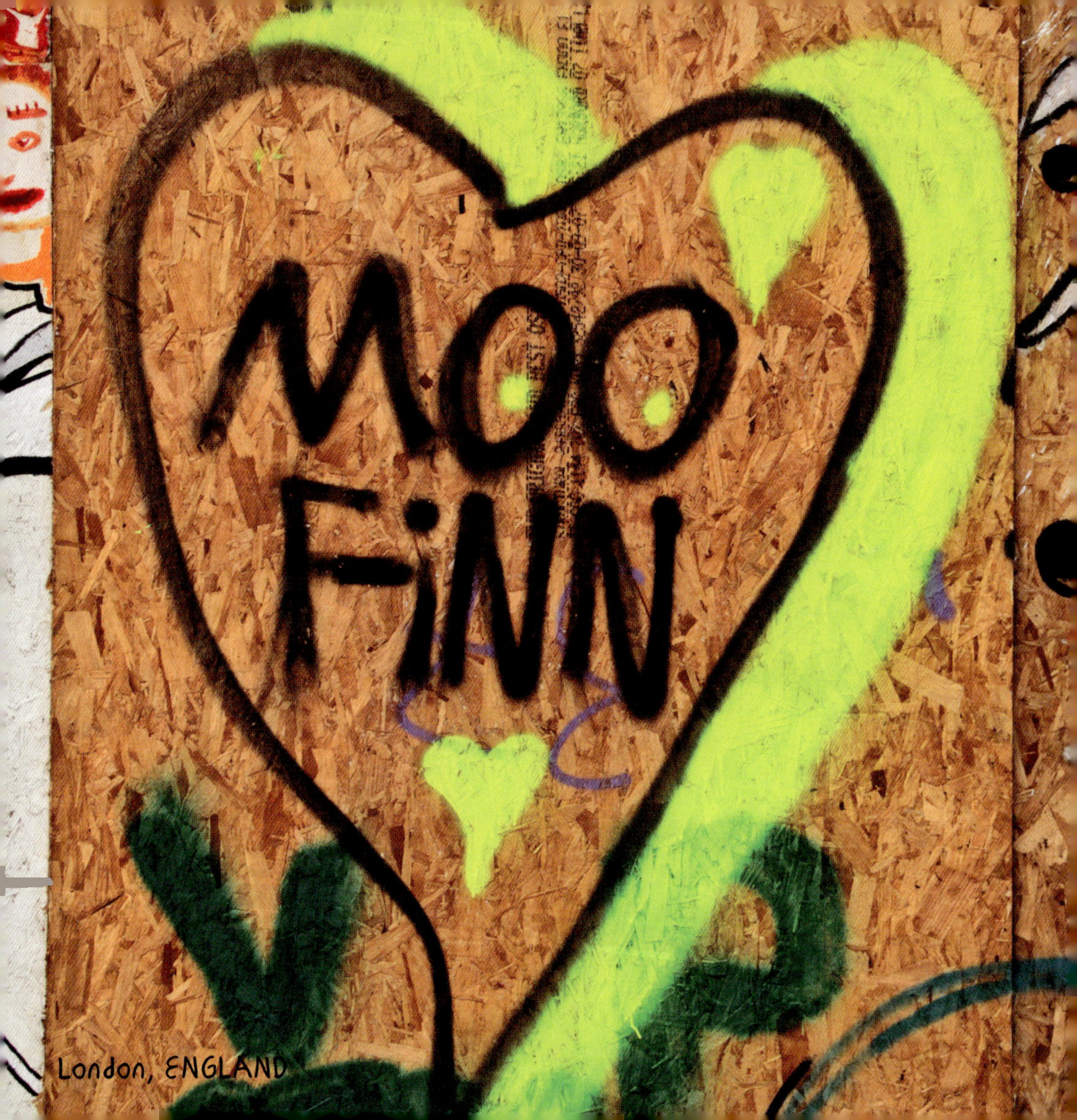

MOO
FiNN
London, ENGLAND

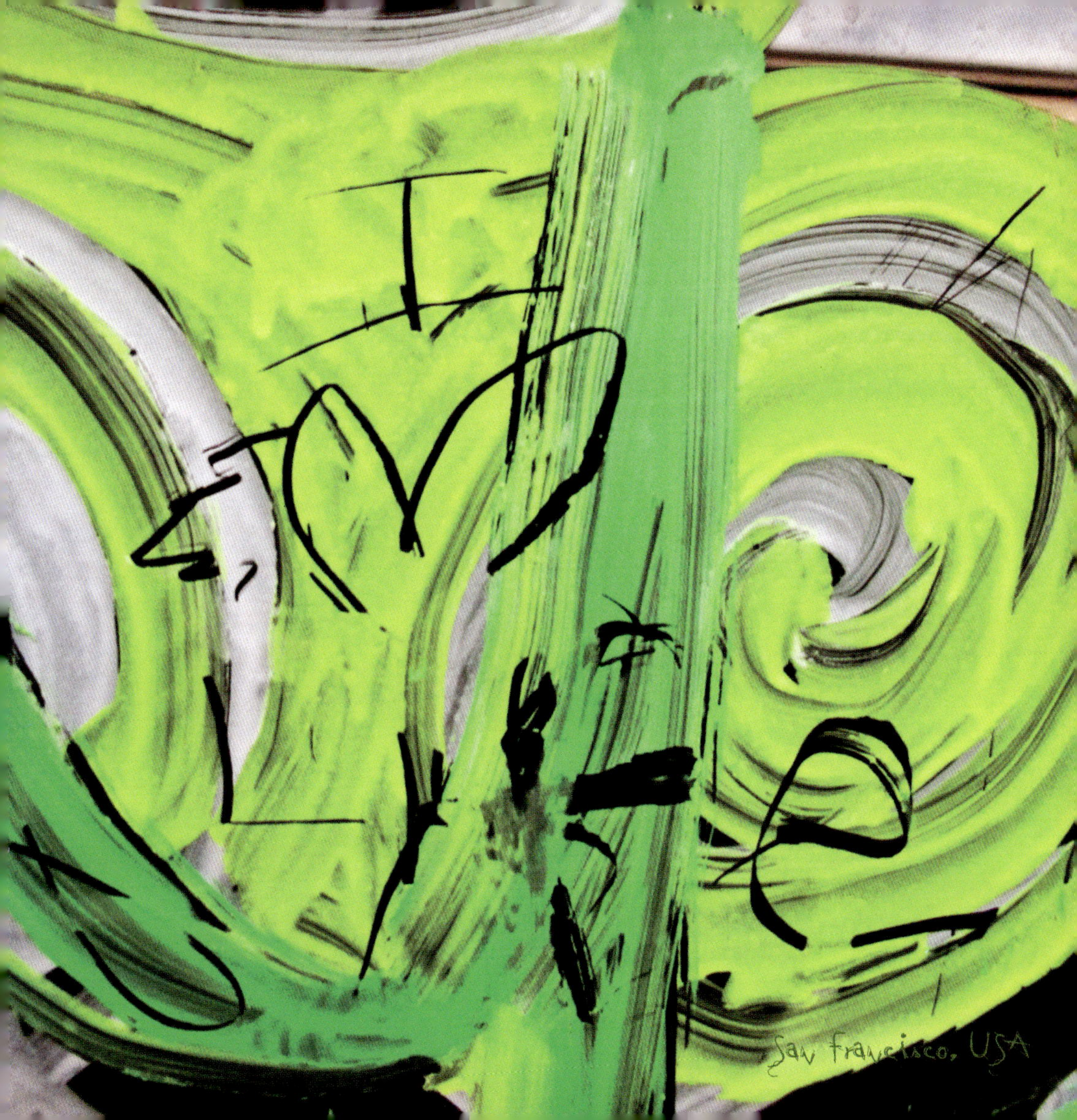
San Francisco, USA

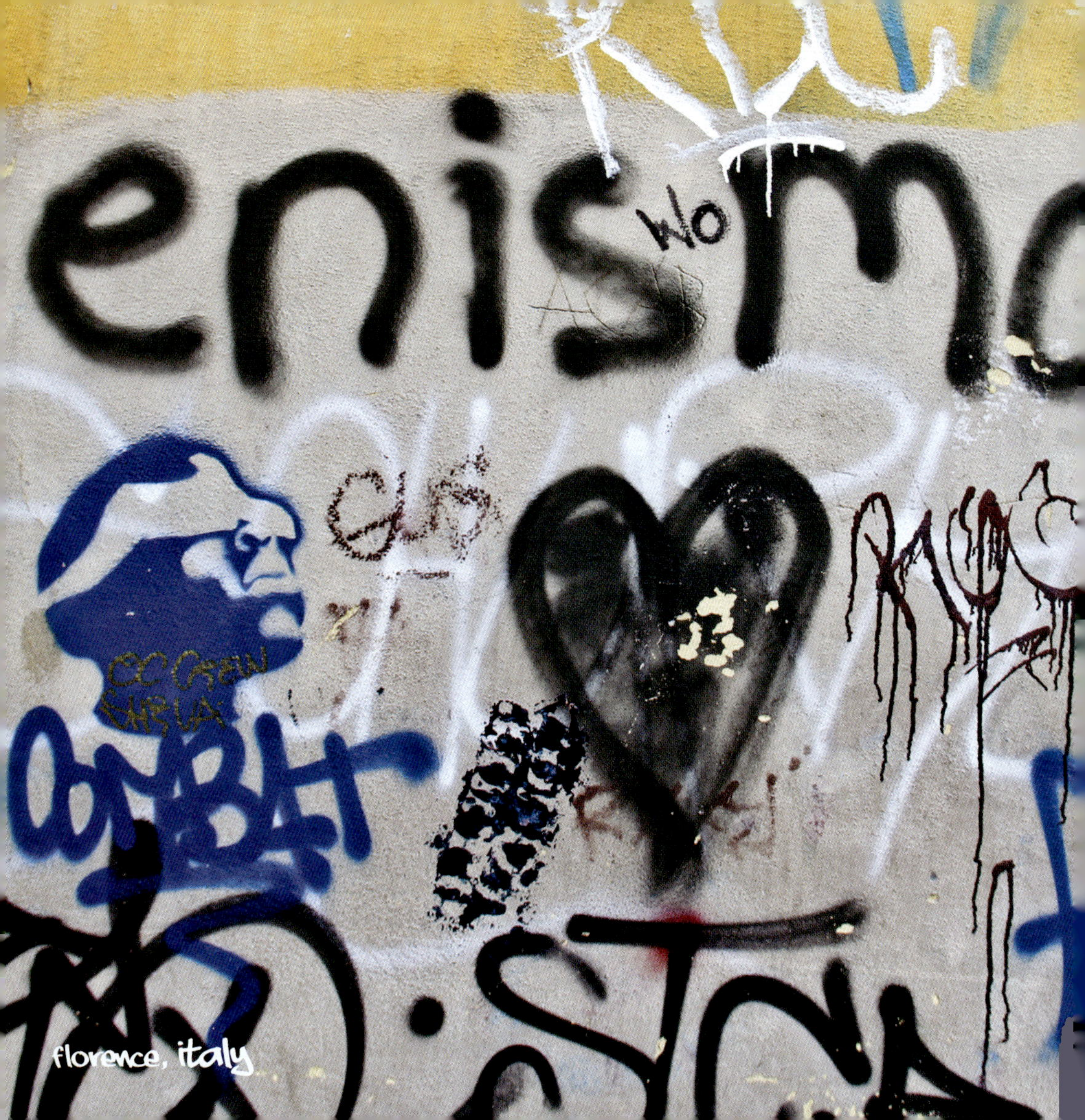
enisma
florence, italy

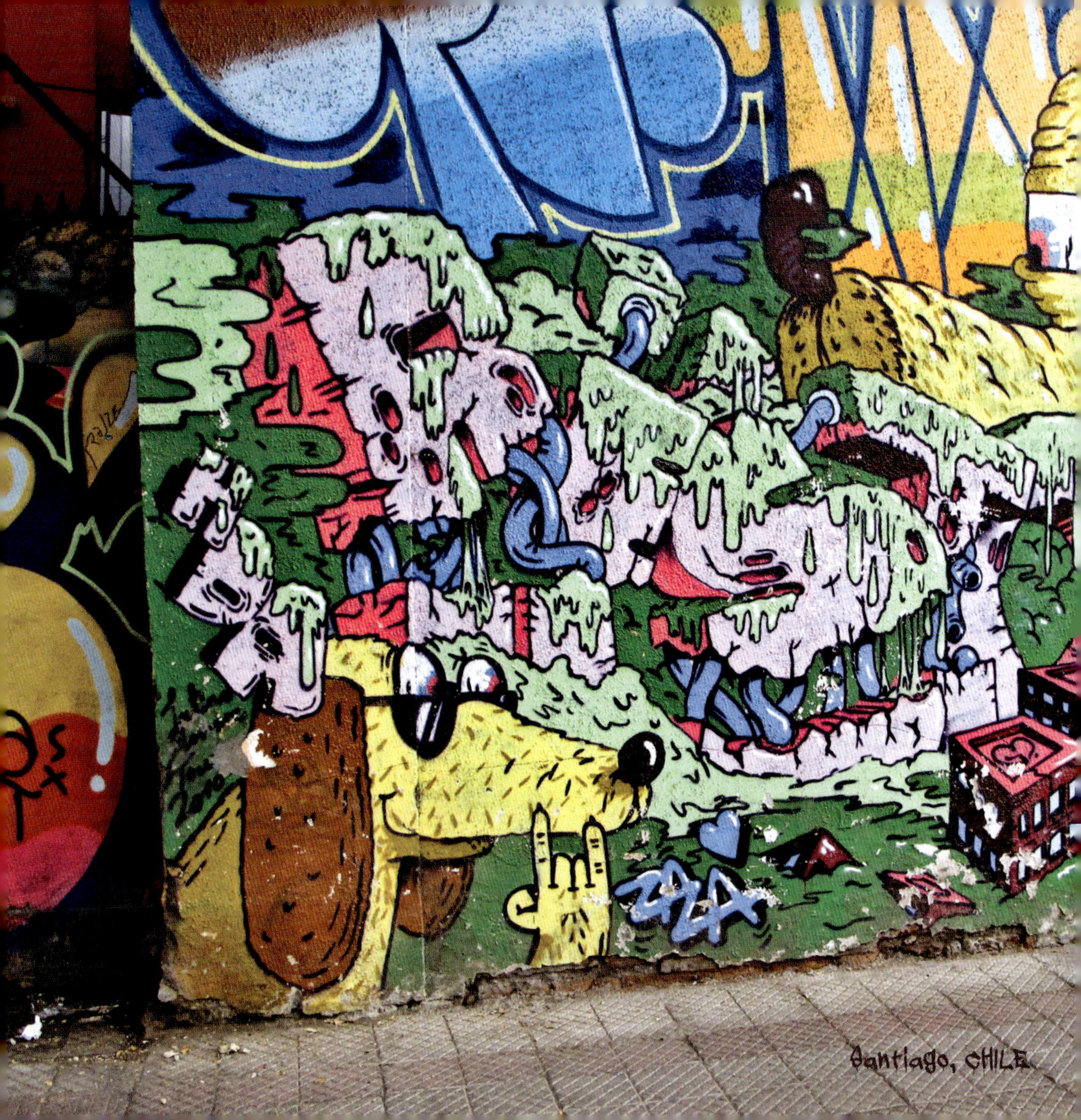
Santiago, CHILE

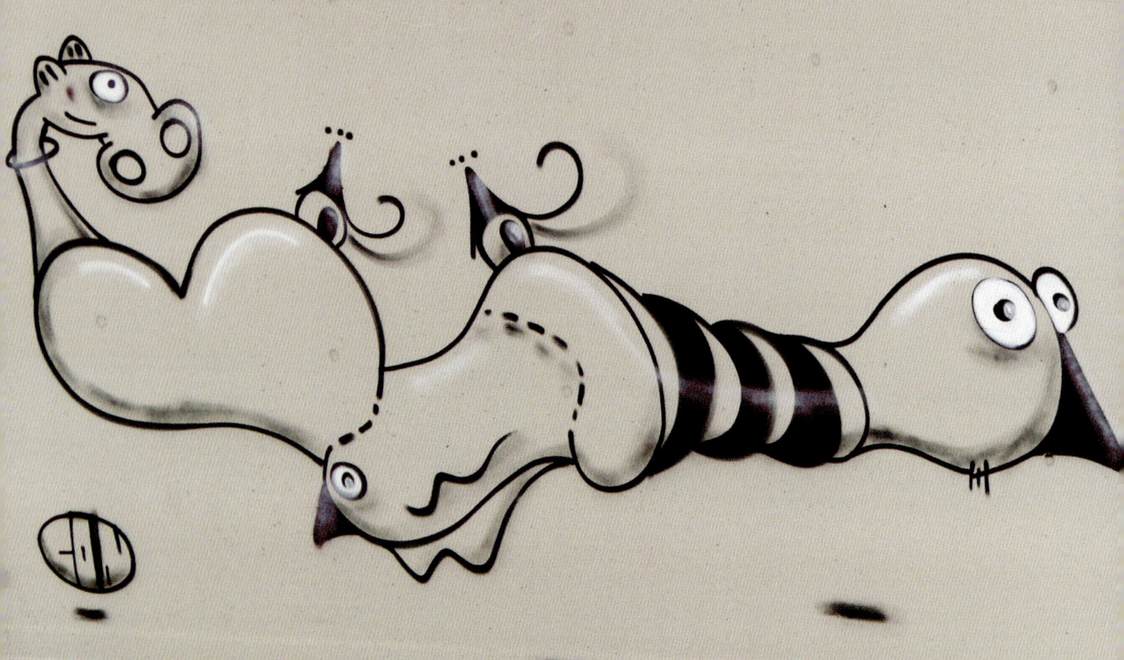
Berlin, GERMANY

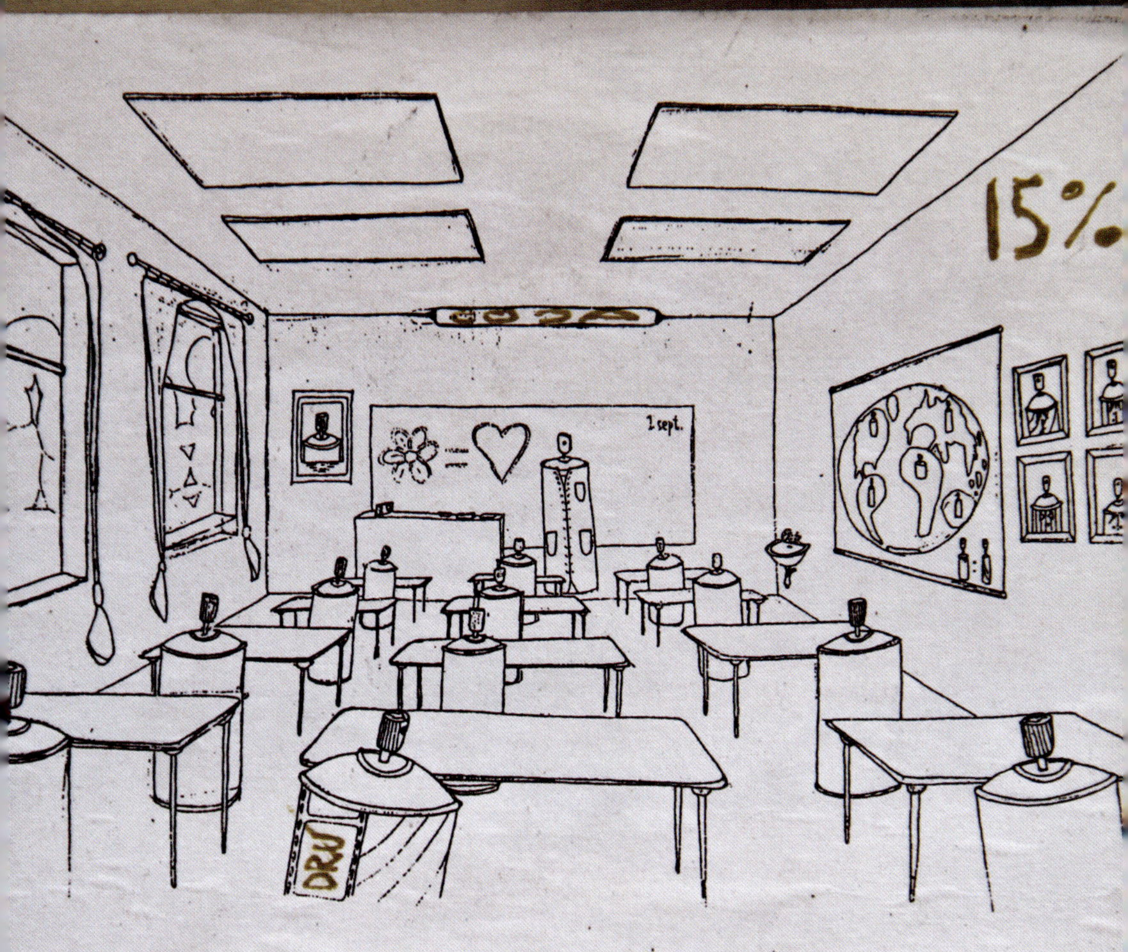

15%
1 sept.
DRU
Bratislava, SLOVAKIA

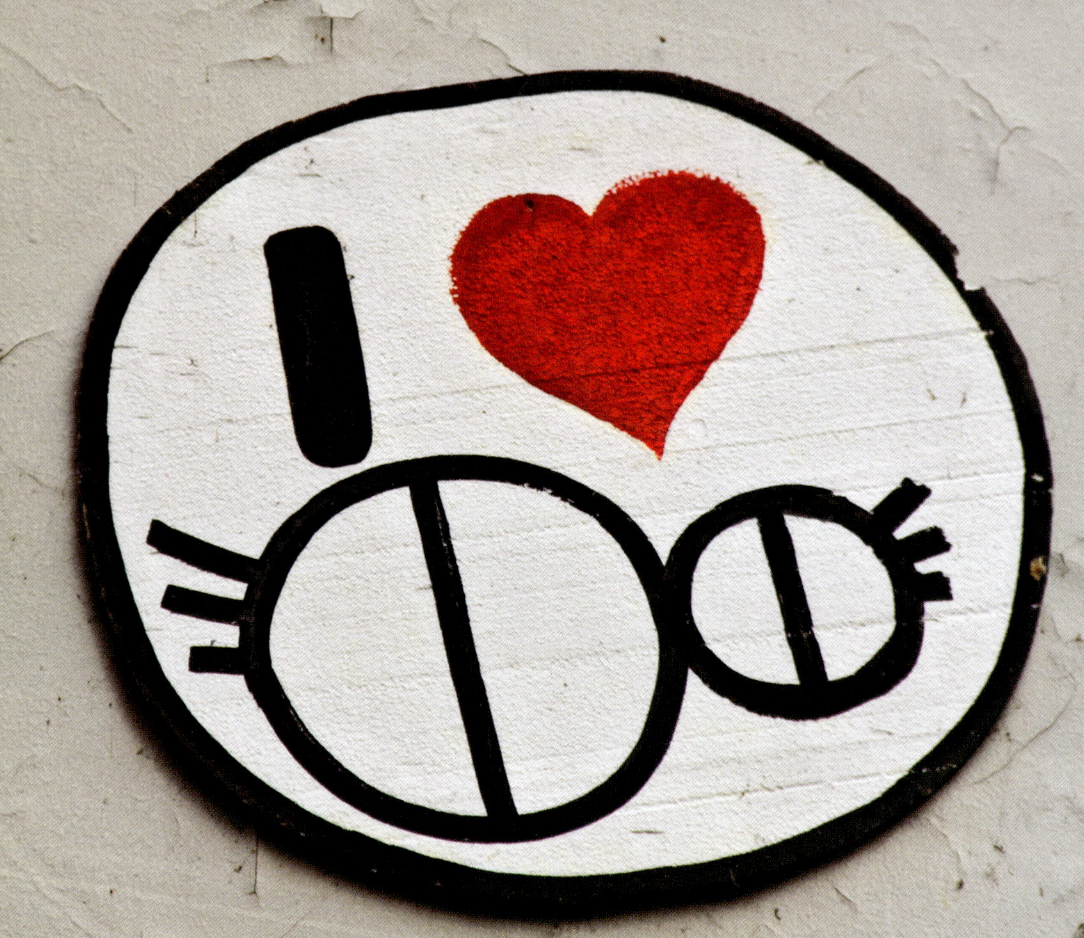

Amsterdam, THE NETHERLANDS

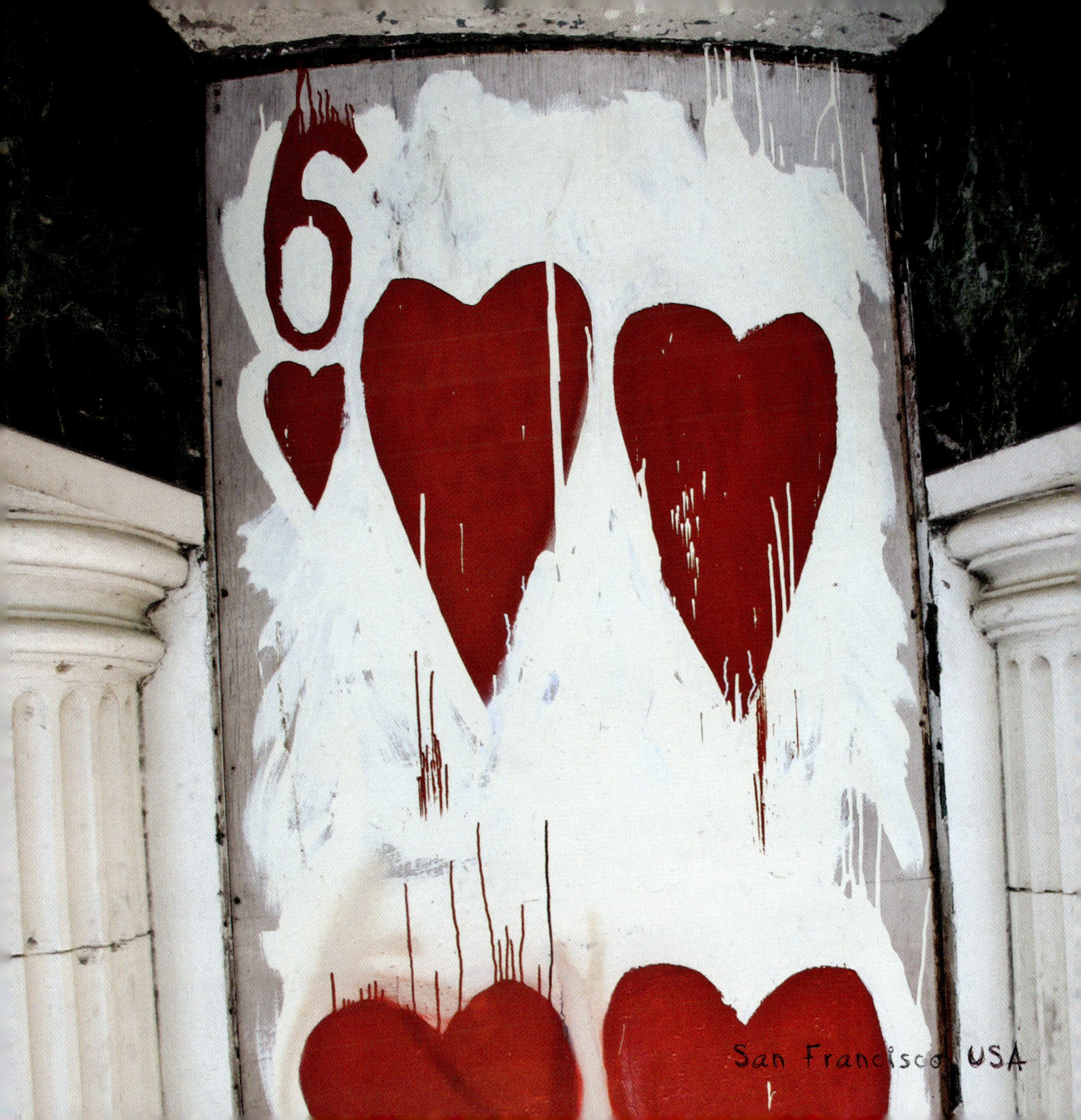
6
San Francisco USA

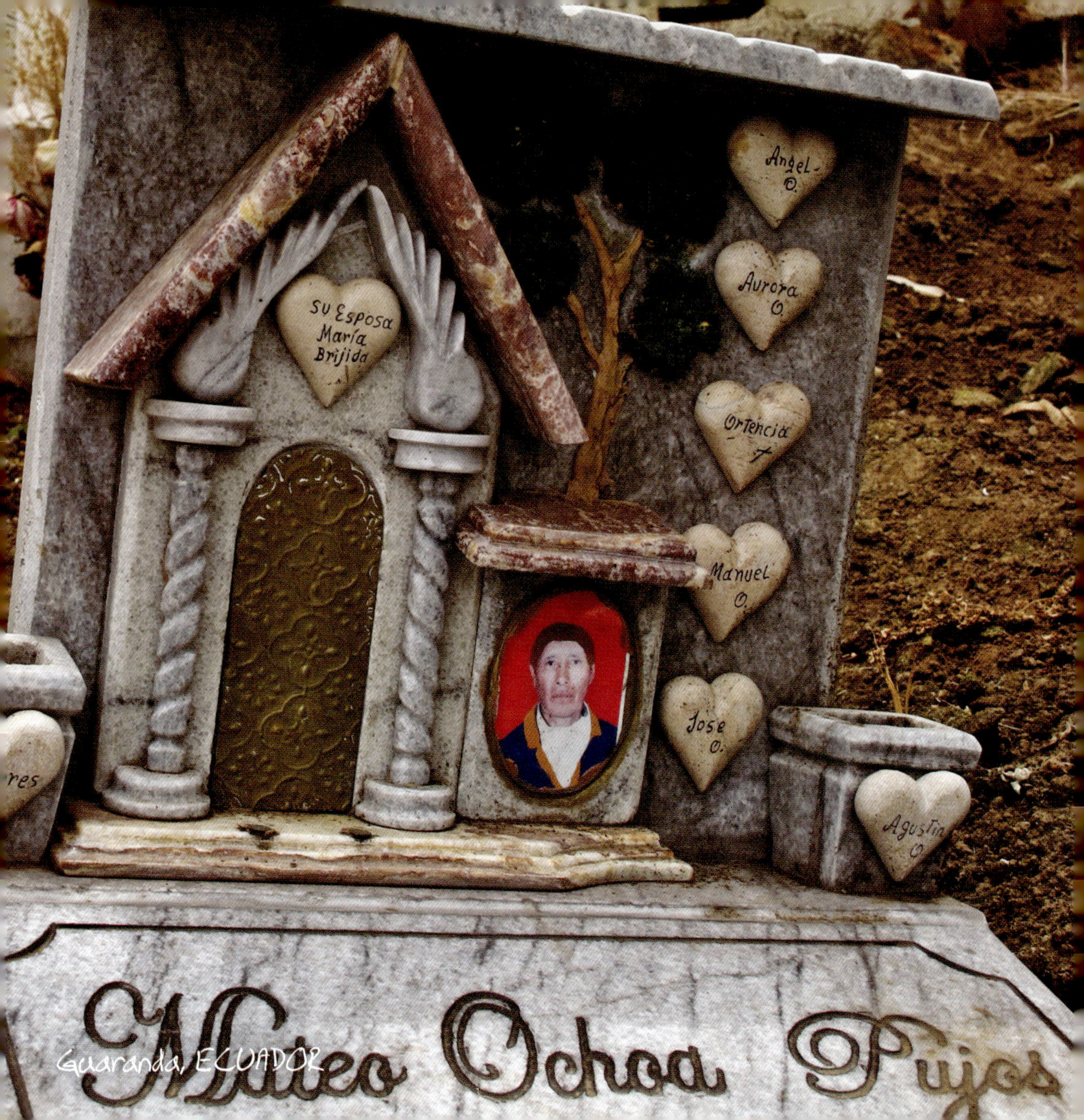

Su Esposa María Brijida
Angel O.
Aurora O.
Ortencia T.
Manuel O.
Jose O.
Agustin O.
Guaranda, ECUADOR
Mateo Ochoa Pujos

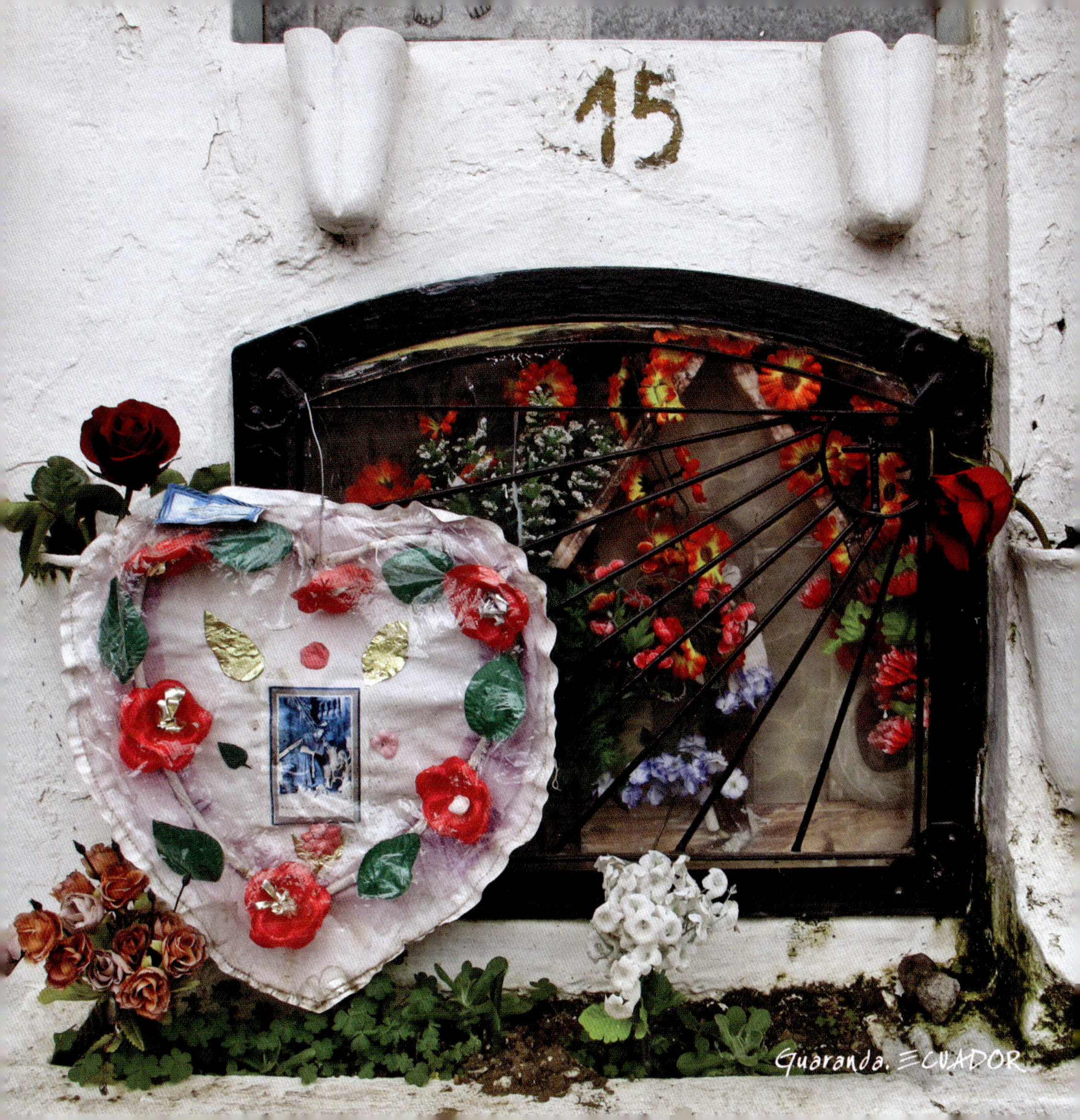

15
Guaranda. ECUADOR

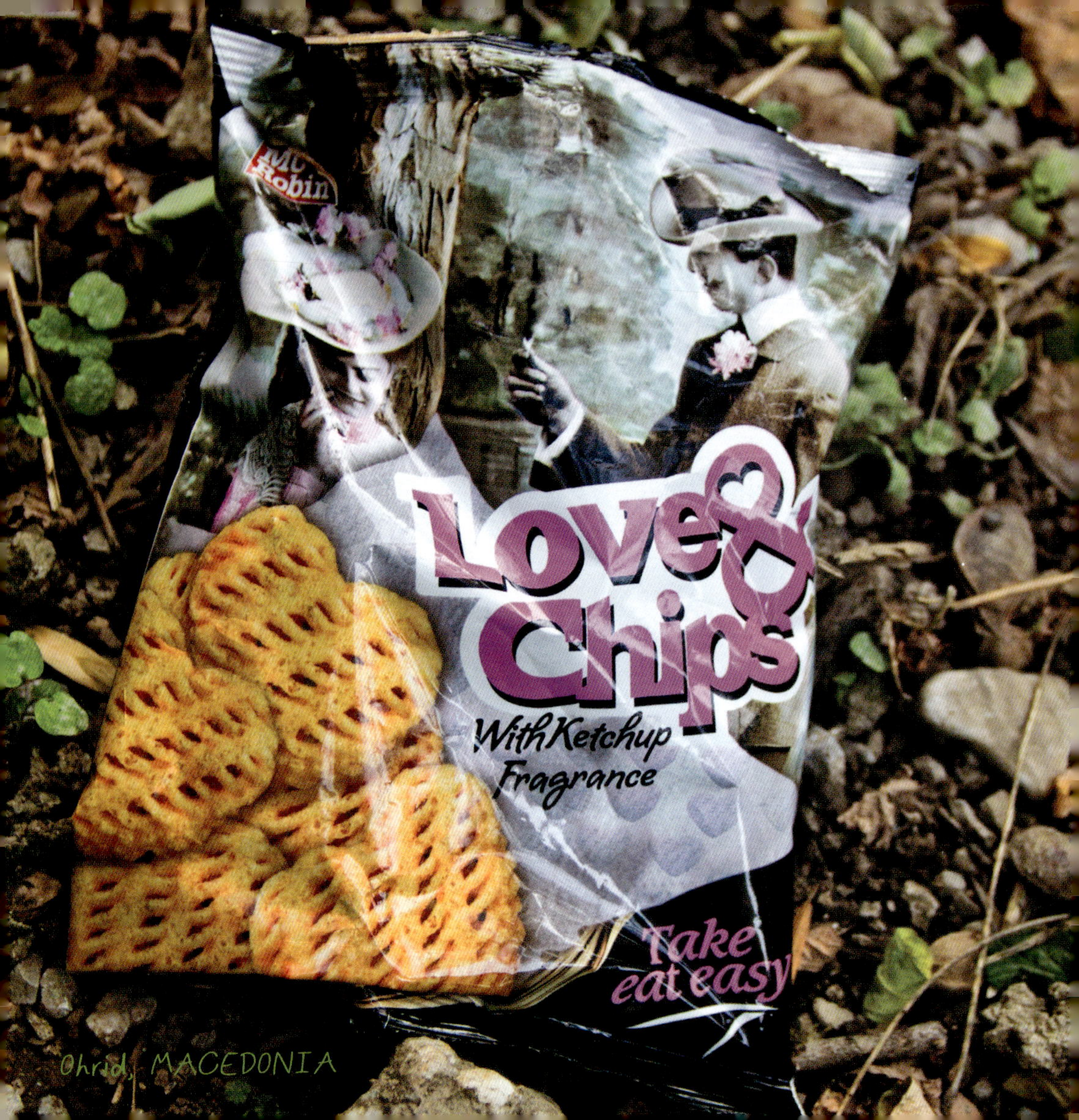

MC Robin
Love Chips
With Ketchup Fragrance
Take eat easy
Ohrid, MACEDONIA

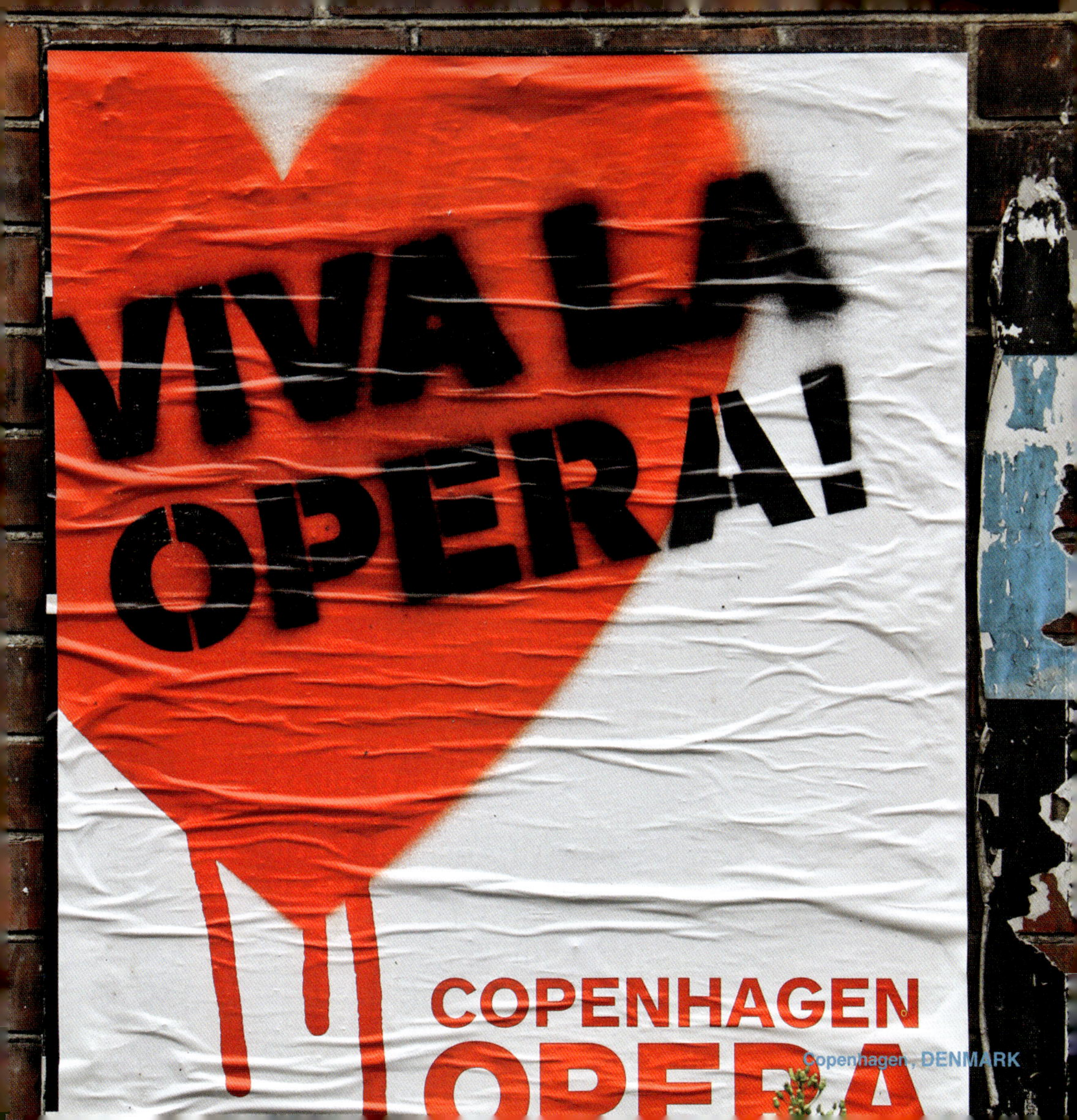

VIVA LA
OPERA!
COPENHAGEN
OPERA
Copenhagen , DENMARK

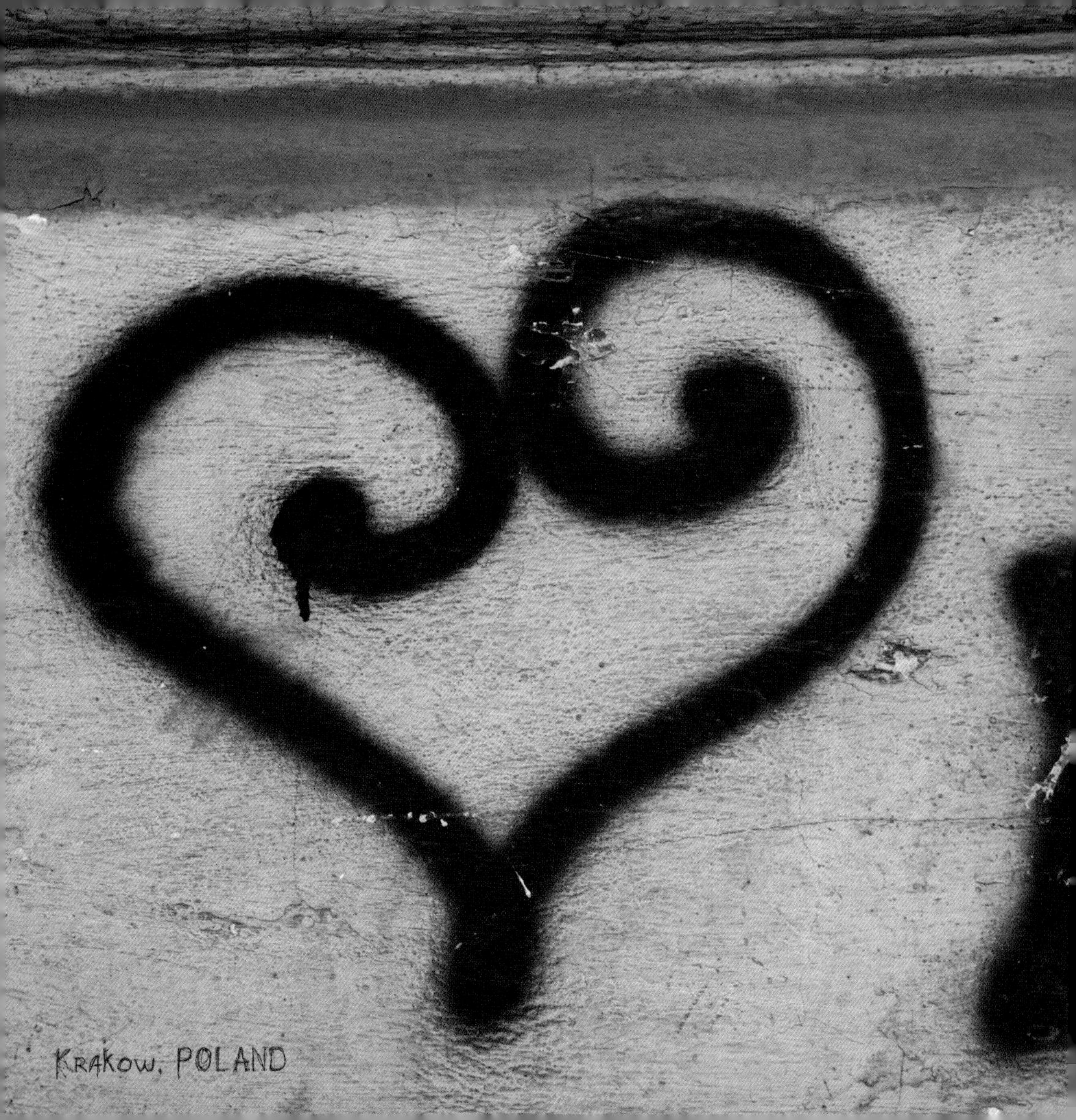
Krakow, POLAND

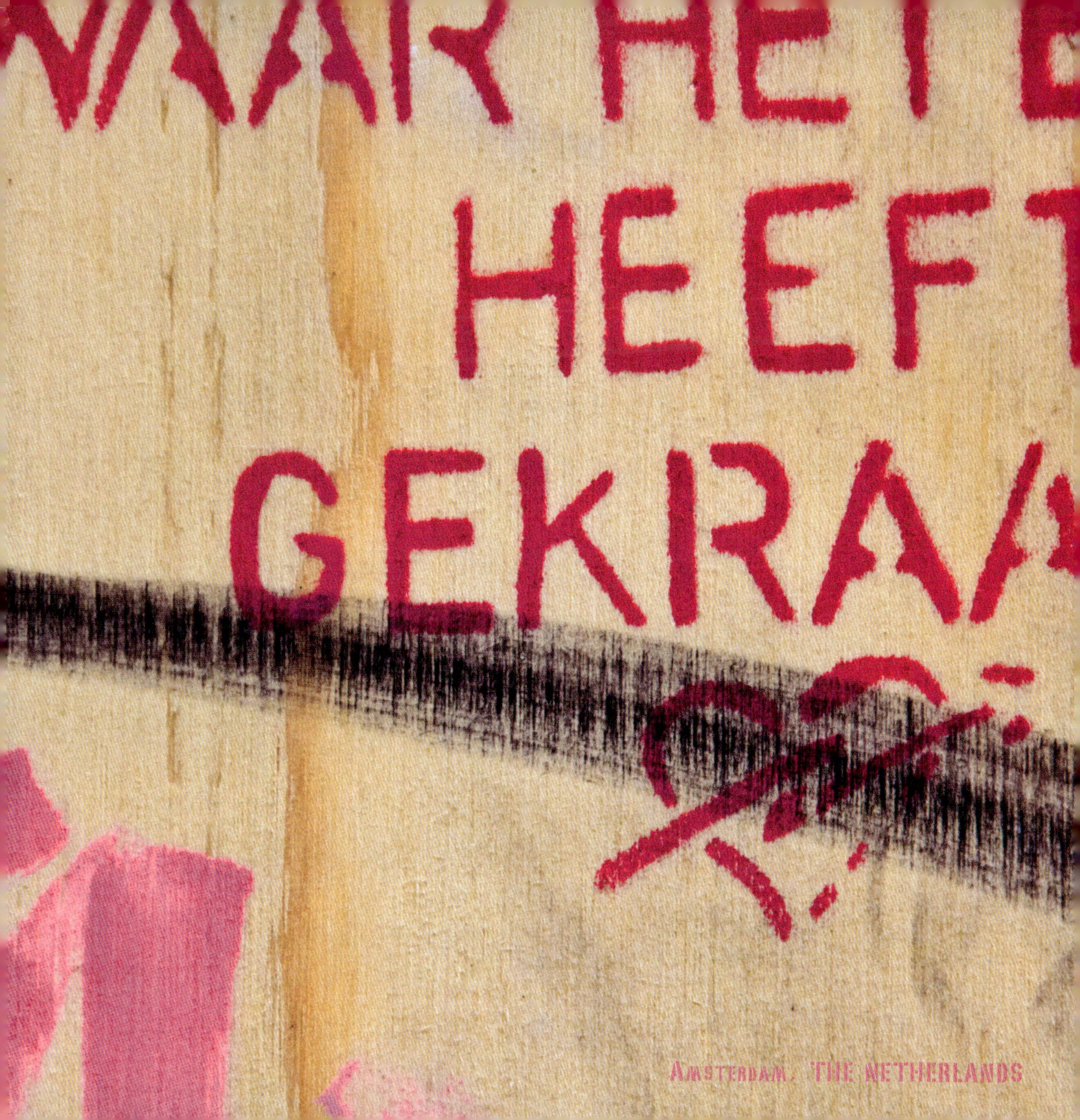
WAAR HET B
HEEFT
GEKRAA

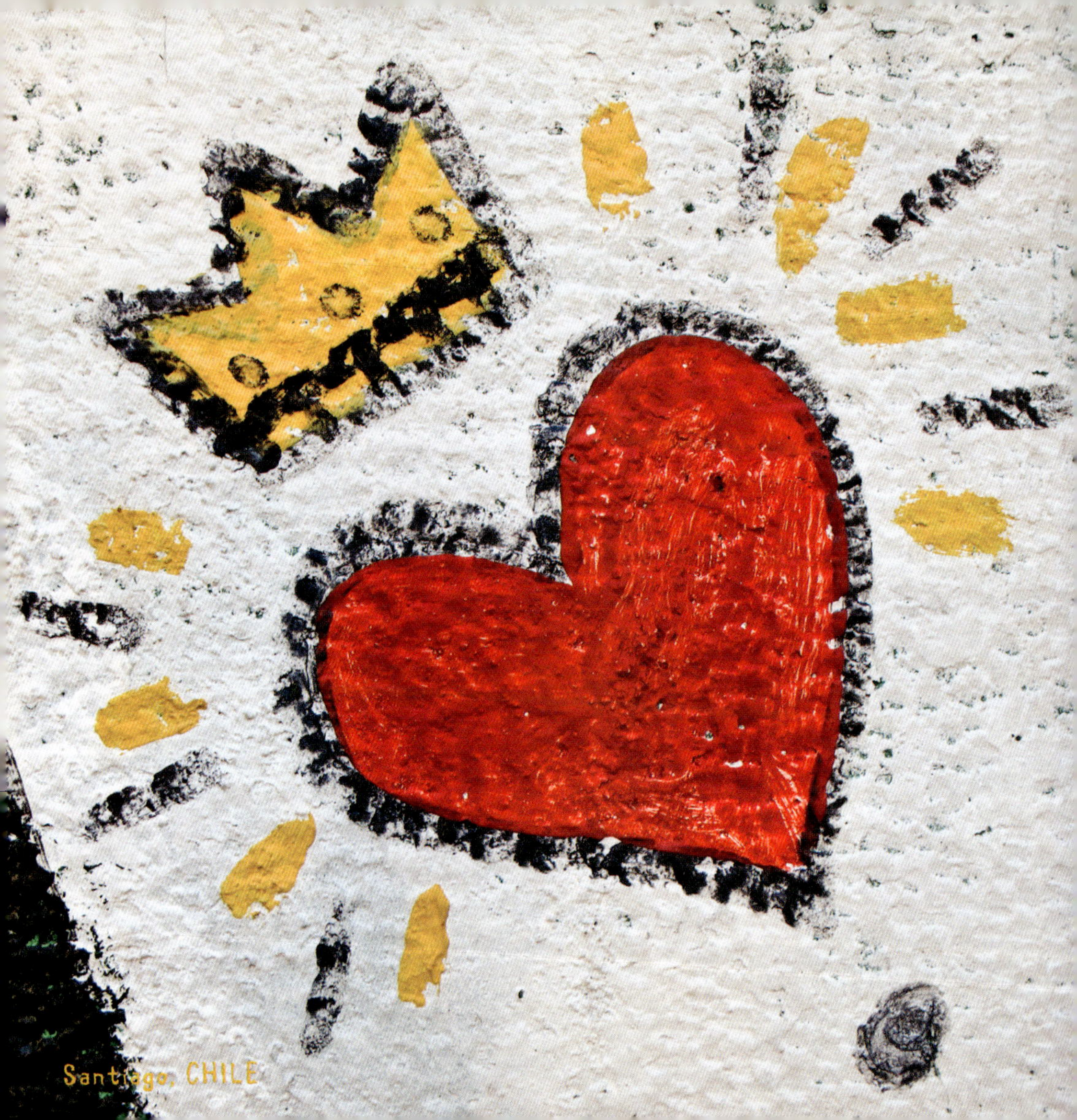
Santiago, CHILE

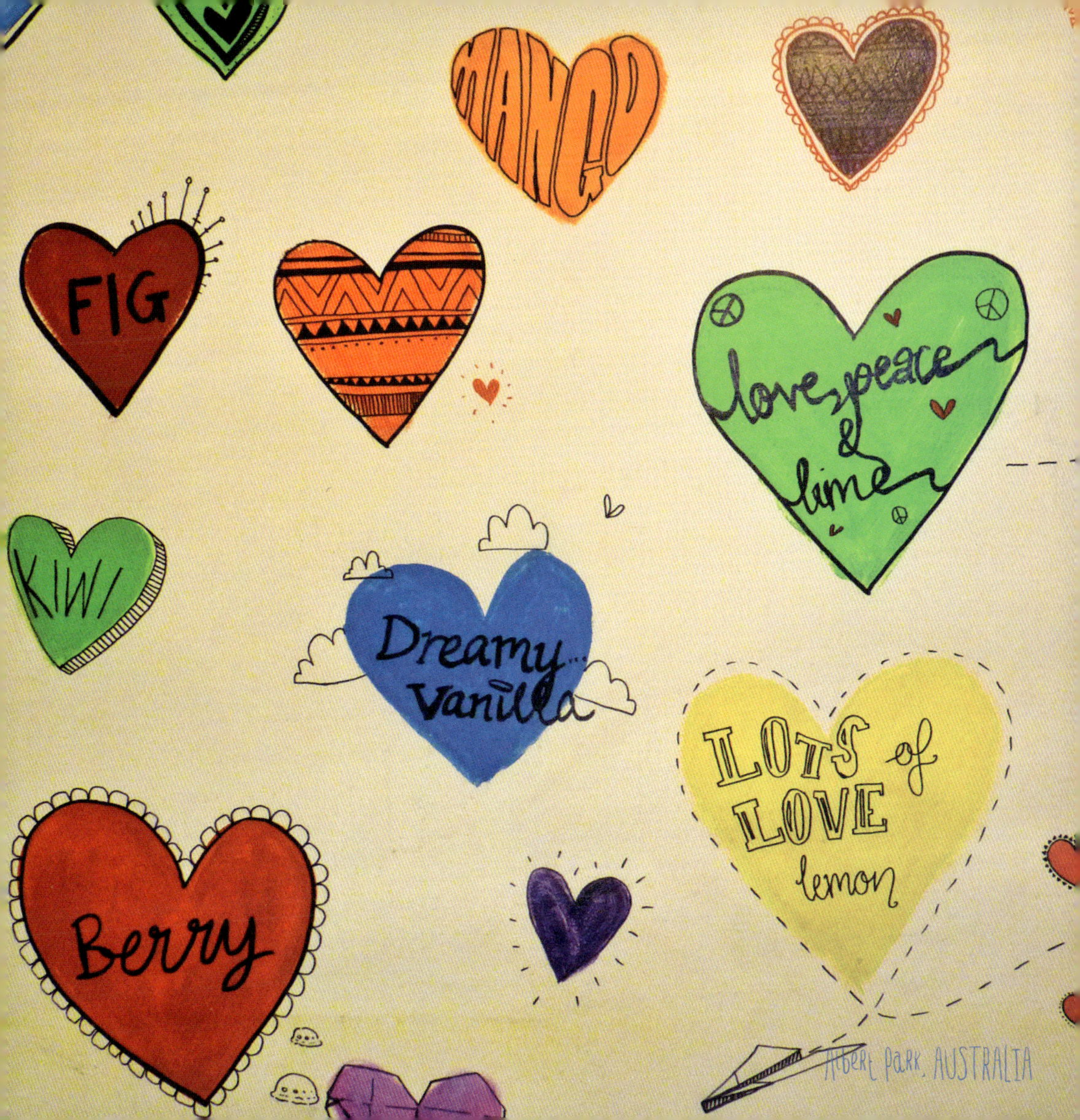

MANGO
FIG
KIWI
love peace & lime
Dreamy... Vanilla
lots of LOVE lemon
Berry
Albert Park. AUSTRALIA

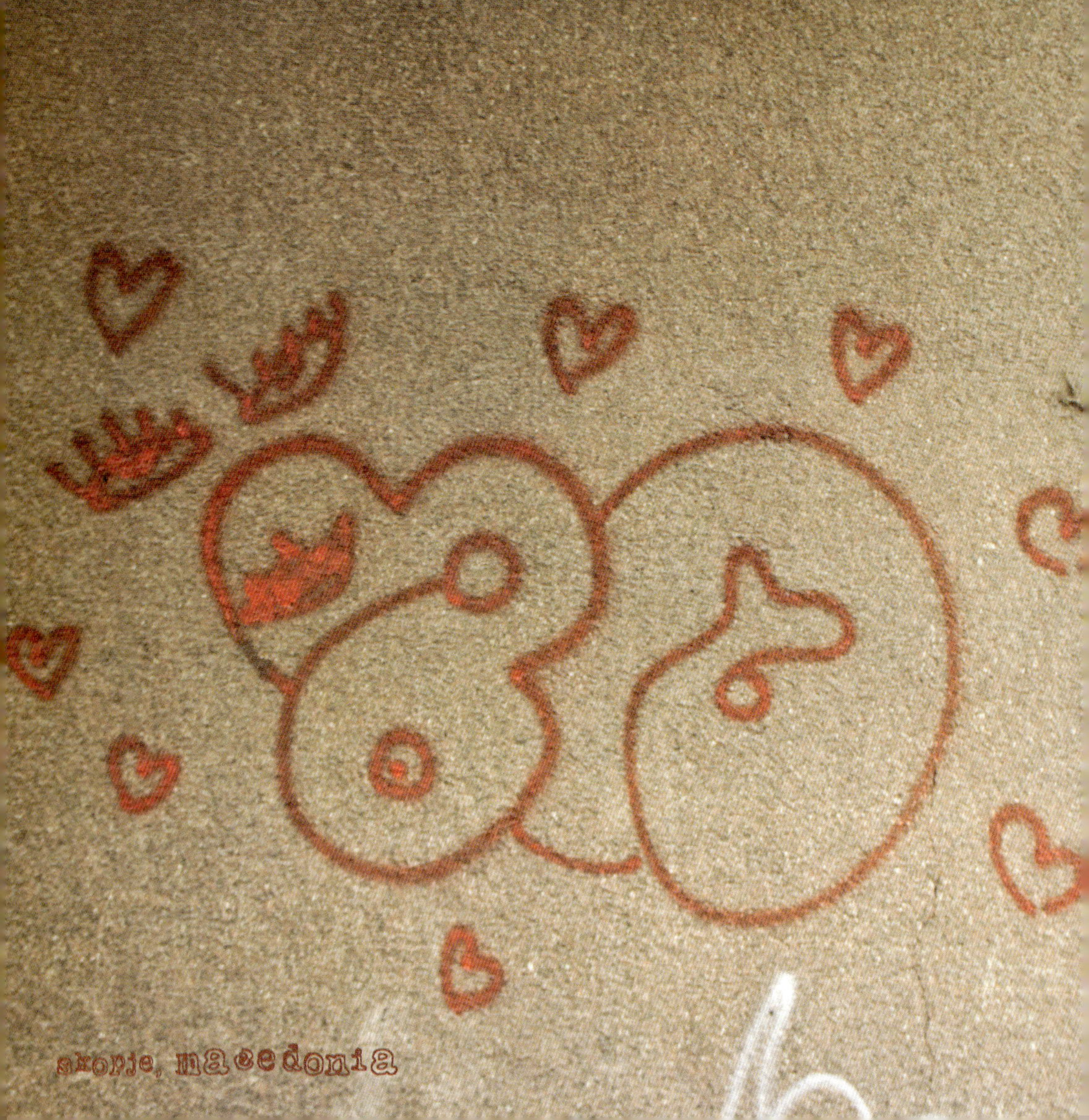

skopje, macedonia

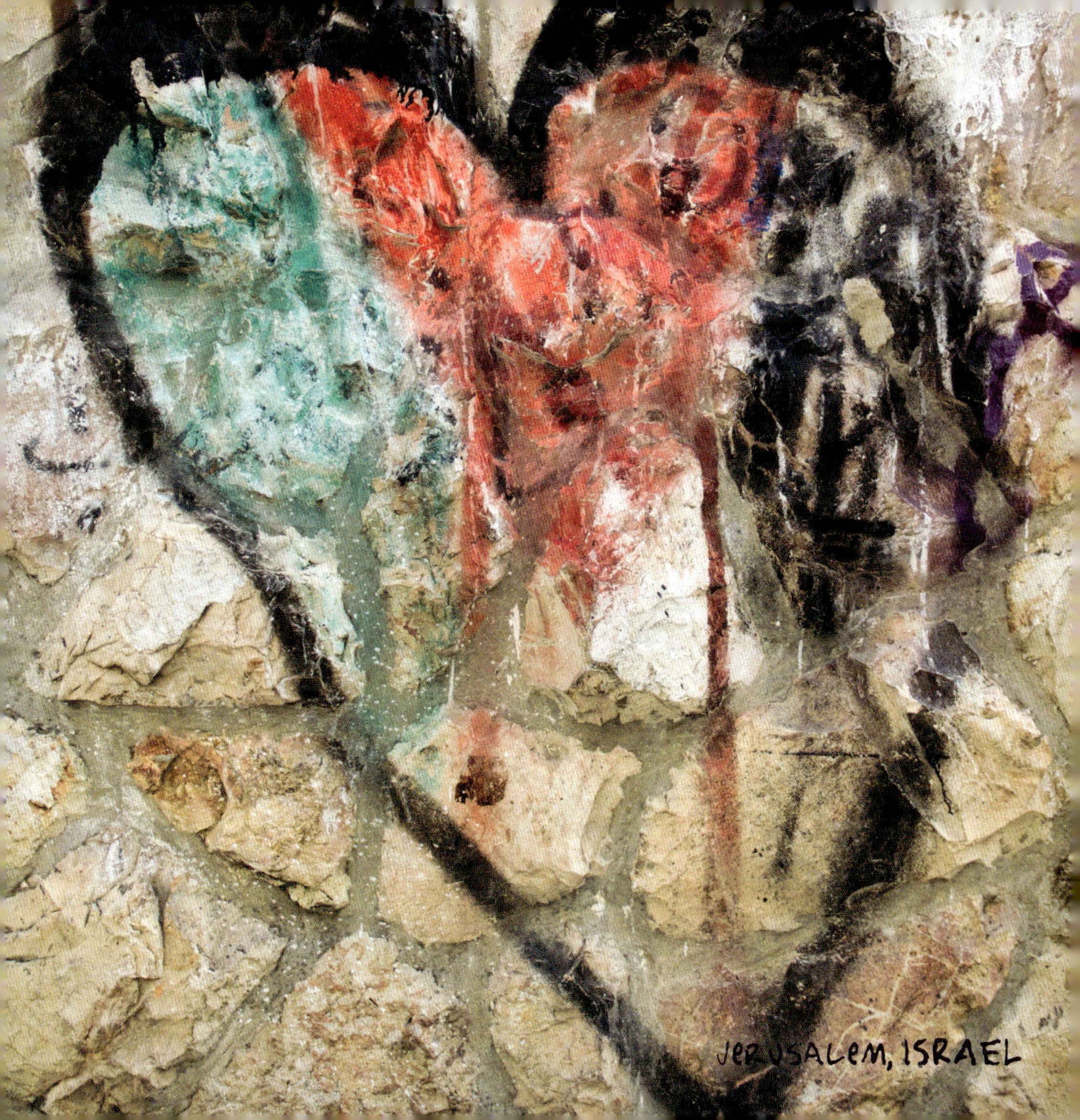
JERUSALEM, ISRAEL

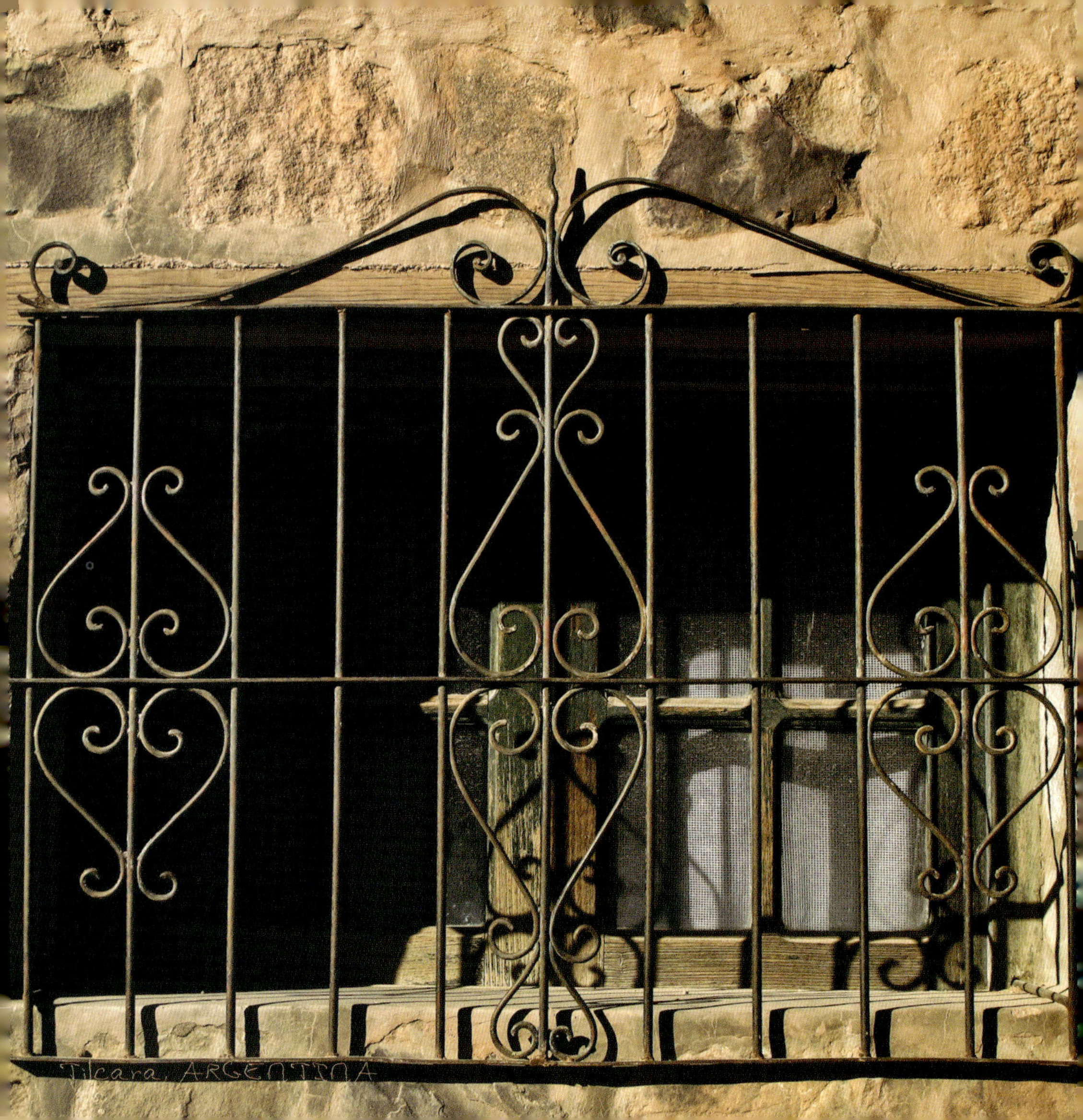
Tilcara, ARGENTINA

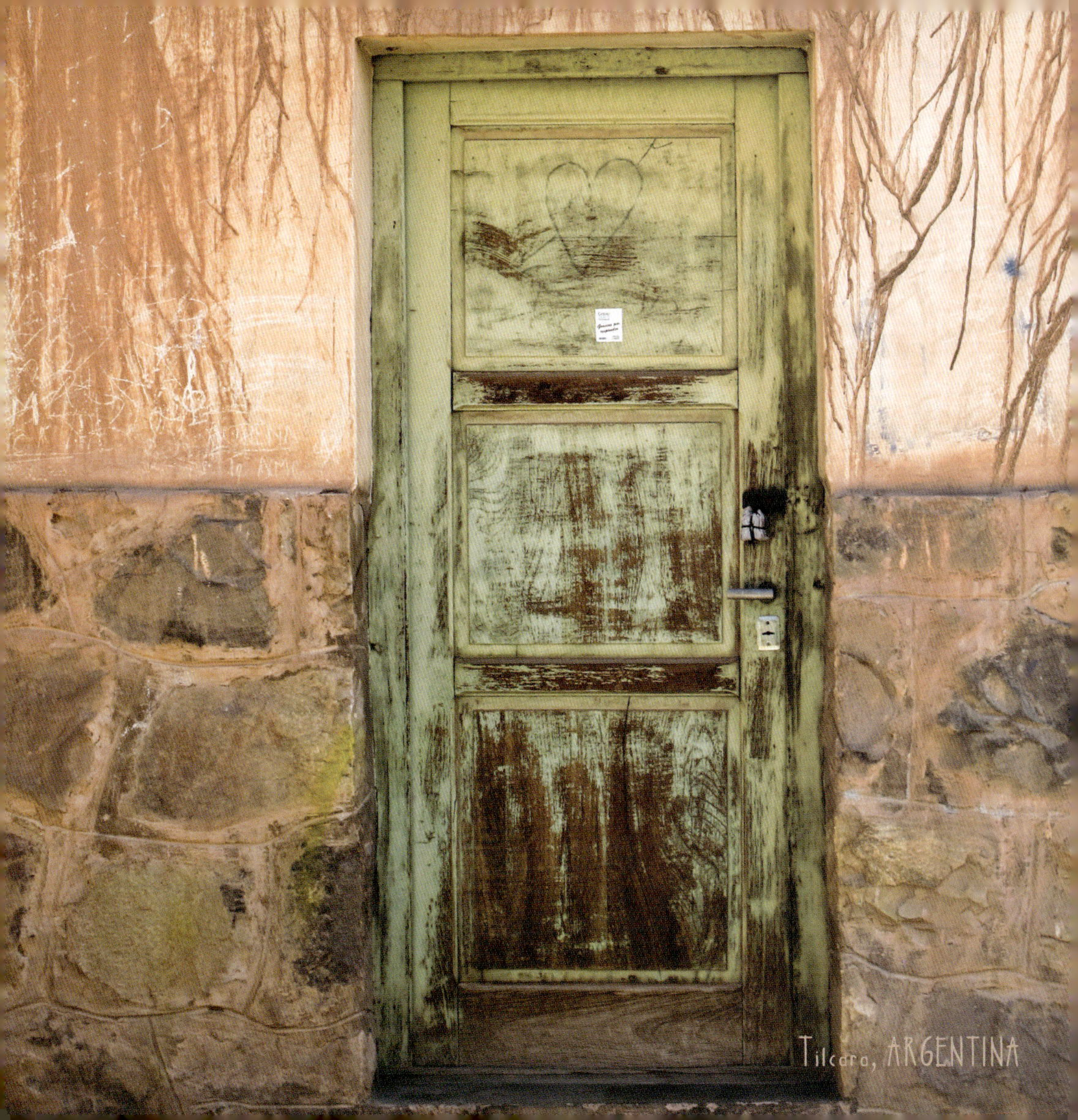

Tilcara, ARGENTINA

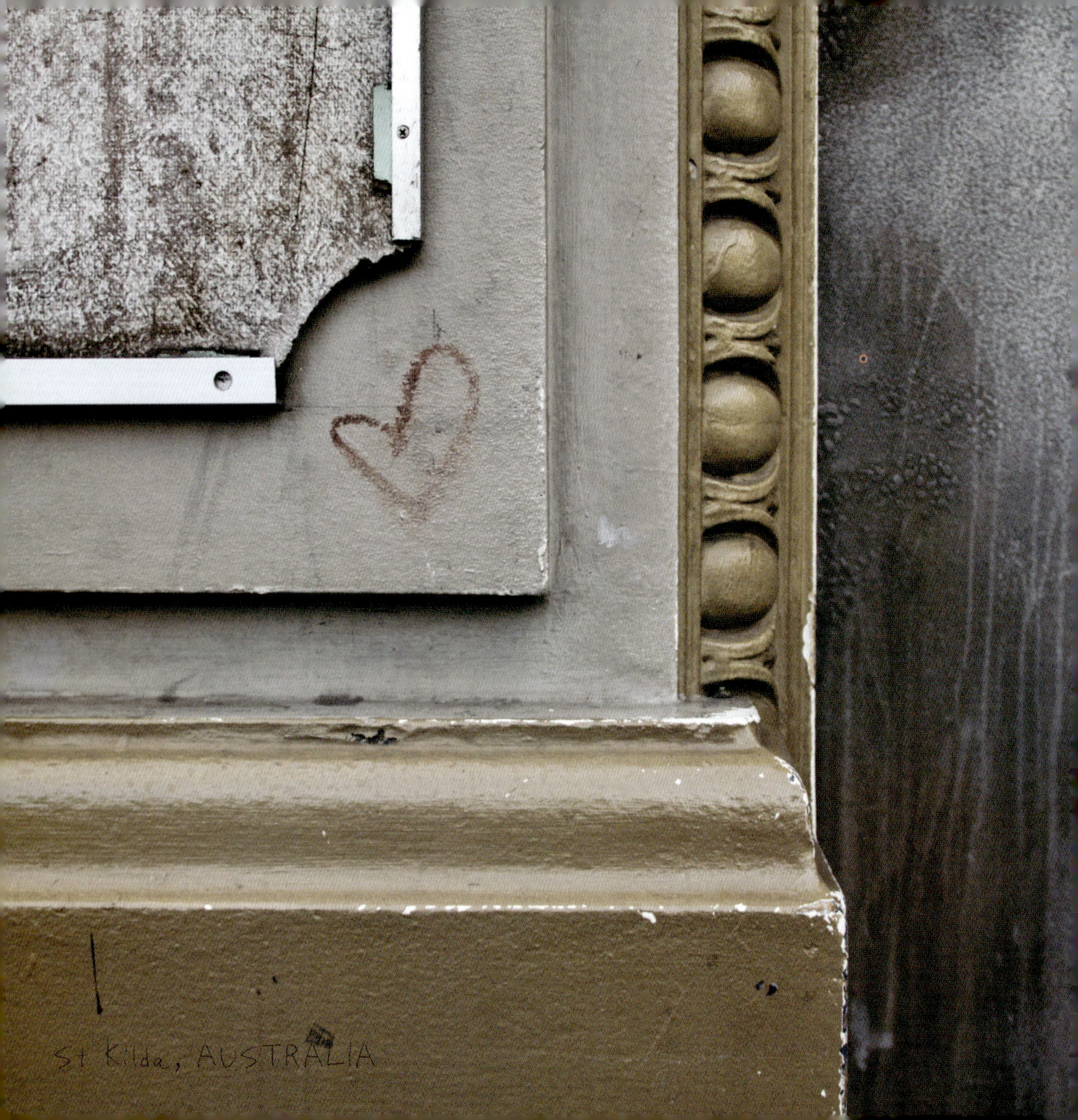
St Kilda, AUSTRALIA

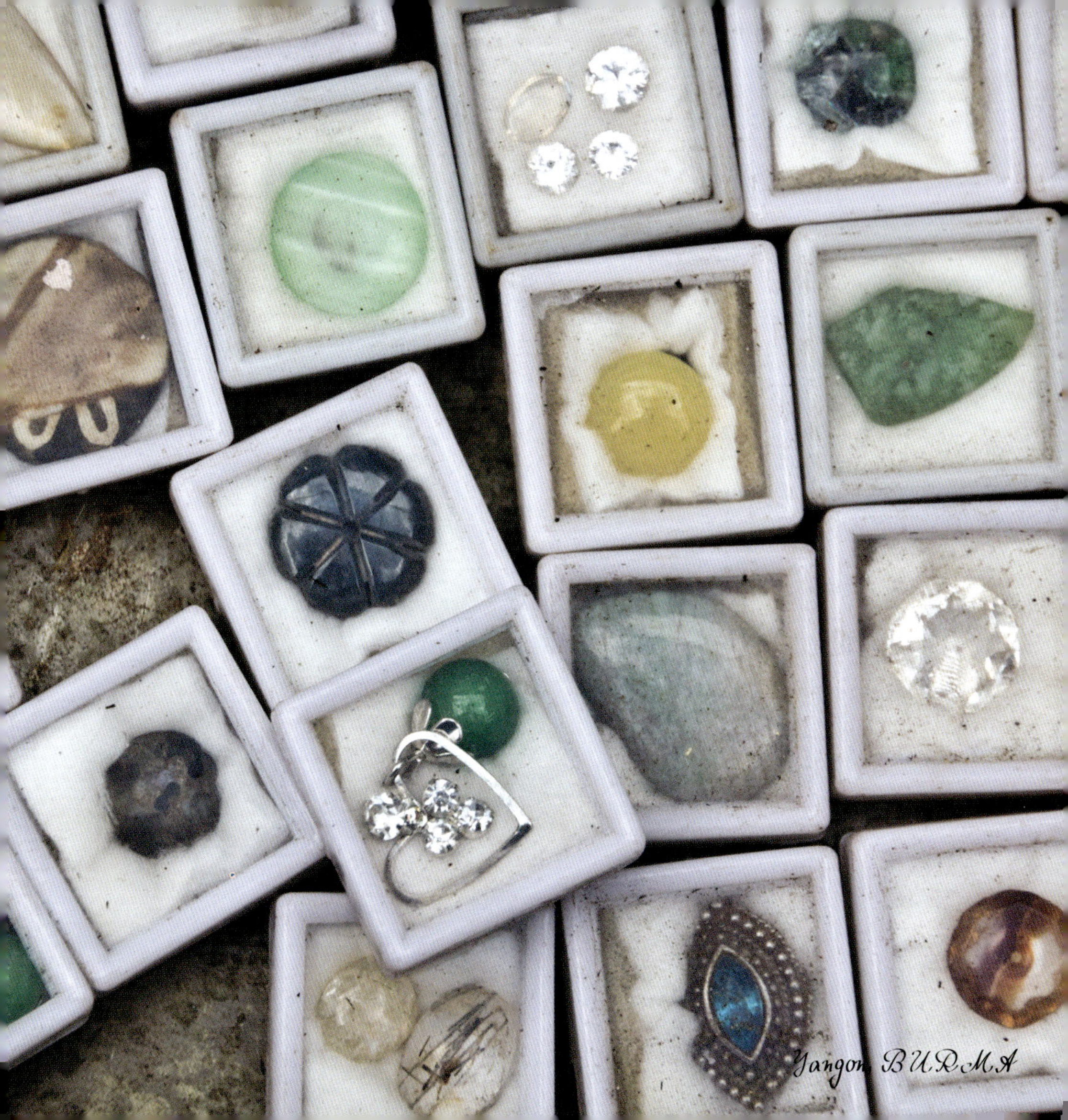
Yangon BURMA

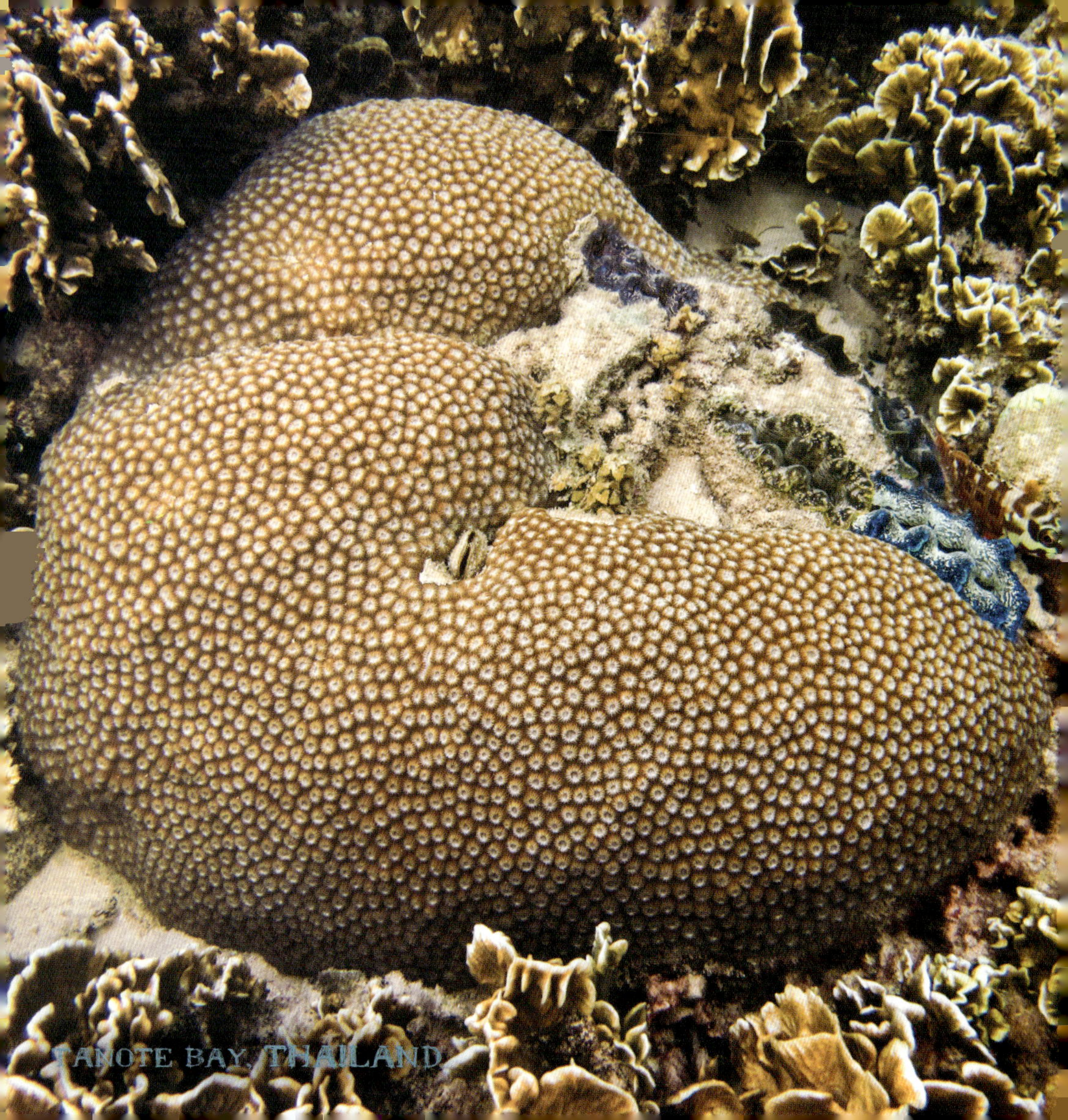
TANOTE BAY, THAILAND

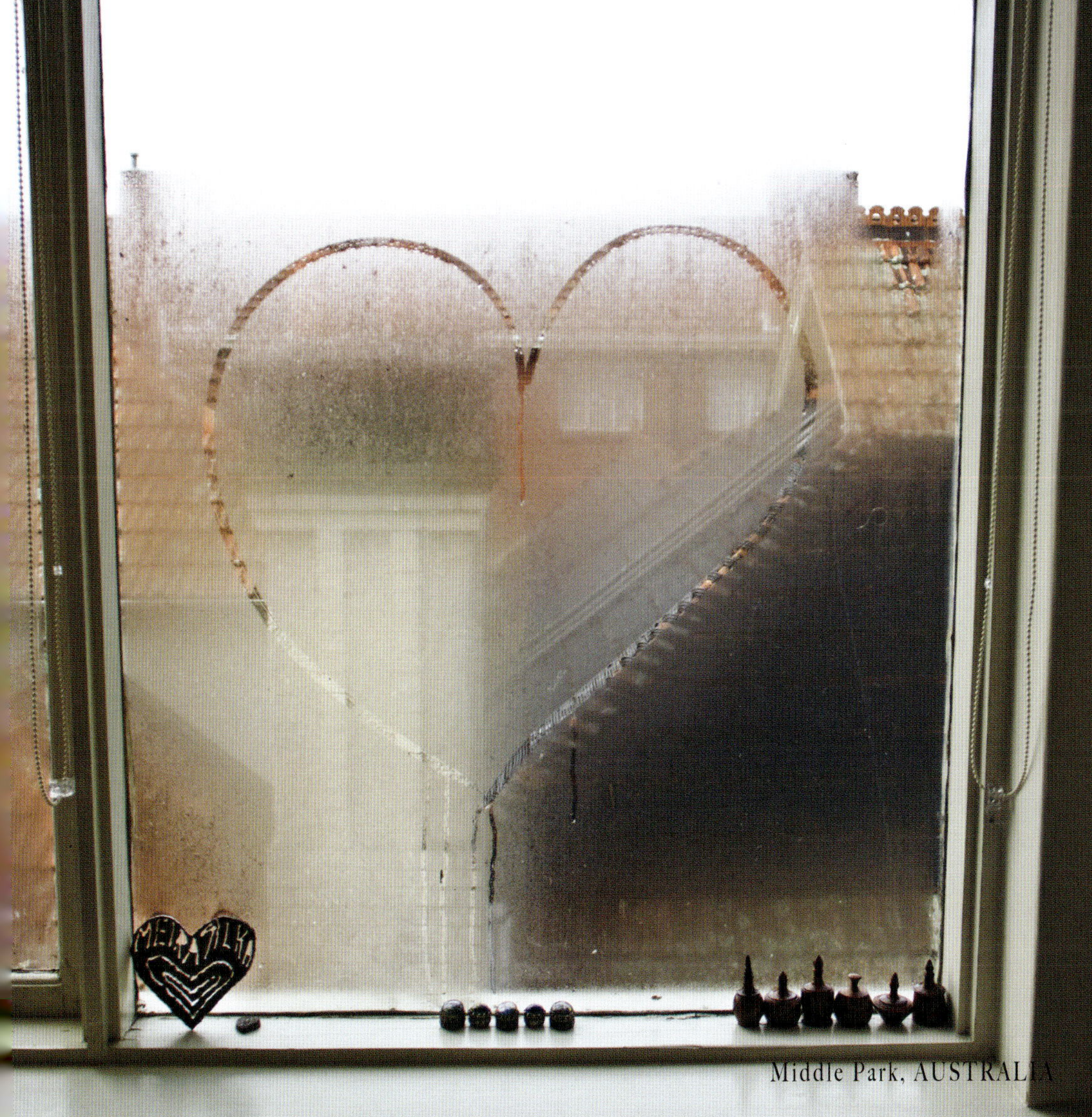
Middle Park, AUSTRALIA

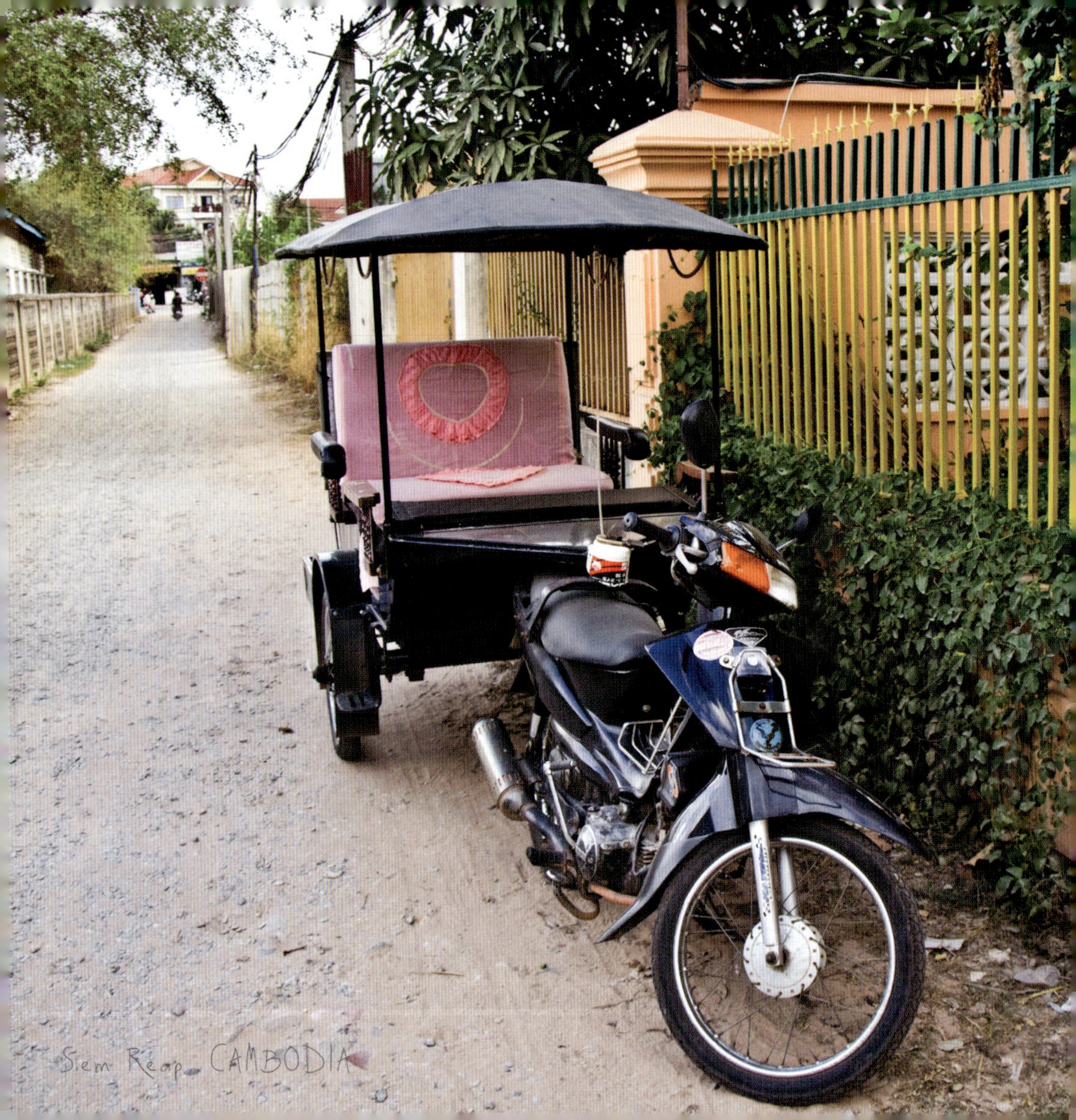

Siem Reap CAMBODIA

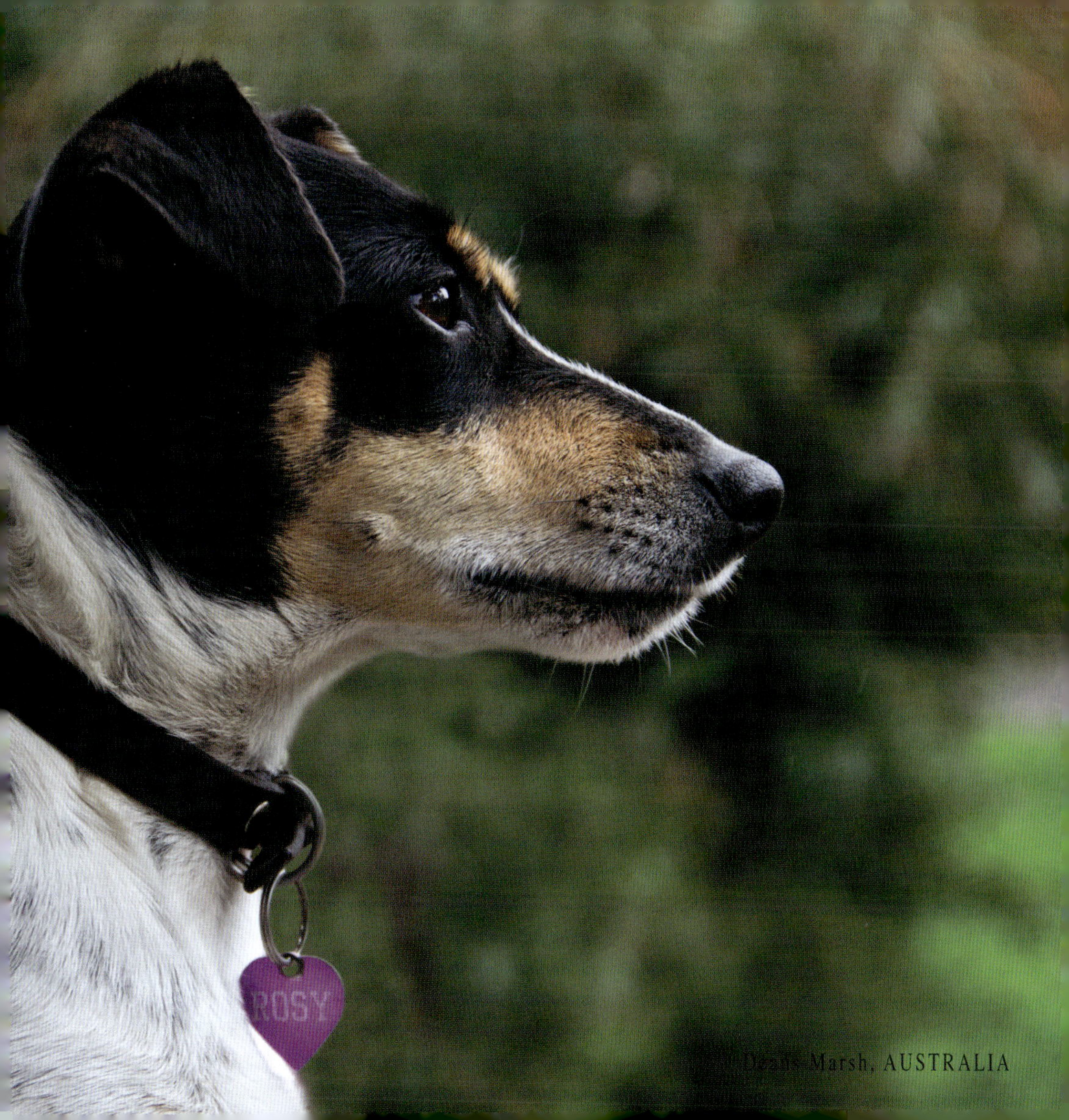
ROSY
Deans Marsh, AUSTRALIA

I want to thank you
from the bottom of
my loving heart for
joining me on this
journey to discover

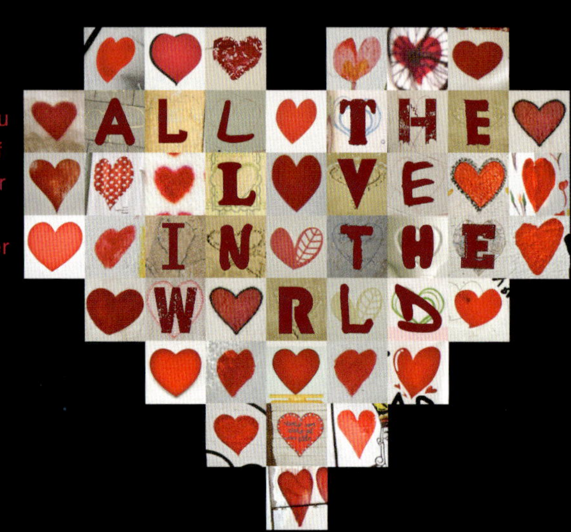

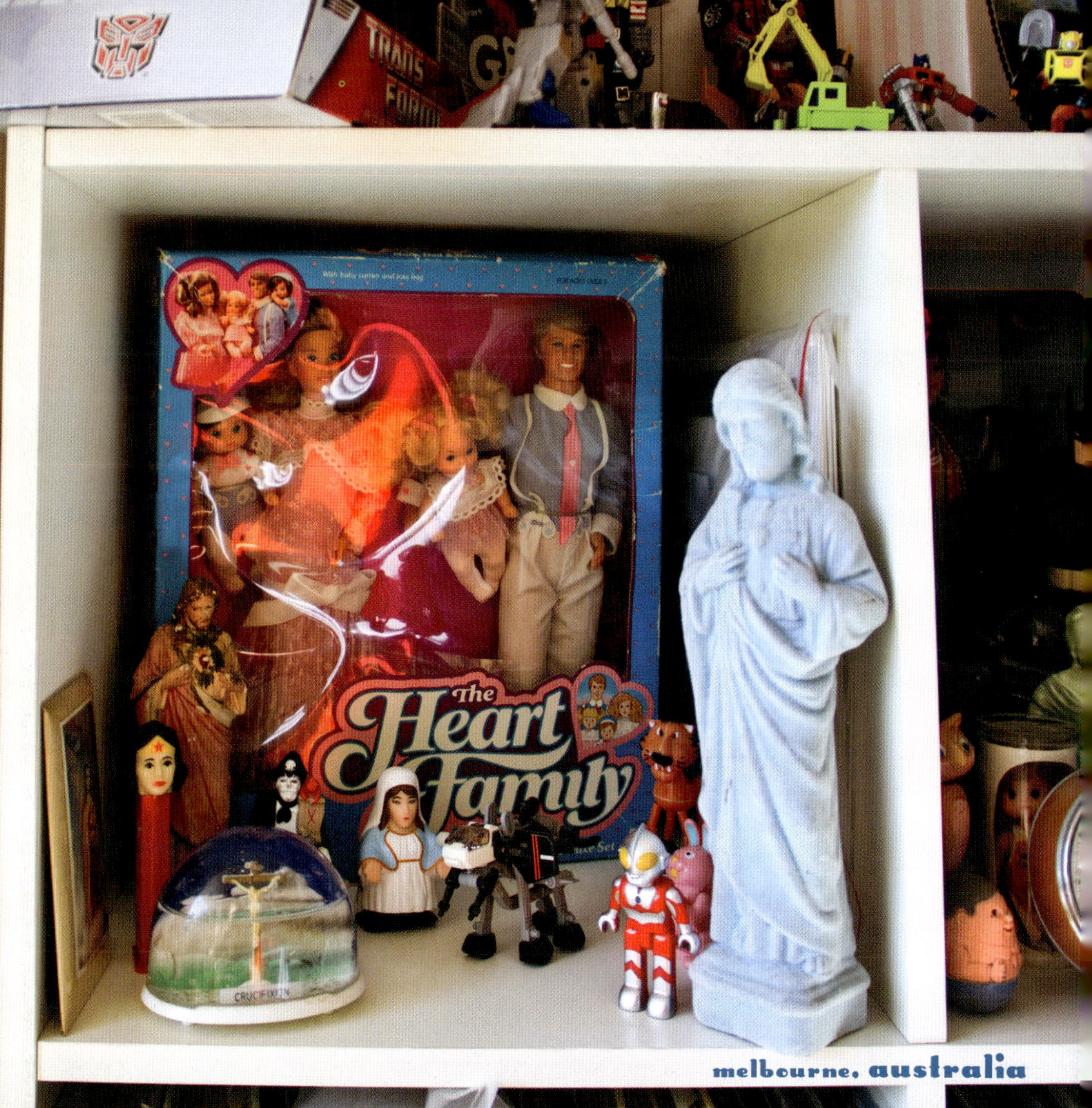

TRANS
FOR
The
Heart
Family
CRUCIFIXION
melbourne, australia

Abundant thanks to
my family and friends
for your constant
love, support and
encouragement
of my creative
endeavours.

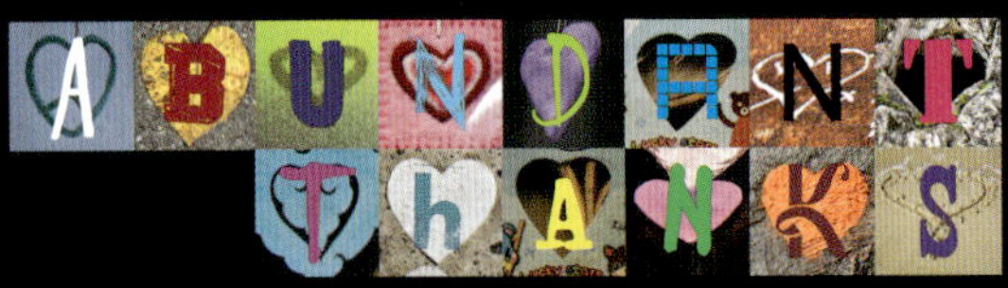

Special thanks
to everyone who
housed or fed
Mikala and I during
our journey around
the world.

Thank you to
everyone who has
shown me love
during my time
on this beautiful
planet we live on.

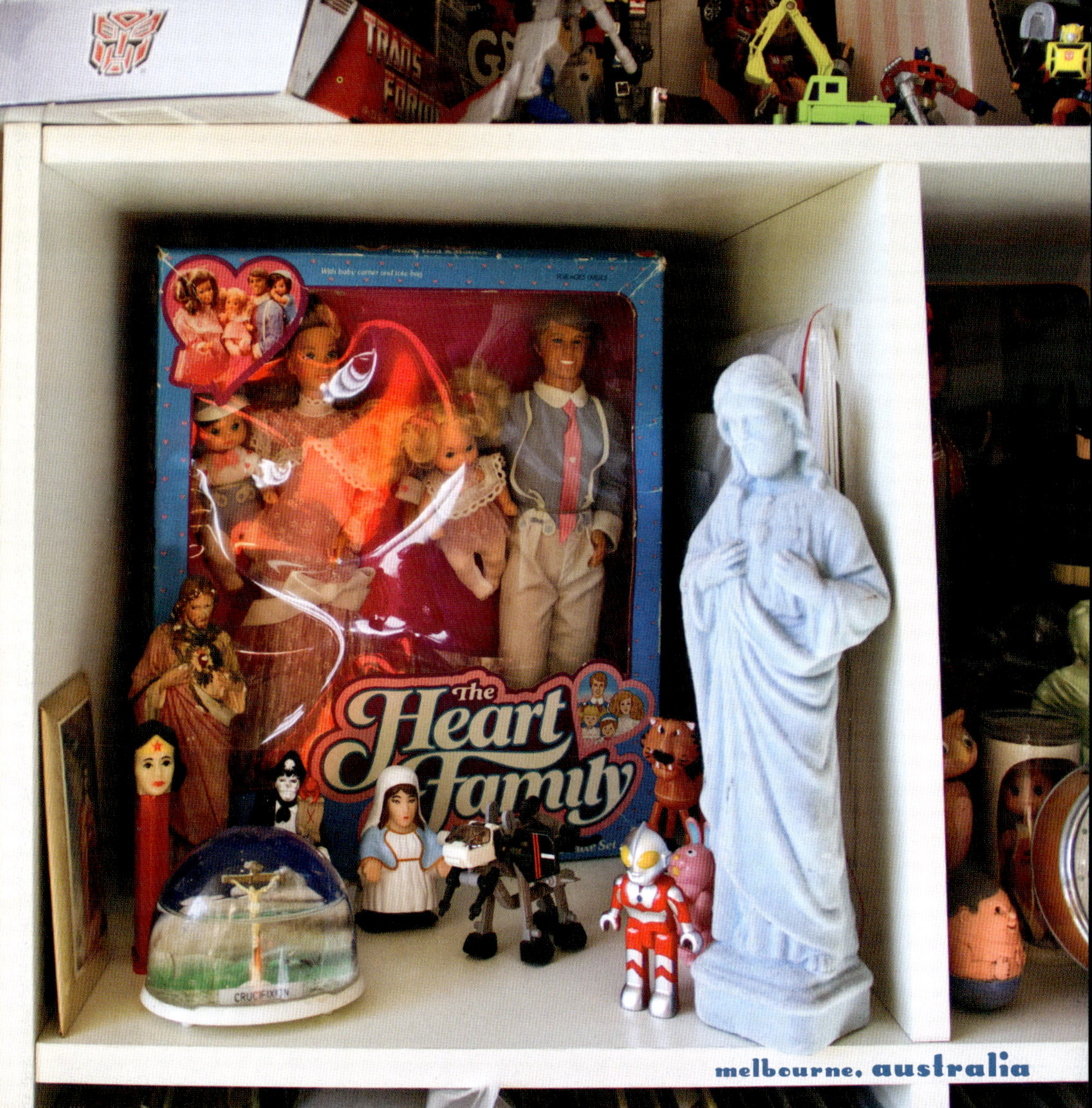
TRANS
FORM
The
Heart
Family
CRUCIFIXION
melbourne, australia

Abundant thanks to
my family and friends
for your constant
love, support and
encouragement
of my creative
endeavours.

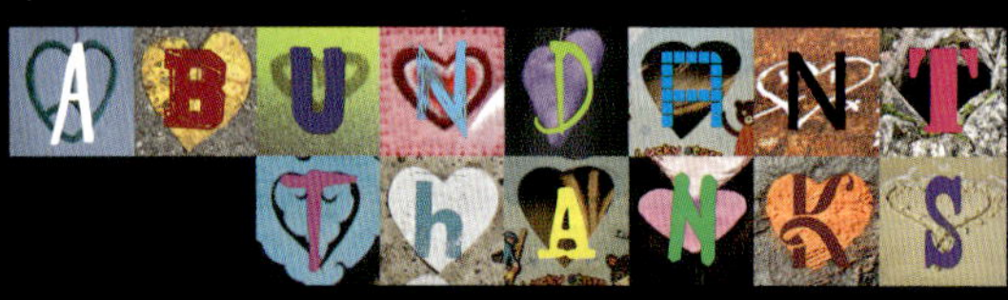

Special thanks
to everyone who
housed or fed
Mikala and I during
our journey around
the world.

Thank you to
everyone who has
shown me love
during my time
on this beautiful
planet we live on.

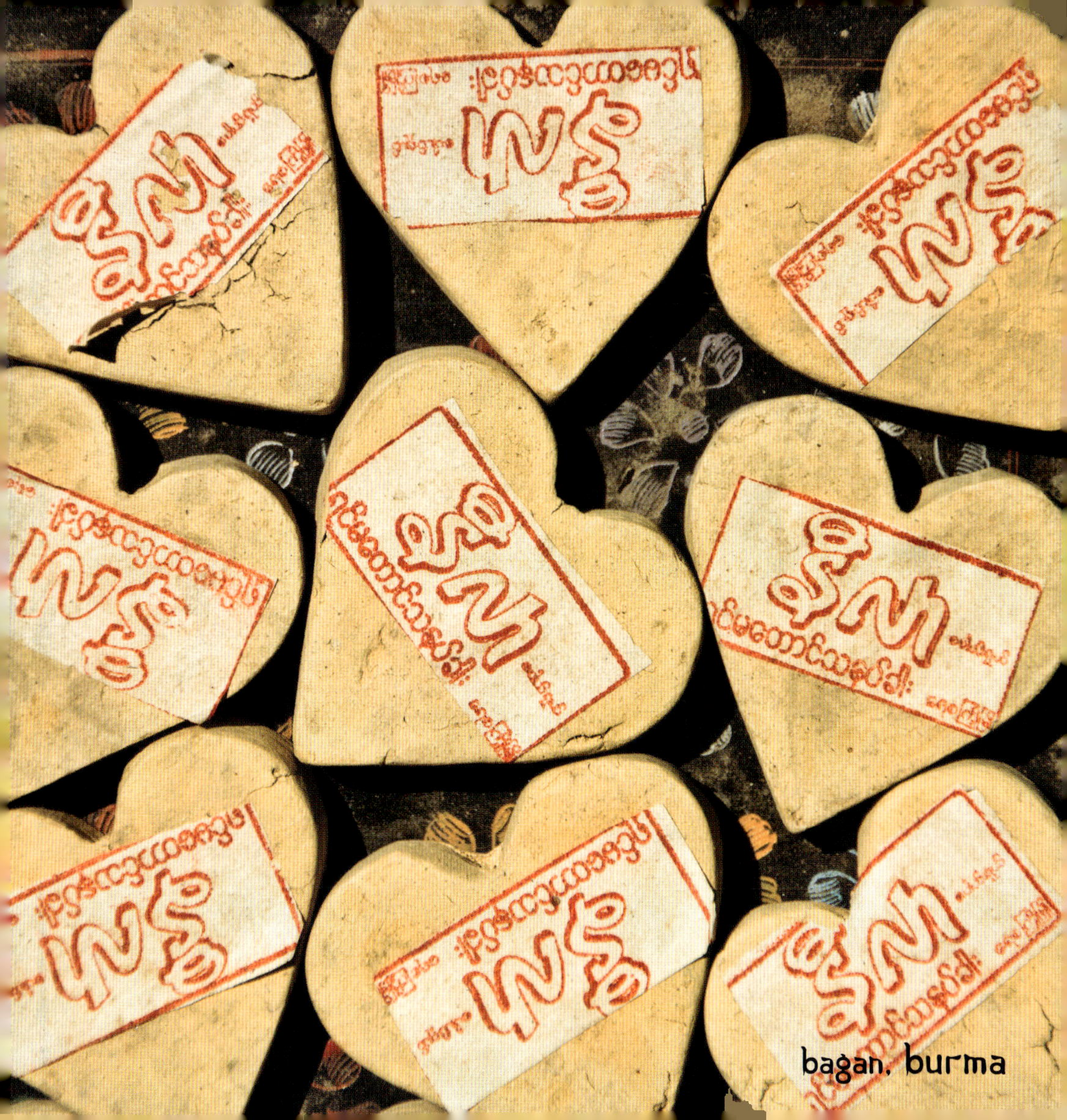

bagan, burma

Where there is Love, there is Peace.

- Jesse Hunter